MW00803233

Microeconometrics of Banking

Microeconometrics of Banking

Methods, Applications, and Results

Hans Degryse
Moshe Kim
Steven Ongena

OXFORD
UNIVERSITY PRESS
2009

Oxford University Press, Inc., publishes works that further
Oxford University's objective of excellence
in research, scholarship, and education.

Oxford   New York
Auckland   Cape Town   Dar es Salaam   Hong Kong   Karachi
Kuala Lumpur   Madrid   Melbourne   Mexico City   Nairobi
New Delhi   Shanghai   Taipei   Toronto

With offices in
Argentina   Austria   Brazil   Chile   Czech Republic   France   Greece
Guatemala   Hungary   Italy   Japan   Poland   Portugal   Singapore
South Korea   Switzerland   Thailand   Turkey   Ukraine   Vietnam

Copyright © 2009 by Oxford University Press, Inc.

Published by Oxford University Press, Inc.
198 Madison Avenue, New York, New York 10016
http://www.oup.com

Oxford is a registered trademark of Oxford University Press

All rights reserved. No part of this publication may be reproduced,
stored in a retrieval system, or transmitted, in any form or by any means,
electronic, mechanical, photocopying, recording, or otherwise,
without the prior permission of Oxford University Press.

Library of Congress Cataloging-in-Publication Data
Degryse, Hans.
    Microeconometrics of banking : methods, applications and results /
Hans Degryse, Moshe Kim, Steven Ongena.
        p. cm.
    Includes bibliographical references and index.
    ISBN 978-0-19-534047-1   1. Banks and banking.   2. Banks and banking—Econometric
models.   3. Microeconomics.   4. Finance—Econometric models.   I. Kim, Moshe.
II. Ongena, Steven.   III. Title.
HG1601.D34 2009

332.1—dc22   2008030336

To
Tom and Hilde Degryse,
Shully, Shelly, and Roni Kim,
and Barbara Beyer.

Acknowledgments

We thank Xavier Freixas for strongly encouraging us to write this book and for helpful comments along the way. We thank Terry Vaughn, who also edited the Freixas/Rochet *Microeconomics of Banking* textbook, for taking on ours as well. Matching the elegance and depth of the Freixas/Rochet *Microeconomics of Banking* textbook is impossible, that much we know. Nevertheless, we hope our book complements theirs adequately enough, so that both books jointly can assist scholars looking for both the theoretical and empirical frontiers in banking to travel there swiftly and along the routes with some of the best viewpoints.

We further thank Santiago Carbó Valverde for thoroughly commenting on the entire manuscript, and Sigbjørn Atle Berg, Antonio Chiccone, Xavier Freixas, David Humphrey, József Molnár, Luc Laeven, Alfonso Novales, María Fabiana Penas, and Günseli Tümer-Alkan for many helpful comments on various chapters. We also thank Günseli Tümer-Alkan for direct input on some of the tables.

We thank the students in the Advanced Studies Program at the Kiel Institute for the World Economy (Degryse), the CentER—Graduate School at Tilburg University (Degryse, Ongena), the Dubrovnik Lectures in Banking and Finance (Kim), the Summer Banking Institute at the Universitat Pompeu Fabra (Kim, Ongena), and the Swedish School of Economics in Helsinki (Kim) who were taught with earlier versions of the various chapters and provided verbal (and visual) feedback during class.

Degryse gratefully acknowledges the support and research atmosphere at CentER—Tilburg University and the University of Leuven. Thanks to my

coauthors for their patience as by now they must be tired of the sentence—
"I am working on the book." Financial support from FWO—the Flemish
National Science Foundation, the Research Council of the University of
Leuven, and the TILEC-AFM Network on Financial Market Regulation is
gratefully acknowledged.

Kim gratefully acknowledges the support, the hospitality, and the
academic atmosphere provided by colleagues and friends at the Universitat Pompeu Fabra, where this book was initiated. Special intellec-
tual and personal indebtedness goes to Xavier Freixas, a colleague and
friend, for encouragement and numerous suggestions. Support from the
Näringslivets Foundation at the Swedish School of Economics in Helsinki
and the Research Department at the Bank of Finland is also gratefully
acknowledged.

Ongena gratefully acknowledges the grace and patience of colleagues
(and coauthors) at CentER—Tilburg University and the hospitality of
the European Central Bank and the Swiss National Bank while writing
this book.

Contents

Microeconometrics of Banking

1

Introduction

1.1. Motivation for the Book

Some books are special. *The Microeconomics of Banking* by Xavier Freixas and Jean Charles Rochet, its first edition published in 1997, is one of those books. Its elegance and depth in addressing modern banking theory continue to inspire scholars who are interested in empirical research in banking, because no hypotheses testing is possible without a profound knowledge of the existing theoretical frameworks. Freixas and Rochet provide the unchallenged and comprehensive treatment of all key theoretical insights in banking theory.[1]

This book is about the second, empirical "wheel on the bike" that constitutes banking research, in the analogy of research as a two-wheeled vehicle (with a theoretical and an empirical wheel that are both needed for steady forward motion)—a compendium to the "spokes and materials used in this second wheel," so to say. Such a compendium was overdue. Indeed, since the publication of the Freixas/Rochet book, work in empirical banking has further blossomed, not only in sheer volume but also in the variety of questions that are tackled, data sets that become available, and methodologies that are being fielded.

---

1. Determining when a field of research started is difficult and ultimately always somewhat fruitless. Modern banking theory and ensuing empirical work find origins in work by Gurley and Shaw (1960), Tobin (1963), Hodgman (1960), Kane and Malkiel (1965), Klein (1971), and Monti (1972), among many others.

Some of these developments are no different from those in finance research in general, where the larger role finance has attained for itself in modern economies is increasingly reflected in larger student numbers and broadened scholarship. At the same time, though, empirical research in banking saw itself additionally spurred by specific academic, institutional, and technological developments. Increasing demands on researchers to advance our knowledge and to provide solutions for many of the critical issues in modern financial markets in general, and in banking markets in particular, necessitate a unified synthesis of existing knowledge, and consequently a determination and emphasis on the important unresolved issues. Where banking sectors continue to play a much larger role among world economies, the new function of the many national central banks within the Eurosystem and elsewhere, and the swift developments in data access, processing technology, and econometric techniques and software provided additional impetus to empirical research in banking.

The credit registers and other data sets that are now "falling open" in Belgium (Degryse and Van Cayseele 2000; Degryse, Masschelein, and Mitchell 2006), Bolivia (Ioannidou and Ongena 2007), Germany (Elsas and Krahnen 1998; Machauer and Weber 1998; Ongena, Tümer-Alkan, and von Westernhagen 2007b), Italy (Sapienza 2002; Focarelli and Panetta 2003), Norway (Kim, Kristiansen, and Vale 2007), Portugal (Farinha and Santos 2002), Spain (Jiménez, Salas, and Saurina 2006), and the United States (Bharath, Dahiya, Saunders, and Srinivasan 2007) seem almost comparable in quantity and quality (e.g., frequency and reliability) to the data sets to which scholars in other areas of finance and economics at large have long been accustomed. The questions broached and methodologies employed followed, as the mocking say, "have data set, write paper."

1.2. Structure for the Book

A compendium to all this activity is therefore overdue. We have closely mirrored the structure in Freixas and Rochet's textbook and have arranged the relevant methodologies, applications, and results according to each of their original chapters in order to have a coherent synthesis between available theory and supporting empirics.

In this book, each chapter contains a modest introduction (where possible and appropriate) and a concise methodology section with one or more relevant methodologies and some illustrative applications. While we discuss a number of econometric methods, we did not have the ambition to provide a review of all relevant econometric techniques (for such a review, we refer the interested reader to excellent econometric textbooks, e.g., Cameron and Trivedi 2005; Greene 2003). Finally, each chapter provides a "muscular" results section that summarizes the main and robust (seminal) findings in the literature and details of many other studies in figures and tables. Table 1.1 graphically represents the structure of this book, underscoring that any linear lineup of a multidimensional phenomenon is bound to "fail" in certain places.

Chapter 2 deals with the question of why financial intermediaries exist. The empirical literature on this topic started with event studies looking at the impact of bank loan announcements on stock market performance of firms. The chapter therefore discusses the event study methodology and also provides a bootstrapping application. The results section highlights loan and bank distress/merger announcement studies and also discusses the long-run impact of bank distress on firm performance.

Chapter 3 outlines the industrial organization approach to banking. While the empirical industrial organization literature has introduced many concepts and methodologies that have been applied either across different industries or initially applied in other industries, we focus on papers bringing these approaches first to financial intermediation. The methodology section in this chapter is substantial and discusses the methodologies employed in the structure-conduct-performance literature, in the studies of bank efficiency and of economies of scale and scope, the Panzar and Rosse (1987) approach, the Boone (2008) competition indicator, the conjectural-variations method, the structural demand models, and other structural models. The results section addresses the evidence on the market structure and conduct nexus in loan markets, deposit markets, and the interplay between markets and the market structure and strategy nexus, as product differentiation and network effects.

Chapter 4 defines and describes the lender–borrower relationship and introduces as methodologies duration, Tobit, count, nested multinomial logit, and heteroskedastic regression models. The chapter then summarizes the evidence on the determinants of characteristics of bank relationships (duration, scope, number, and intensity), for example, the impact of relationships on the cost and availability of credit and firm performance. The results section also deals with bank strategy and its orientation and specialization.

Chapter 5 focuses on the equilibrium and rationing in the credit markets, with evidence regarding the importance of location for the availability of credit and the conduct and strategy of the banks.

Table 1.1. Structure of the book

Ch.	Topic	Methodology	Main Findings (Text)	Also Other Findings
2	Existence	Event Study Methodology Bootstrapping	Loan Announcements Bank Distress/Merger Announcements Bank Distress and Firm Performance	Table 2.1 Table 2.2 Table 2.3
3	Industrial Organization	*Traditional Industrial Organization* Structure-Conduct-Performance Bank Efficiency Economies of Scale and Scope *New Empirical Industrial Organization* Panzar and Rosse (1987) Boone (2007) Conjectural Variations Models Structural Demand Models Other Structural Models	*Market Structure and Conduct* Loan/Deposit Markets and Interplay *Market Structure and Strategy*	Tables 3.2 and 3.3
4	Relationships	Duration Analysis Tobit and Count Models Nested Multinomial Logit Heteroskedastic Regression	*Characteristics of Bank Relationships* Duration, Scope, Number, Intensity *Impact of Bank Relationships* Bank Orientation and Specialization	Tables 4.1 to 4.8 Tables 4.9 to 4.13 Figure 4.3, Table 4.14
5	Rationing		*Conduct* Spatial Rationing and Pricing, Segmentation *Strategy* Branching, Entry and Mergers and Acquisitions	Table 5.1

Table 7.1

6	Macro	Growth Regression Instrumental Variables Interaction Variables	Banks and Growth Causality? Banks, Financial Markets, and Growth
7	Bank Runs		Determinants Implications Regulation Contagion
8	Managing Risks	Value at Risk and Credit Risk Measurement	Default or Credit Risks Liquidity Risks Market Risks
9	Regulation	Difference-in-Difference	Market Structure Bank Conduct Bank Strategy Financial Stability and Development
10	Conclusion		Summary of Main Findings Issues for Future Research
11	Epilogue		Liquidity and the 2007–2008 Crisis

In this book, each chapter contains a concise methodology section with one or more relevant methodologies and some illustrative applications. We summarize the main findings in the literature in the text, but provide the details of many other studies in figures and tables.

Chapter 6 discusses the macroeconomic consequences of financial imperfections through the set of empirical models used in this literature dealing with the finance–growth nexus and thus discusses the instrumental variable technique for the assessment of the direction of causality between banking to growth and the channels involved in such. The evidence section introduces and summarizes the papers investigating banks and growth, the direction of causality, and the role financial markets play in addition.

Chapter 7 looks at individual bank runs and systemic risk featuring the evidence on the determinants of banking crises: market and economic conditions, implications of banking crises and their results, regulation and banking crises, and interbank market exposure and contagion.

Chapter 8 discusses the empirical management of risks in the banking firm. In terms of methodology the chapter broaches the assumptions, estimation approaches, and issues of the value at risk and credit risk measurement models. Evidence on default or credit risk, liquidity risk, and market risk is consecutively discussed.

Chapter 9 delves into the regulation of banks. From a methodology point of view, we introduce the difference-in-difference methodology. We group further results in subsections on regulation and market structure, bank conduct, strategy, and financial stability and development. Finally, chapter 10 concludes by summarizing the existing evidence and by providing a laundry list of topics for further research, and chapter 11 provides an epilogue on the banking crisis of 2007–2008. This banking crisis is a source for research for many years to come.

2

Why Do Financial Intermediaries Exist?

2.1. Introduction

Modern theory of financial intermediation argues that it is a bank's ability to reduce information asymmetries between borrowers and savers that makes a bank unique relative to other financial institutions (Leland and Pyle 1977; Diamond 1984; Ramakrishnan and Thakor 1984; Fama 1985; Boyd and Prescott 1986).[1] A bank may learn a substantial amount of information when it initially screens the borrower for the loan, but also later on as the bank has the ability to closely monitor repayment and other behavior of firm management over the course of the loan (duration), the bank may gain proprietary knowledge of the borrowing firm through deposit and other services (scope), or the bank can even influence decisions made by firm management (control). The fact that the bank has such wide access to private information about its borrowers leads Fama (1985), for example, to label the bank an "inside debt holder." The informational advantage of inside banks compared to outside banks may imply that firms face informational switching

---

1. Our discussion is based partly on Ongena and Smith (2000a). Other sources of reviews on financial intermediation include Berger and Udell (1998), Berger (2003), Bernanke (1993), Bhattacharya and Thakor (1993), Davis (1996), Degryse and Ongena (2004), Freixas and Rochet (1997), Gertler (1988), Goddard, Molyneux, Wilson, and Tavakoli (2007), Gorton and Winton (2003), Greenbaum (1996), Hellwig (1991), Mayer (1996), Nakamura (1993a), Neuberger (1998), Scholtens (1993), Swank (1996), Thakor (1995, 1996), and Van Damme (1994).

costs when willing to borrow from outside banks or other providers of
finance.

Motivated by Fama (1985)'s conjectures regarding the uniqueness of
bank loans, James (1987) studies the average stock price reaction of firms
that publicly announce a bank loan agreement or renewal. The results in
his seminal paper are key in our current thinking of the role banks play
in credit markets. Before summarizing the results in James (1987), and
the many papers it spawned, we first discuss event study methodology in
a stylized setting similar to James (1987). Event study methodology is a
standard toolbox in finance and has been heavily employed to evaluate the
value added of bank–firm relationships. We add an example of a bootstrap
application.

2.2. Methodology

2.2.1. Event Study Methodology

Event studies in empirical banking often involve the analysis of stock price
reactions of relevant firms and/or banks to certain events of interest, the
announcement of a bank loan, or the announcement of bank distress, for
example (for a general overview, see Thompson 1985). Associating stock
price reactions with changes in investors' assessments requires market efficiency and a correspondingly short time window around the events that are
material, unanticipated, and not confounded by other events (McWilliams
and Siegel 1997). Stock price reactions are benchmarked with a pricing
model to determine if the stock returns are abnormal. A number of other
operational choices need to be made in this regard, such as the length and
placement of the estimation and event windows.

Imagine we want to study the impact of the announcements (in the
financial press) that firm j obtained a bank loan on their (end-of-day)
stock prices $P_j, j = 1, 2, \ldots J$. In practice, J has ranged between 50 and
>1,000. Adjusting for dividends and stock splits, we calculate the daily
stock returns, r_{jt}:

$$r_{jt} = \frac{P_{jt} - P_{jt-1}}{P_{jt-1}} \tag{2.1}$$

We then estimate daily abnormal returns by using a market model regression.
We regress the daily returns for firm j, r_{jt}, on a measure of the market return,
r_{mt}, and a set of daily event dummies, δ_{jkt}, that take the value of 1 when

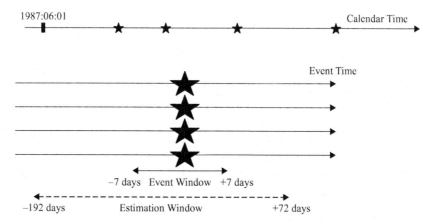

Figure 2.1.   Event and estimation windows in calendar and event time. Stars represent events.

day t is inside the event window and 0 otherwise. Dates inside the event window are indexed by k. The regression could, for example, be

$$r_{jt} = \alpha_j + \beta_j r_{mt} + \sum_{k=-7}^{7} \gamma_{jk} \delta_{jkt} + \varepsilon_{jt}. \qquad (2.2)$$

Figure 2.1 displays an example of events (stars) in calendar and event time. It also displays an example of estimation and event windows.

The estimation window can span a full year (of stock market activity) and start, for example, 185 days before the event window to end 65 days after the final day of the event window. The event window itself contains up to 15 trading days (for events with more information leakage, e.g., public bank merger announcements, a longer preevent window, may be appropriate, e.g., 60 days). The market model is estimated over a 265-day period starting 192 days before the event and ending 72 days after the event (t is expressed in event time, not calendar time, and consequently runs from -192 to $+72$). Employing a similarly sized estimation window that ends 20 days or so prior to the start of the event window constitutes a solid robustness check. The coefficients γ_{jk} measure daily abnormal returns during the event period and the β_j values are assumed to be time invariant (a good robustness check is to alter the estimation window).

A standard setup probably includes a value-weighted index of all domestic stocks as a proxy for the market return. Three leads and lags of the index can be added as a Scholes and Williams (1977) correction for nonsynchronous trading that occurs in thinner markets. In addition, stocks that are traded too infrequently within the estimation and event period (e.g., <100 of 265 estimation days and <7 of 15 event days) can be removed. Replacing the index with a fixed-weighted index of all domestic stocks and a world index (the fixed-weighted Morgan Stanley All Country World Index, e.g.) is crucial to check robustness. More complex market models may include multiple indices (a domestic *and* a world index, e.g.) and additional factors, such as a domestic interest rate and inflation.

For each firm j, we calculate cumulative abnormal returns (CARs) by adding daily abnormal return estimates $\hat{\gamma}_{jk}$. The 3-day CAR, for example, would equal

$$CAR(-1, +1) = \sum_{k=-1}^{1} \hat{\gamma}_{jk}. \tag{2.3}$$

The *statistical significance* of this estimated CAR can be assessed using a standard F-test of a sum. Given the abnormal returns are already in percent and the model is linear, evaluating the *economic relevance* of the estimates requires no further calculations. It is important to stress at this point the importance of assessing the magnitude of the effects that are measured. In general, assessing economic relevance relies on the magnitude of the coefficients and the size of the estimated effects given the range over which the independent variable of interest can be thought to vary. One or two standard deviations around the mean, or minimum to maximum values of the independent variable can be used to assess economic relevance. In other cases, stylized facts or even economic theory can be used to define reasonable ranges over which the independent variable should be allowed to vary to measure the effect on the dependent variable.

Typically, CARs are computed for multiple event windows, preferably as short as possible to be compatible with the underlying market efficiency hypothesis and to minimize the effect of confounding events:

$$CAR(-x, +y) = \sum_{k=-x}^{y} \hat{\gamma}_{jk} \tag{2.4}$$

Reasonable choices of event windows, that is, of x and y, for loan announcements are, for example, $(-3, -1)$, $(0, 1)$, and $(-3, +3)$. The leakage of information about preparatory negotiations before and the further revelation of crucial details after the public announcement of a merger deal necessitate the use of longer event windows in case of a merger announcement.

Calculating the CARs up to a couple of months before and after the merger announcement is sometimes justifiable.

2.2.2. Bootstrapping

Imagine now that we wanted to analyze the impact of loans not on firm stocks but on bank stocks and that the loans are granted by a syndicate of banks, that is, syndicated loans offered by multiple banks operating in a syndicate. Abstracting from syndicate hierarchy, to summarize the CARs across a given set of banks, we would have to group the bank stocks into different (syndicated) loan announcements portfolios and calculate sample averages of the CARs across the banks in a given portfolio. The standard errors for these sample averages would have to be calculated using a bootstrap method to account for contemporaneous correlation across bank stocks in an event portfolio, and possibly for events that overlap in time. We describe here such a bootstrapping procedure.

To obtain a distribution for the average CAR across all events that account for the cross-sectional (and cross-event) correlation in bank error terms, we first regress the realized daily return of the stock for each bank i, r_{it}, on the realized daily return on the market index in period t, r_{mt}, and 15 event dummies, δ_{jkt}:

$$r_{it} = \alpha + \beta_i r_{mt} + \sum_{k=-7}^{7} \gamma_{ik} \delta_{jkt} + \varepsilon_{it} \qquad (2.5)$$

Again, $t = -192, -191, \ldots, 72$ and $i = 1, 2, \ldots, I$. ε_{it} is an error term. Let I_j represent the number of banks involved with the syndicated loan event j and $I = \sum_{j=1}^{j} I_j$ (to keep things simple, we assume the loan shares to be equal). Denote the estimated coefficients as $\hat{\alpha}$, $\hat{\beta}$, and $\hat{\gamma}_{ik}$ and note that the CAR is the sum of the daily abnormal return estimates over the event window.

The goal of the bootstrapping exercise is to break up the correlation structure and to obtain standard errors on the coefficients which reflect this correlation. We draw our bootstrapped data by first drawing with replacement 265 integer index values (to be used to select the residuals) from a uniform distribution defined over the interval $-192, -191, \ldots, 72$.

For each draw, we store the results in a vector. These independent draws determine the dates of the original errors that will be used to sequentially fill in the new time series of 265 daily observations. Based on this vector, we will then draw the ordinary least squares (OLS) residuals corresponding to the index values for each of the I_j banks involved in the event. Basically, we draw index numbers for the entire sample period, which starts on the first day of the first estimation period and ends on the last day of the last estimation period. Then, we take the index numbers allocated to each estimation period. By drawing the bootstrapped data in this manner, we preserve both the within-event and cross-event error dependencies in the data. Note, however, that we otherwise assume that the data are independently distributed through time.

For one completed draw of data, we then calculate for each bank the bootstrapped daily return of the stock, $\hat{r}^1_{it}$:

$$\hat{r}^1_{it} = \hat{\alpha}_i + \hat{\beta}_{in}r_{mt} + \sum_{k=-7}^{7} \hat{\gamma}_{ik}\delta_{jkt} + \hat{\varepsilon}^1_{i\tau}, \qquad (2.6)$$

where $t = -192, -191, \ldots, 72$; $\tau = \tau^j_{-192}, \tau^j_{-191}, \ldots \tau^j_{72}$; $i = 1, 2, \ldots I$. $\hat{\varepsilon}^1_{it}$ is the tth OLS residual order according to the index values drawn above, and the superscript 1 refers to the first draw of data.

Once the new set of returns has been created, we can run regressions similar to equation 2.5 to estimate daily bank-level abnormal returns, bank-level CARs, and average CARs across banks. We repeat this procedure then say between a 100 and 10,000 times to generate a distribution of the estimates. From this distribution we can compute the empirical p-values. A similar procedure can then also used to bootstrap distributions for the estimated coefficients in cross-sectional regressions.

2.3. Evidence

2.3.1. Loan Announcements

Following work by Mikkelson and Partch (1986), James (1987) studies the average price reactions of firm stocks following the public announcement of bank loan agreements or renewals employing the previously discussed event study methodology. The second row of table 2.1 summarizes his findings (the first row lists the original results from Mikkelson and Partch 1986).[2]

---

2. Our discussion is based partly on Degryse and Ongena (2008).

Table 2.1. Loan Announcement Studies

Paper	Country, Period	Average (Median) Firm Size	Announcement (Number of Events)	Two-Day Mean Abnormal Return, % (is difference significant?)
Mikkelson and Partch (1986)	United States, 1972–1982	NA	Credit Agreements (155)	0.89***
James (1987)	United States, 1974–1983	Liabilities: 675 (212)	Bank Loan Agreement (80)	1.93***
Slovin, Sushka, and Hudson (1988)	United States, 1982–1985	Market Equity:[b] 7,303	Commercial Paper Offering (35) through Note Issuance Facility (18) or Letter of Credit Backed (17)	1.39**
Lummer and McConnell (1989)	United States, 1976–1986	NA	Bank Credit Agreement (728): Revised (357)/New (371)	0.61*** 1.24***/−0.01 (NA)
Slovin et al. (1992)	United States, 1980–1986	Market Equity: 281 (68 for initiations)	Loan Agreement (273) Renewals (124)/Initiations (149) Small Firms (156)/Large Firms (117)	1.30*** 1.55***/1.09*** (NA) 1.92***/0.48 (NA)
Best and Zhang (1993)	United States, 1977–1989	NA	Bank Credit Agreement (491) Renewals (304)/New (187) Renewals and Noisy[a] (156)/ New and Accurate[a] (187)	0.32** 1.97**/0.26 (no) 0.60**/−0.05 (*)
Billett et al. (1995)	United States, 1980–1989	Market Equity: 316 (79)	Loan (626) Renewals (187)/New Banks (51) Banks' Rating: AAA (78)/<BAA (29)	0.68*** 1.09***/0.64* (no) 0.63***/−0.57 (no)

(continued)

Table 2.1. (Continued)

Paper	Country, Period	Average (Median) Firm Size	Announcement (Number of Events)	Two-Day Mean Abnormal Return, % (is difference significant?)
Johnson (1997)	United States, 1980–1986	Market Equity: 290 (100)	Bank Credit Agreement (222) Small Bank (53)/Large Bank (54) Poorly Capitalized Bank (55)/Well Capitalized Bank (56)	1.18*** 0.90*/1.78*** (no) 0.59/2.17*** (no)
Preece and Mullineaux (1996)	United States, 1980–1987	Assets: 1,087 (188)	Credit Agreement (446) No Syndicate (121)/Syndicates (325) 2 and 3 Banks (60)/15 or More Banks (38)	1.00*** 1.78***/0.78*** (**) 1.43***/0.15 (NA)
Hadlock and James (1997)	United States, 1980–1993	Assets: 2,181 (238) 3,252 (485)/315 (143)	Bank Loan (120) Public Debt: With (64)/Without (56)	0.91*** 1.50*/0.19 (*)
Shockley and Thakor (1998)	United States, 1989–1990	NA	Loan Commitments Purchase (189) Usage Fees: With (137)/Without (52)	1.95*** 2.47*/0.54 (***)
Kracaw and Zenner (1998)	United States, 1980–1989	Market Equity: 296 (65)	Bank Loan (378) Clear and Potential Strong Interlocks (32)/No (346)	NA −0.89/0.96 (*)
Hadlock and James (2002)	United States, 1980–1993	Market Equity: 773 (93)	Bank Loan, Clean (144)	1.45***
Fields et al. (2006)	United States, 1980–2000	Market Equity: 4,615 (113) Assets Book: 1,111 (176)	Bank Loan Renewal (454) 1980–1990 (179)/1991–2000 (275)	0.80*** 1.31***/0.48 (NA)
Ross (2007)	United States, 2000–2003	NA	Bank Loan (1,064) New (74)/Favorable Revision (274)/Mixed Revision (44)	1.03*** 0.72/0.74***/4.39***

Study	Country, Period	Size	Type of announcement	Return
Aintablian and Roberts (2000)	Canada, 1988–1995	NA	Corporate Loan Announcement (137) Renewal (35)/New (69)/Restructuring (18)	1.22*** 1.26***/0.62 ***/3.45***
Andre et al. (2001)	Canada, 1982–1995	NA	Bank Credit Agreement (122) Lines of Credit before 1988 (13)/after 1988 (33) Term Loans before 1988 (22)/after 1988 (54)	2.27*** 4.82/0.32 1.14/3.30***
Mathieu, Robb, and Zhang (2002)	Canada, 1980–1999	NA	Bank Credit Agreement (456) Lines of Credit before 1990 (107)/ after 1990 (172) Term Loans before 1990 (69)/after 1990 (52)	1.73*** 2.50***/0.08 1.12**/2.70***
Fery et al. (2003)	Australia, 1983–1999	NA	Signed Credit Agreements (196) Published: Single Bank Relationship h18)/Multiple (22) Nonpublished: Single Relationship (56)/ Multiple (89)	0.38* 1.62**/0.89 0.02/0.25
Huang and Zhao (2006)	China, 2001–2006	Assets: 316 (154)	Bank Loan Announcements (261)	−0.38*

The table lists the main findings of event studies tracing the impact of bank loan announcements on the stock prices of announcing firms in order of publication date. The second column reports the country affiliation of the firms announcing the bank loans and the period during which the announcements were made. The third column lists both the size measure and the average (median) size of the firms in parentheses by the number of events. The fourth column reports the type of announcement followed in parentheses by the number of events. The second and third rows in each cell provide a breakdown of the announcements in key categories reported in the paper. The final column provides a 2-day mean percent abnormal return, in most cases over the [−1, 0] interval. The column also reports in parentheses whether the differences in mean abnormal returns between reported groups of announcements are significantly different from zero. NA, not available.
*** Significant at 1%, ** significant at 5%, * significant at 10%.
[a] Prediction.
[b] Their table 1b does not specify which firm size measure is used (the usage of market equity is possibly implied in the text).

Source: Updated from Ongena and Smith (2000a).

James finds that bank loan announcements are associated with *positive* and statistically significant firm stock price reactions that equal 193*** basis points (bp) in a two-day window,[3] while announcements of privately placed and public issues of debt experience zero or negative firm stock price reactions. This result holds independently of the type of loan, the default risk, and size of the borrower. The positive stock-price reaction supports the Fama (1985) argument that a bank loan provides accreditation for a firm's ability to generate a certain level of cash flows in the future.

Results in James (1987) spawned numerous other event studies. Table 2.1 exhibits many of the studies. As one example, Lummer and McConnell (1989) divide bank loan announcements into first-time loan initiations and follow-up loan renewals. Because loan initiations are loans to new borrowers while renewals are loans to established borrowers, the difference in stock price reactions between the two categories should act as a measure of the value of an established lending relationship. Consistent with this argument, Lummer and McConnell (1989) find that stock price reactions to bank loan announcements are driven by renewals. The abnormal returns in the event period associated with announcements of loan initiations are not statistically different from zero, while loan renewals are positive and statistically significant. With the exception of Aintablian and Roberts (2000), who use Canadian bank loan announcements and whose reported statistics imply that mean excess returns on new loans and renewals differ at a 10 percent level of significance, no study has duplicated the results in Lummer and McConnell (1989).

Slovin, Johnson, and Glascock (1992), Best and Zhang (1993), and Billett, Flannery, and Garfinkel (1995), for example, document positive and significant price reactions to both initiation and renewal announcements, but find no significant difference in price reactions between the two categories. Best and Zhang (1993) do find that price reactions to renewal announcements are significantly larger than initiations when analyst uncertainty about the loan customer is high. In their study, Billett et al. (1995) argue that the Lummer and McConnell (1989) results may be driven by their system for classifying loans into initiation and renewal categories. Overall, the positive wealth effect of loan announcements seems to hold, but the evidence on the differential wealth effects of loan renewals versus loan initiations is inconclusive.

---

3. As in the tables, asterisks by the coefficients indicate their significance levels: ***significant at 1%, **significant at 5%, *significant at 10%.

In addition, some other qualifications should be made as the entire literature on loan announcements suffers from a few clear but difficult to address shortcomings. First, the literature may be suffused with insidious reporting issues (James and Smith 2000) as both firms and newspaper editors may push only "positive news" stories; Australian evidence by Fery, Gasborro, Woodliff, and Zumwalt (2003) is suggestive in this regard. Even more basic selection issues may arise in the firm selection of financier (Cantillo and Wright 2000), the firm loan application, the bank offer, and the firm acceptance (Hadlock and James 2002). Second, it is not clear that initiations or renewals in the United States still result in excessive returns during the 1990s, a point made clear by Fields, Fraser, Berry, and Byers (2006) but also present in samples studied by Andre, Mathieu, and Zhang (2001) and Ongena, Roscovan, and Werker (2007a), raising some doubt about the robustness of the initial findings. Finally, there may be substantial differences across countries in loan announcement returns (Boscaljon and Ho 2005), though it remains unclear why exactly this is the case.

Despite these issues, loan announcement studies continue to inspire researchers and to inform the academic debate. Research is further pushed forward in multiple directions. Waheed and Mathur (1993) and DeGennaro, Elayan, and Wansley (1999), for example, study the impact of bank loan announcements on bank stocks, while Ongena et al. (2007a), for example, analyze the impact of the loan announcements on firm bond (and equity) returns. They find that though bank certification reduces information asymmetry, there is also a transfer of bondholder's welfare to the shareholders as a result of claim dilution. Their analysis then provides the first estimates of the *net* impact on firm value of bank loan announcements.

2.3.2. Bank Distress/Merger Announcements

Another important event study containing evidence on the value of bank relationships and hence the existence of switching costs is an innovative paper by Slovin, Sushka, and Polonchek (1993). They examine the influence of the 1984 impending insolvency of Continental Illinois on the stock price of firms with an ongoing lending relationship with that bank. Slovin et al. (1993) report an average abnormal 2-day return of -420^{***} bp around the insolvency announcement and an abnormal increase of 200^{**} bp upon the announcement of the FDIC rescue. They argue that such large price changes are estimates of the potential value tied directly to this specific firm–bank relationship. The existence of these quasi rents implies that borrowers are bank stakeholders.

There are many event studies that considered bank distress/merger announcements and have sought to replicate or extend the initial results by Slovin et al. (1993).[4] We summarize the results in table 2.2. All studies focus on countries other than the United States, and many trace the impact on the borrowers' stock prices of bank events other than distress such as scandals, transfers, and bank mergers that could also be unsettling to the borrower–bank relationship. (Dahiya, Saunders, and Srinivasan [2003] complement these results by studying the reaction of banks stocks following firm distress.)

Most studies find smaller and seemingly more temporary effects than the initial −420*** bp documented by Slovin et al. (1993). In addition, the three studies that actually check whether returns differ between firms related to the affected banks and all other firms find that the differences are not significant (Ongena, Smith, and Michalsen 2003; Brewer, Genay, Hunter, and Kaufman 2003; Miyajima and Yafeh (2007). Of course, the different results across the various studies may stem from heterogeneity in the value of the specific bank relationships that are being considered or because the banks that failed were many or large. Indeed, if a large bank (or many banks) fails because of an exogenous shock, its many borrowers may find it easy to find a new bank, even when not identifiable as former customers of the failed bank, because the improvement of the borrower pool may ameliorate adverse selection, allowing other banks to ease their lending standards (Detragiache, Garella, and Guiso 2000; Hainz 2005; a related argument with respect to new borrowers is in Dell'Ariccia and Marquez 2006).

2.3.3. Long-Run Impact of Bank Distress on Firm Performance

Complementary to event studies—which look at immediate stock price reactions—are methods that investigate the long-term performance of firms whose banks are affected by distress or default (table 2.3). Kang and Stulz (2000) show that Japanese firms with relatively more debt stemming from bank loans in 1989 (a year during which Japanese banks in general were negatively affected) performed worse from 1990 to 1993 and also invested less than other firms did. Similarly, Yao and Ouyang (2007) find that Japanese firms in which the main bank owned a larger proportion of equity also performed worse (but surprisingly borrowed and invested more) than other

---

4. See, e.g., Becher (2000) for a summary of the studies of the effects of bank mergers on the stocks of the merging banks and their rivals.

Table 2.2. Bank Distress and Bank Merger Announcements

Paper	Country, Period	Average (Median) Firm Size	Announcement (Events), Affected Borrowers	Two-Day Mean Abnormal Return, % "Which firms suffer the least?" (Difference)
Slovin et al. (1993)	United States, 1984	E: 1,085 (692)	Continental Illinois Distress (1) 29 Firms (Direct Lender/Lead Manager)	−4.16*** Firms with low leverage and other banks
Hwan Shin, Fraser, and Kolari (2003)	Japan, 19.08.99	S: 790 (716)[a]	Three-Way Alliance (1) 570	−0.31*** Main bank, high debt, profitable
Chiou (1999)	Japan, 1997–98	A: 3,913 (1,110)	Daiwa Bank Scandal (1) 32 Main Bank Firms	−0.98*** Large firms and with No Main Bank
Brewer et al. (2003)	Japan, 1997–98	A: 1,450	Three Bank Failures (3) 327	0.17; −1.32***; −0.49** Firms with alternative financing (no)
Miyajima and Yafeh (2007)	Japan, 1995–01	A: 2,293[a]	Actions (11), Downgrading (5), Mergers (3) $9,250 + 4,016 + 2,606$	NA; −3.1[NA]; 0 Large, profitable, technology, low debt, bonds (No)
Bae, Kang, and Lim (2002)	South Korea, 1997–98	BA: 404	Negative Bank News (113) 486	−1.26*** Healthy, unconstrained firms
Sohn (2002)	South Korea, 1998	A: 324[a]	Closure/Transfer of Five Banks (1) 118	−4.85*** Firms with no prior relationship
Bonin and Imai (2007)	South Korea, 1997	NA	Two Banks/Foreign Sales Events 106	−2** Profitable, liquid, less bank-dependent firms
Karceski, Ongena, and Smith (2005)	Norway, 1983–00	S: ± 500	Completed Bank Mergers (22) 342 Acquirers, 78 Targets, 1,515 Rivals	0.29, −0.76**, 0.06 Firms with relationship with acquiring banks

(continued)

Table 2.2. (Continued)

Paper	Country, Period	Average (Median) Firm Size	Announcement (Events), Affected Borrowers	Two-Day Mean Abnormal Return, % "Which firms suffer the least?" (Difference)
Ongena et al. (2003)	Norway, 1988–91	S: 400	Bank Distress (6) 217 Main Bank Firms	−1.7** Equity-issuing firms with undrawn credit (No)
Djankov, Jindra, and Klapper (2005)	Indonesia, Thailand, South Korea, 1997–99	NA	Closures (52) Foreign Sales (209) Domestic Mergers (92) Nationalizations (94)	−3.94*** −1.05* −1.27 3.14*** Large Firms (No)

The table lists the main findings of event studies tracing the impact of bank distress or bank merger announcements on the stock prices of borrowing firms. The papers are listed according to country size and sample period (the most recent samples are ranked first). The second column reports the country affiliation of the affected firms and the period during which the announcements were made. The third column lists both the size measure and the average (median) size of the firms in millions of U.S. dollars. A, assets; BA, book assets; E, equity; S, sales. The fourth column reports the type of announcement and the number of events (first row) and the number of affected borrowers (second row). The final column provides on the first row a 2-day mean percent abnormal return, in most cases over either [−1,0] or [0, 1] interval. If 2-day CARs are not reported over either interval, the shortest reported interval including either one of these 2-day periods is used. The second row provides a breakdown of the announcements in key categories reported in the paper (in parentheses we report whether the differences in mean abnormal returns between reported groups of announcements are significantly different from zero) or key results from any cross-sectional exercises reported in the paper as an answer to the question "Which firms suffer the least?" Between brackets we report if abnormal returns differ between affected and unaffected firms (i.e., firms not borrowing from the affected bank at the time of the announcement). NA, not available.

[a] Our calculations.

*** Significant at 1%, ** significant at 5%, * significant at 10%.

Source: Updated from Ongena and Smith (2000a).

Table 2.3. Studies on the Impact of Bank Failures and Distress on Borrowing Firm Performance

Paper	Country, Period	Average (Median) Firm Size	Type of Default/Distress, Number of Banks, Number of Affected Borrowers	Impact on Performance Measure, % "Which firms suffer the least?" Difference Affected/Unaffected Firms
Hori (2005)	Japan, 1995–00	Sales: 16 (5) Employees: 39 (16)	Failure of Hokkaido Takushoku Bank 1 2,247 Main Bank/3,662 2nd Bank	Profit/Capital: −1.0% Highly rated; transferred to other bank No Difference
Gan (2007)	Japan, 1994–98	All Publicly Listed Firms	Bank Real Estate Exposure (Price Decrease) ? 7,452	Investment / Capital: −0.5%*/% Bank Real Estate Assets Liquid, growth firms without real estate holdings Significant
Yao and Ouyang (2007)	Japan, 1990–92	Sales: 2	1990–1992 Shock Period "All" 449 (Main Bank Ownership > Median)	Firm's 3-Year Cumulative Return: −8% Firms with less bank loans/debt Significant
Ongena et al. (2003)	Norway, 1988–91	Sales: 400	Bank Failures 6 217 Main Bank Firms	Firms That Leave: −5.8% Profits, −8.7% Tobin's-Q Firms That Stay NA

(continued)

Table 2.3. (*Continued*)

Paper	Country, Period	Average (Median) Firm Size	Type of Default/Distress, Number of Banks, Number of Affected Borrowers	Impact on Performance Measure, % "Which firms suffer the least?" Difference Affected/Unaffected Firms
Joeveer (2007)	Estonia, 1998	Sales: 2 (0.5)	Bank Failure 1 119 (114 in Control Group)	Probability of Survival: −13% NA Significant
Habyarimana (2006)	Uganda, 1998–99	Employees: 134	Closure of Banks (Imprudent Practices) 4 70	Annual Growth: −2.3%*** Firms not owned by insiders, low debt Significant

The table lists the main findings of studies tracing the impact of bank failures on the performance of borrowing firms. The papers are listed according to country size and sample period (the most recent samples are ranked first). The second column reports the country affiliation of the affected firms and the period during which the bank defaults occurred. The third column lists both the size measure and the average (median) size of the firms in millions of U.S. dollars. The fourth column reports the type of default (first row), number of banks (second row), and number of affected borrowers (third row). The final column provides the percent impact on a performance measure (first row), key results from any cross-sectional exercises reported in the paper as an answer to the question "Which firms suffer least?" (second row), and whether performance differs between affected and unaffected firms (i.e., firms not borrowing from the affected bank at the time of the announcement; third row).

*** Significant at 1%, ** significant at 5%, * significant at 10%.

firms. Even more direct evidence is provided by Gan (2007), who reports that firms that maintained a borrowing relationship with Japanese banks with substantial real estate exposure were more negatively affected in their investments (compared to unaffected firms) following the dramatic real estate price deflation in Japan. Joeveer (2007) also finds that the default of their bank increased the probability of default of related Estonian firms, while Habyarimana (2006) finds that growth of small Ugandan firms was stunted by the closure of their bank.

Hori (2005), on the other hand, finds no difference between firms affected by the failure of Hokkaido Takushoku Bank and other unaffected firms, while Ongena et al. (2003) find that Norwegian firms that switched distressed banks in the long run actually underperformed those firms that stayed (as virtually all Norwegian banks failed, they could not compare affected with unaffected firms).

Consequently, the existing evidence suggests that firms perform worse in the long run after their relationship with a distressed bank comes under pressure. However, the results are still mixed and (to some extent) preliminary. More research seems warranted to isolate those firm and institutional characteristics that could be responsible for negative long-run effects of bank distress on firm performance.

3

The Industrial Organization
Approach to Banking

3.1. Introduction

In this chapter we review the different methodological approaches taken to address competition in general and banking in particular. We discuss the "traditional" and "new" empirical methods employed in industrial organization (IO), specifically applied to banking, and provide a detailed illustration in each section.[1] Again, we want to highlight that we do not discuss the first application of a particular method within the field of IO but highlight its first application to banking research.

We first discuss the traditional studies of structure-conduct-performance (SCP), bank efficiency, and economies of scale and scope. We then turn to the new empirical IO approaches taken by Panzar and Rosse (1987), Boone (2008), the conjectural variations, structural demand, and other structural models (sunk costs and entry). We highlight the strengths and weaknesses of these different approaches and are naturally drawn to focus on the differences in data requirements and treatment of endogeneity in each method.

Table 3.1 shows how research on banking competition has evolved over time. The table highlights that in the early 1990s an important change took place in modeling competition, measuring concentration and conduct, and arriving at fruitful applications. The literature basically abandoned the

---

1. For general overviews, see also Berger, Demirgüç-Kunt, Levine, and Haubrich (2004a) and Shaffer (2004). We mention more specific reviews in the text.

Table 3.1. Evolution of research on the impact of bank concentration and competition on bank performance.

Element	Time Period	
	Early 1990s	Current
Model	SCP Hypothesis	Various Models of Competition
Measures of Concentration	Herfindahl-Hirschman Index or Concentration Ratio for n banks	Bank Size and Type (Foreign, State) Broader Measures of Competition
Measures of Conduct	Bank Prices Bank Profitability	Bank Efficiency, Service Quality, Risk Firms' Access to Credit Banking System Stability
Empirical Models	Static Cross Section Short Run	Dynamic Effects over Time of Bank Consolidation
Data	U.S. Metropolitan Statistical Areas or Non-MSA Counties	Differently Defined U.S. Markets Other Countries

The table shows changes that took place in the literature investigating the impact of bank concentration and competition on bank performance and contrasts the models, the measures of concentration, the measures of conduct, the empirical models, and the data sources that were used in the early 1990s with those that are used today. HHI, Herfindahl-Hirschman Index.

Source: Berger et al. (2004a).

traditional SCP paradigm, stating that banks in less concentrated markets behave less competitively and capture more profits.

The literature has pushed in two directions since. One strand of the literature embarked on modeling market structure as endogenous. We review this part of the literature in this chapter. A second push in the literature intended to capture the "special nature of banking competition" by also looking at nonprice dimensions of banking products. Theoretical work tackled, for example, the availability of credit and the role bank–firm relationships play in overcoming asymmetric information problems. Consequently, in following chapters we focus our discussion of the methodologies and empirical findings in the literature dealing with competition and bank—firm relationships in chapter 4, competition and location in chapter 5, and competition and regulation in chapter 9.

3.2. Methodology: Measuring Banking Competition and Market Power

We start with a review of the different methodological approaches that have been employed to investigate banking competition.[2] This empirical

2. Our discussion is based partly on Degryse and Ongena (2008).

research can be subdivided into the more traditional IO and the new empirical IO (NEIO) approaches. Within the traditional methods, we distinguish between the structure-conduct-performance (SCP) analyses, studies of efficiency, and studies of scale and scope economies. The NEIO methods aim to measure the degree of competition directly. We differentiate between the approaches taken by Panzar and Rosse (1987), the Boone (2008) indicator, the conjectural variations models, structural demand models, and other structural models (sunk costs and entry) (for a review, see Bresnahan 1989). The usefulness of the different approaches hinges on data availability and the questions being addressed. The special nature of banking markets prompted the introduction of alternative and complementary approaches. For brevity's sake, we do not introduce these approaches in this methodology section (but we return to some of these developments in later sections).

3.2.1. Traditional Industrial Organization

3.2.1.1. Structure-Conduct-Performance

The SCP model is originally developed by Bain (1956). SCP research was quite popular until the beginning of the 1990s. Table 3.1 summarizes the characteristics of SCP research. The SCP hypothesis argues that higher concentration in the banking market causes less competitive bank conduct and leads to higher bank profitability (but lower performance from a social point of view). To test the SCP hypothesis, researchers typically regress a measure of bank performance, for example, bank profitability, on a proxy for market concentration, that is, an n-bank concentration ratio or a Herfindahl-Hirschman Index (HHI).[3] A representative regression specification equals

$$\Pi_{ijt} = \alpha_0 + \alpha_1 CR_{jt} + \sum_k \gamma_k X_{k,ijt} + \varepsilon_{ijt}, \tag{3.1}$$

where Π_{ijt} is a measure of bank i's profitability, in banking market j at time t, CR_{jt} is the measure of concentration in market j at time t, and $X_{k,ijt}$ stands for a k-vector control variables that may affect bank profits (e.g., variables that control for the profitability implications of risk taking). Banks operating in more concentrated markets are able (within the SCP paradigm) to set higher loan rates or lower deposit rates as a result of noncompetitive behavior or

---

3. See Alegria and Schaeck (2008) for a derivation of analytical relationships between the various concentration measures.

collusion. Hence, the SCP hypothesis implies that $\alpha_1 > 0$, that is, that higher market concentration implies more market power and higher bank profits. The market structure itself, however, is assumed to be exogenous.

The specification taking the market structure as exogenous and the resulting use of the HHI, for instance, have been criticized by Berg and Kim (1998), who estimate a multioutput conjectural variation type of a model to show that concentration must not preclude substantially competitive conduct. In fact, their study of multioutput oligopolies shows that the (Norwegian) retail loan market is plagued by market power whereas the wholesale loan market lacks such power, contrary to the HHI, which produces opposite results.[4]

Numerous studies document, for example, a positive statistical relationship between measures of market concentration and bank profitability. As Gilbert (1984) and Berger et al. (2004a) wrote excellent critical reviews of this early approach, there is no need to make another attempt in this setting (but we discuss some of the results later in this chapter). However, to illustrate SCP research in general, we briefly discuss Berger and Hannan (1989). While many studies focus on the *profitability*–concentration link, Berger and Hannan (1989) actually study the *deposit rate*–concentration link. Nevertheless their study is representative for the SCP approach given their measurement of concentration, reduced-form estimation, and interpretation.

Berger and Hannan (1989) study U.S. retail deposit markets. Their analysis covers 470 banks operating in 195 local banking markets offering six different deposit products. Using quarterly data from 1983Q3 to 1985Q4, they estimate the following specification:

$$r_{ijt} = \alpha_0 + \alpha_1 CR_{jt} + \sum_k \gamma_k X_{k,ijt} + \varepsilon_{ijt}, \tag{3.2}$$

where r_{ijt} is the interest rate paid on the retail deposit by bank i in banking market j at time t. The SCP hypothesis implies that $\alpha_1 < 0$, that is, that higher market concentration implies more market power and lower deposit rates.[5]

---

4. The calculated HHI of Berg and Kim (1998) for the Norwegian retail and wholesale loan markets averaged between 866 and 2,155, respectively, for the period 1990–92. The U.S. Department of Justice guidelines consider HHI < 1,000 as "unconcentrated" market and HHI > 1,800 as "highly concentrated" (Salop 1987).

5. In the *relative* market power hypothesis in Shepherd (1982) only banks, with large market shares and well-differentiated products enjoy market power in pricing.

Researchers have employed many different concentration measures to capture noncompetitive behavior. Berger and Hannan use both a three-bank concentration ratio (CR3) and the HHI.[6] Their results overall show a negative impact of market concentration on deposit rates, independent of the concentration measure being used. For example, moving from the least concentrated market toward the most concentrated market in their sample yields a reduction of about 47–52 basis points (bp) on money market deposit accounts.

While the early SCP approach was successful in documenting the importance of market structure for various bank interest rates, Berger et al. (2004a) surely presents the consensus view when they write that the empirical banking literature "has now advanced well past this simple approach." We summarize the notable differences between the SCP and more recent studies both within an SCP framework and beyond in table 3.1.

3.2.1.2. Studies of Bank Efficiency

The efficiency hypothesis provides an alternative explanation for the positive link between bank profitability and concentration or market share. The efficiency hypothesis (see Demsetz 1973; Peltzmann 1977) entails that more efficient banks will gain market share. Hence market concentration is driven (endogenously) by bank efficiency. Two types of efficiency can be distinguished (Berger 1995). In an *X-efficiency* narrative, banks with superior management and/or production technologies enjoy higher profits and as a result grow larger market shares. Alternatively, some banks may produce at more *efficient scales* than others, again leading to higher per unit profits, larger market shares, and higher market concentration.

The positive relationship between structure and performance reported in the SCP literature is spurious in the two versions of the efficiency hypothesis, as both structure and performance are determined by efficiency. Initially, the empirical literature aimed to disentangle the SCP and efficiency hypotheses through the following regression specification:

$$\Pi_{ijt} = \alpha_0 + \alpha_1 CR_{jt} + \alpha_2 MS_{ijt} \sum_k \gamma_k X_{k,ijt} + \varepsilon_{ijt}, \qquad (3.3)$$

6. As control variables, they include time dummies, the 1-year growth in market deposits, the proportion of bank branches in total number of branches of financial institutions (including savings and loan branches), a wage rate, per capita income, and a metropolitan statistical area dummy variable.

with MS_{ijt} the market share of bank i in market j for period t (the notation for the other variables remains the same).

SCP implies that $\alpha_1 > 0$, whereas both efficiency hypotheses imply that $\alpha_2 > 0$. Most studies find a positive and statistically significant α_2, but an α_1 close to zero and insignificant. These findings support both efficiency hypotheses, that is, larger market shares go together with higher profitability.

Berger (1995) goes one step further than the standard bank efficiency study and aims to further differentiate between the SCP and efficiency hypotheses by including direct measures of both X-efficiency and scale efficiency into the regression specification (as additional variables in the $X_{k,ijt}$ vector). He argues that after controlling for efficiency, MS_{ijt} captures the relative market power of banks. Berger derives both efficiency measures from the estimation of a translog cost function. X-efficiency is separated from random noise by assuming that X-efficiency differences will persist over time while random noise will not. The X-efficiency measure for bank i then equals the ratio of the predicted costs for the most efficient bank in the sample to the predicted costs for bank i for any given vector of outputs and inputs. Berger (1995) also computes scale efficiencies on the basis of the translog cost function by taking the ratio of the minimum predicted average costs for bank i to the actual predicted average costs for bank i given output mix and input prices. By construction, both measures range between 0 and 1.

Berger (1995) estimates a cost function using data from 4,800 U.S. banks during the 1980s. Mean scale inefficiencies amount to > 15 percent. Including both computed efficiency measures in the performance equation that also contains market share and concentration, Berger finds that in 40 out of 60 regressions, market share actually retains its positive sign. However, the economic significance of market share seems very small: a 1 percent increase in market share boosts return on assets by < 0.1 percent. Nevertheless, Berger interprets these findings as evidence in favor of the relative market power hypothesis: market share does represent market power of larger banks, and their market power may be grounded in advertising, local networks, or business relationships. Results further show that X-efficiency also contributes positively in explaining profits, whereas the results on scale efficiency are mixed and never economically important.

Studies of operational efficiency of financial institutions are also related to the efficiency hypotheses. Operational efficiency requires (1) optimization of the input mix to avoid excessive input usage (technical X-inefficiency) or suboptimal input allocation (allocative X-inefficiency), and (2) production at an optimal scale and in an optimal mix to achieve economies of scale and scope.

Berg and Kim (1994) criticize the way optimal scale and efficiency measures have been estimated and applied as described in the aforementioned studies. They document the different scale estimates emanating from different market structures implicitly assumed in the models estimated. Moreover, using a "thick frontier" applied to virtually all (173) Norwegian banks in 1988 they show that the measured inefficiency, as well as its ranking, is not behavior/conduct independent. Thus, the major point they stress is that conduct has an important effect on both (in)efficiency and scale measurements and therefore the estimation of such should not be carried out independently of market structure and conduct.

For more on X-efficiency studies analyzing financial institutions, we refer the reader to surveys by Allen and Rai (1996), Molyneux, Altunbas, and Gardener (1996), Berger and Humphrey (1997), or work by Turati (2001). We turn to economies of scale and scope in the next subsection.

3.2.1.3. Studies of Economies of Scale and Scope

Studies of economies of scale and scope in banking address the question whether financial institutions produce the optimal output mix both in terms of size and composition. In an early paper, Kim (1986) develops cost function separability restrictions amenable for testing the existence of a consistent banking output aggregate. He concludes that such an aggregate fails to exist and thus the specification of a multioutput technology and its resulting economies of scope measure is necessary.

Allen and Rai (1996), for example, estimate economies of scale and scope while controlling for X-efficiency. In particular, they estimate the following equation:

$$\ln(TC_{it}) = f(y_{it}, p_{it}) + \varepsilon_{it}, \tag{3.4}$$

where TC_{it}, y_{it}, and p_{it} are total costs, outputs, and input prices of bank i in at time t, respectively. They consider only one market (hence, j is dropped as a subscript). ε_{it} is a composite error term that can be decomposed into statistical noise and X-inefficiency. Allen and Rai pursue two identification strategies. First, they follow the so-called *stochastic cost frontier* approach (see also, e.g., Mester 1993), whereby the error term is assumed to consist of random noise and a one-sided inefficiency measure. Second, they estimate a *distribution-free model*, whereby X-efficiency differences are assumed to persist over time while random noise is not.

Allen and Rai (1996) estimate a translog cost function with total costs due to labor, capital, and borrowed funds, employing data from 24 countries for the period 1988–92. They obtain the price of labor by dividing staff expenses by the total number of employees; the price of fixed capital by dividing capital equipment and occupancy expenses by fixed assets; and interest costs by taking total interest expenses over total interest-bearing liabilities.

They distinguish between countries with and without universal banking (i.e., so-called *separated* banking occurs in countries that prohibit the functional integration of commercial and investment banking) and between small and large banks (smaller or larger in asset size than the median bank in each country).

Allen and Rai (1996) find evidence of significant scale economies for *small* banks in all countries. Large banks in separated markets on the other hand show significant diseconomies of scale amounting to 5 percent of optimal output levels. They do not find any evidence of significant economies of scope.[7] Many other papers present comparable results on economies of scale and scope (for detailed reviews, see Berger and Humphrey 1997; Cavallo and Rossi 2001).

3.2.2. New Empirical Industrial Organization

A fundamental criticism leveled against the SCP and the efficiency hypotheses relates to the embedded—assumed—one-way causality from market structure to performance. In other words, most SCP studies do *not* take into account the conduct of the banks in the market and the impact of performance of the banks on market structure. In fact, studies that have attempted to determine the degree of competition relying on various indexes of concentration such as the C4, the HHI, and the like, reach conflicting and troublesome results. Carbo, Humphrey, Maudos, and Molyneux (in press) document that the coefficients of determination among these various indexes for both the within and between countries are very weak (most < 40 percent). They use cross-country European data for the 1995–01 period. The

---

7. Work by Vander Vennet (2002) revisits the issue employing a large European data set. He distinguishes between universal banks, financial conglomerates (institutions that offer the entire range of financial services), and specialized banks. In contrast to previous studies, he nicely allows for heterogeneity in bank types within each country. In line with Allen and Rai (1996), he finds large unexploited *scale* economies for the small-specialized banks. But, in addition Vander Vennet (2002) also reports unexploited *scope* economies for the smallest specialized banks and for the largest financial conglomerates and universal banks.

implication of these results is that the SCP nexus may not generate consistent results which make the assessment of the competitive state of the banking sector difficult to determine.

New empirical industrial organization (NEIO) circumvents this problem and does not try to infer the degree of competition from "indirect proxies" such as market structure or market shares, or argue that market structure is the result of the degree of competition. Indeed, NEIO aims to infer firms' conduct directly—without even taking into account market structure— employing a variety of alternative methodologies with sometimes substantially different data requirements. We highlight a number of approaches.

3.2.2.1. Panzar and Rosse (1987)

Panzar and Rosse (1987) present a reduced form approach using industry or bank-level data to discriminate between perfect competition, monopolistic competition, and monopoly. The Panzar and Rosse methodology investigates the extent to which changes in factor input prices are reflected in equilibrium industry or bank-specific revenues. In particular, bringing the empirical Panzar and Rosse methodology to banking can be obtained by the following revenue equation:

$$\ln(INTR_{it}) = \alpha + \sum_f \beta_f \ln(P_{f,it}) + \sum_k \gamma_k X_{k,it} + \varepsilon_{it}, \qquad (3.5)$$

where $INTR_{it}$ is the ratio of total interest revenue to total assets of bank i at time t. $P_{f,it}$ and $X_{k,it}$ denote the (price of) factor input f and control variable k, respectively, of bank i at time t. The application may consider one market only, or many markets (in which case j should be added as subscript). Moreover, some authors use variables that are not scaled and/or total revenues (including non-interest-rate revenues) as left-hand-side variables. The Panzar and Rosse (1987) H-statistic can be computed as

$$H = \sum_f \beta_f. \qquad (3.6)$$

Hence, H is the sum of the elasticities of the (scaled) total interest revenue of the banks with respect to their factor input prices. In most studies, three different input prices are considered: (1) the deposit rate, measured by the ratio of annual interest expenses to total assets; (2) wages, measured by the ratio of personnel expenses to total assets; and (3) price of equipment or fixed capital, measured by the ratio of capital expenditures and other expenses to total assets.

A monopoly situation yields an H-statistic that can be negative or zero. What will happen to a monopolist's revenues when all factor prices increase with 1 percent? For a monopolist such increase in factor prices leads to lower revenues (since the price elasticity of demand exceeds one). In other words, the sum of the elasticities should be negative. Perfect competition implies an H-statistic equal to 1. Indeed, an increase in input prices augments both marginal costs and total revenues to the same extent as the original increase in input prices. Monopolistic competition yields values of H between 0 and 1. Banks will produce more but less than would be optimal in each individual case, leading to an H-statistic between 0 and 1. It is worth stressing, though, that the interpretation of competition based on the H-statistic requires that the banking sector be in a long-run equilibrium (Nathan and Neave 1989).

Many studies bring the Panzar and Rosse (1987) methodology to banking. Bikker and Haaf (2002) offer a broad review of the results of many other studies (their table 4). By far the most comprehensive application to date of the Panzar and Rosse (1987) methodology is a paper by Claessens and Laeven (2004). They compute the Panzar and Rosse H-statistic for 50 countries for the period 1994–01. They exclude countries with less than 20 banks or 50 bank-year observations but still end up with 35,834 bank-year observations in total.

The empirical results by Claessens and Laeven (2004) show that most banking markets are actually characterized by monopolistic competition with H-statistics ranging between 0.6 and 0.8. In addition, Claessens and Laeven aim to identify factors that determine banking competition across countries by regressing the estimated country H-statistics on a number of country characteristics. They find no evidence of a negative relationship between bank system concentration and H, but find that fewer entry and activity restrictions result in higher H-statistics and hence more competition.

Typically, researchers have employed a scaled variant of the interest rate revenues, INTR (i.e., interest rate revenues to total assets), in the implementation of the Panzar and Rosse methodology as well as scaled right-hand-side variables. This approach has been criticized by Bikker, Spierdijk, and Finnie (2006), who argue that scaling changes the nature of the model as it transforms the revenue equation into a pricing equation, leading to a systematic distortion in the measurement of competition. Their results employing unscaled variables show that the adjusted Panzar and Rosse results are more tilted toward monopoly compared to the regressions employing the scaled variables.

The Panzar and Rosse methodology seems well designed to compare competition across banking markets. Data requirements are quite low, and the necessary data are readily available in many countries. And as already discussed, Claessens and Laeven (2004) nicely exploit this attractive feature of the methodology and document that entry barriers, not market structure, determine competition in most banking markets.

3.2.2.2. The Boone (2008) Competition Indicator
Boone (2008) introduces a new way to measure competition. He starts from the notion that in a more competitive market firms are punished more harshly in terms of profits for being inefficient. Boone develops a concept that wants to capture the two ways in which competition in a market can be intensified. The first way is a fall in entry barriers. The lower the entry barriers, the more firms should enter and the more competitive the industry should be. This intuition underlies the use of concentration indices like the HHI.

The problem with concentration measures is that they cannot distinguish with the second idea being more aggressive conduct by incumbents. As firms behave more aggressively and competition increases, firms leave the market and concentration increases. Boone's indicator allows for both forces at work in his measure of competition. To this end, he develops the idea of the elasticity of profits toward marginal costs or "profit elasticity". Boone, van Ours, and van der Wiel (2007) argue that profit elasticity picks up both forms of changes in competition correctly. In particular, they postulate the following specification:

$$\ln \pi_i = \alpha - \beta \ln(c_i), \tag{3.7}$$

where β gives the profit elasticity, that is, the percentage drop in profits of bank i as a result of a percentage increase in bank i's marginal costs. The larger is β, the more intense the competition. Boone et al. (2007) review how several theoretical models show that both changes in entry conditions and strategic behavior influence in the correct way the profit elasticity.

The interested reader may observe that the profit elasticity is reminiscent of the Panzar and Rosse H-statistic that was based on factor price elasticities, discussed above. The Boone indicator has some advantages and disadvantages compared to the H-statistic. First, while the H-statistic allows to exclude certain states of competition, an increase cannot be unambiguously interpreted as more competition. This does not hold for Boone's profit elasticity indicator. Second, both measures of competition have different data requirements. Often data on input factor prices are not available, whereas measures about costs may be available or can be estimated.

Van Leuvensteijn, Bikker, van Rixtel, and Sørensen (2007) bring equation 3.7 to the data for several countries. They introduce two modifications, however. The first is that they employ a translog cost function to estimate the marginal cost c_i, while Boone et al. (2007) employed average variable costs as a proxy. Second, van Leuvensteijn et al. (2007) use the bank's market shares as a left-hand-side variable instead of profits. They apply this methodology for several product categories for the time period 1994–04.

They find that competition in the bank loan market varies considerably across countries. In particular, the bank loan market in the Euro area is less competitive than the U.S. market—where $\hat{\beta}$ equals 5.41***—but more competitive than in the United Kingdom ($\hat{\beta} = 1.05^{***}$) and Japan ($\hat{\beta} = 0.72^{***}$). Within the Euro area, the German and Spanish market seems most competitive ($\hat{\beta}$ equals 3.38*** and 4.15***, respectively) and least competitive in France ($\hat{\beta} = 0.90^{***}$). Further work may be required to address the appropriateness of the Boone competition indicator. For example, it may be interesting to investigate whether this indicator is not correlated with other not controlled for determinants.

3.2.2.3. Conjectural-Variations Method

Another methodology to infer the degree of competition was introduced by Iwata (1974), Bresnahan (1982), and Lau (1982). This methodology is often referred to as the conjectural-variations method. It is based on the idea that a bank when choosing its output takes into account the "reaction" of rival banks. The equilibrium oligopoly price is then characterized by the following first-order condition:

$$P(Q, Y; \alpha) + \lambda Q P(Q, Y; \alpha) = C(Q, Z; \beta), \tag{3.8}$$

where P is the market's equilibrium price, $P(Q, Y, \alpha)$ is the market inverse demand function, Q the market level quantity, and $C(Q, Z, \beta)$ is the market marginal cost. α and β are vectors of unknown parameters associated with demand and costs, respectively. Y and Z are a vector of variables that affect demand and costs, respectively. λ is the conjectural elasticity of total bank industry output to variation of bank i output; that is, $\lambda = \frac{\partial Q}{\partial Q_i} \frac{Q_i}{Q}$. In other words, λ is the perceived response of industry output to a change in quantity by bank i (for more on this methodology, see Vives 1999).

One can also compute the conjectural elasticity or conduct parameter as

$$\lambda = \eta(P) \left[\frac{P - MC}{P} \right], \tag{3.9}$$

where $\eta(P)$ is the price elasticity of demand, and $MC[= C(Q, Z; \beta)]$ the marginal cost. This implies that λ is the elasticity-adjusted Lerner index. An attractive feature of the conjectural variations model is the possibility to write different types of competition compactly. It nests the joint profit maximization ($\lambda = 1$), perfect competition ($\lambda = 0$), and the Cournot equilibrium or zero-conjectural variations model ($\lambda = 1/I$ with I the number of firms in the market; that is, the perceived variation of other participants in the industry to changes in bank i's output is zero).[8]

Shaffer (1993) applies this methodology to banking (see also Berg and Kim 1994; for an earlier application, see Spiller and Favaro 1984). He approximates the demand function as

$$Q = a_0 + a_1 P + a_2 Y + a_3 PZ + a_4 Z + a_5 PY + a_6 YZ + e, \tag{3.10}$$

with Z is an additional exogenous variable such as the price of a substitute for banking services, and e an error term.[9] He derives the unobserved marginal cost from estimating a translog cost function:

$$\ln TC = \beta_0 + \beta_1 \ln Q + \beta_2 (\ln Q)^2 + \beta_3 \ln W_1 + \beta_4 \ln W_2 + \beta_5 (\ln W_1)^2 / 2$$
$$+ \beta_6 (\ln W_2)^2 / 2 + \beta_7 \ln W_1 \ln W_2 + \beta_8 \ln Q \ln W_1 + \beta_9 \ln Q \ln W_2, \tag{3.11}$$

where TC is total cost, Q is output, and W_1, W_2 are input prices. Assuming that banks are input price-takers, the supply relation becomes

$$P = \left[\frac{-\lambda Q}{a_1 + a_3 Z + a_5 Y} \right] + MC. \tag{3.12}$$

---

8. The conjectural variations approach has been subject to a number of important criticisms. Corts (1999), e.g., argues that the conduct parameter λ may not only hinge on the firm's static first-order condition, but also on the dynamics, i.e., the incentive compatibility constraints associated with collusion. In the dynamic case, the estimated λ may be biased when the incentive compatibility constraints are a function of demand shocks.

9. Shaffer introduces interaction terms between the price P and the exogenous variables Y and Z, as well as between these exogenous variables, in order to capture the rotation of the demand curve to identify λ.

An important issue is whether banks can be viewed as price takers in the input market. The "price taking" assumption is especially problematic in deposit markets, where banks may enjoy market power. If this is indeed the case then the estimated degree of market power λ will be overestimated, as some of the "input market power" will wrongly be attributed to market power on the asset side.

Shaffer (1993) applied this specific conjectural variations method to the Canadian banking sector, using annual data from 1965 to 1989. The application is attractive as "Canada . . . had but twelve chartered banks in 1980 [and] six of these banks have dominated the Canadian financial sector since the 1930s" (p. 50). The low number of players for a long time raised concerns about competition in the Canadian financial sector. And that was (is) also increasingly the case in other parts of the world where bank consolidation gathered momentum.

In his study, Shaffer (1993) follows the so-called intermediation approach of banking. According to this view, banks use labor and deposits to originate loans. The quantity of output Q is the dollar value of assets and the price P is the interest rate earned on assets. Input prices are the annual wage rate and the deposit rate.[10] The exogenous variables are output and the 3-month Treasury bill rate. The regression results show that λ is not significantly different from zero, implying that the estimates are consistent with perfect competition. Shaffer (1989) actually shows that U.S. banking markets are even more competitive than Cournot competition (λ is again close to zero and not statistically significant).

Shaffer's paper focuses on one "aggregate" market and to implement his approach it suffices to have aggregate data. In this aggregate setting λ captures the "average industry" market power. Shaffer's methodology has been extended to allow for heterogeneity within and between different sectors and countries and to include bank heterogeneity. The potential to include bank heterogeneity and estimate specific λ_{ij} is an attractive feature of the conjectural variations methodology.

The aforementioned attractiveness of estimating λ for different output segments or sectors is reflected in a study by Berg and Kim (1998). They estimate λ jointly for both the retail and wholesale segments of the loan market. Employing panel data pertaining to all Norwegian banks between 1990 and 1992, they clearly document the market for retail loans to exhibit strong

---

10. In certain specifications, researchers also include the price of capital, since this price may vary over time.

market power whereas the market for wholesale loans is characterized by a competitive structure. It is emphasized that these findings are in sharp contrast to those arrived at when using the HHI of concentration, which again brings up the troublesome use of market structure indices emanating from the SCP nexus for assessing the competitive nature of the banking sector.

3.2.2.4. Structural Demand Models

Another strand of the NEIO uses characteristics-based demand systems. Dick (2002), for example, estimates a demand model for deposit services following a methodology prevalent in the discrete choice literature.[11] Consumers choose for a particular bank based on prices and bank characteristics. In particular, Dick starts from a consumer's utility function to derive a demand model and introduces product differentiation through bank heterogeneity, and then adds a model of firm conduct in order to define the price-cost margin. She defines the relevant banking market as geographically local, be it either a metropolitan statistical area (MSA) or a non-MSA rural county. Her study considers only commercial banks but incorporates other financial institutions as providing the outside good in the demand model. Market shares are computed on the basis of dollar deposits at each bank branch in the United States.

Consumers c and banks i populate markets j. The utility a consumer c derives from depositing at bank i stems both from individual and product characteristics. Formally, consumer c derives indirect utility from choosing bank i's services in market j. The consumer utility includes both the mean utility from buying at bank i in market j, δ_{ij}, and a mean zero random disturbance, ε_{cij}:

$$u_{cij} \equiv \delta_{ij} + \varepsilon_{cij} \equiv p_{ij}^d \alpha^d - p_{ij}^s \alpha^s + X_{k,ij}\beta + \xi_i + \varepsilon_{cij} \qquad (3.13)$$

p_{ij}^d represents the deposit rate paid by bank i in market j; p_{ij}^s are the service charges on deposits by bank i in market j; $X_{k,ij}$ is a vector capturing k observed product characteristics for the (singular) product offered by bank i in market j; ξ_i are the unobserved bank product characteristics. The taste parameters to be estimated are α^d, α^s, and β.

A consumer c chooses a bank i in market j if and only if $u_{cij} \geq u_{crj}$, for $r = 0$ to I_j, with 0 the outside good and I_j the number of banks in

---

11. See also, e.g., Molnár, Nagy, and Horvath (2007) and Molnár (2007) for an application of discrete choice models to banking.

market j. Making assumptions on the distribution of ε_{ci} then allows obtaining a closed form solution for the market share of bank i. A multinomial logit specification is obtained when assuming that ε_{ci} is identically and independently distributed (i.i.d). extreme value, yielding bank i's market share s_i in market j:

$$s_i = \frac{\exp(\delta_i)}{\sum_{r=0}^{I_j} \exp(\delta_r)}. \tag{3.14}$$

Other assumptions may yield a nested logit model.[12]

Dick (2002) estimates this discrete choice model on U.S. data for the period 1993–99. Her results indicate that consumers respond significantly to changes in deposit rates but to a lesser extent to changes in account fees. Bank characteristics such as geographic diversification, density of the local branch network, bank age, and size increase the attractiveness of a bank to consumers. The computed price elasticities in the logit model are around 6 for the deposit rate but <6 for the account fees. The implied price cost-margin is 10 percent for the deposit rate and 25 percent for the service fees.

3.2.2.5. Other Structural Models

3.2.2.5.1. *Sunk-Cost Models*   Sutton (1991) finds that some product markets remain concentrated even when growing in size. Vives (2000) introduces endogenous sunk costs models to banking. He argues that investments in information technology become more important when markets grow. When the level of these "quality investments" can be chosen by individual banks and a bank's market share is sufficiently responsive to these investments, then a new global marketplace with only a few global players may arise. The outcome of this "competition through endogenous sunk costs" is that the number of "dominant" banks in the market remains approximately the same and that only the number of "fringe" banks will increase in market size.

Dick (2007) investigates a cross-sectional sample of U.S. MSAs. As endogenous sunk costs, Dick takes bank branch and automatic teller

---

12. The idea in the nested logit model is that consumer tastes are correlated across bank products i. Making a priori groups G, a product i belonging to one of the groups then provides a utility to consumer c equal to $u_{ij} \equiv \delta_{ij} + \zeta_{cg} + [1 - \sigma]\varepsilon_{cij}$, where ζ_{cg} denotes the group specific component for individual c.

machine (ATM) networks, advertising, and branding expenses. She defines banks that hold jointly more than 50 percent of market deposits as the dominant banks. All other banks are her fringe banks. She finds that there is a lower bound to concentration and that markets remain concentrated across all market sizes. She also reports in line with Sutton (1991) that the number of dominant banks remains unchanged in market size and is independent of the total number of banks in the MSA. Finally, she finds that the level of bank quality investments increases in market size, and dominant banks offer higher quality than fringe banks.

A further illustration can be found in Dick (2006). In this paper, she explores the impact of the Riegle-Neal Interstate Banking and Branching Efficiency Act of 1994 on various aspects of banking markets. In particular, she examines the effects of the Act on bank market concentration, structure, and service quality, by comparing markets in 1993 and 1999. She finds that market concentration at the regional level increased dramatically, but that market structure at the MSA level, that is, the presence of a few dominant banks, remained unchanged. However, nationwide branching did lead to increases in product quality as consumers can now enjoy expanded branch and ATM network coverage.

3.2.2.5.2. *Structural Models of Entry* A number of papers aim to infer competitive behavior from observed industry structure that produces insights about unobserved firm profitability. The underlying idea in these so-called "structural models of entry" is that the entry decisions of potential competitors and the continuation decisions of the incumbent firms only occur in case these decisions are actually profitable. The entry decision hinges on the level of fixed costs, the nature of postentry competition, and the (future) entry or continuation decisions of other firms. A crucial advantage of the structural entry models is that detailed data on prices and volumes are not necessary for the analysis. We refer the interested reader to Bresnahan and Reiss (1991, 1994) for more on this methodology. Important starting assumptions are that (1) markets are nonoverlapping; that is, consumers do not buy from banks outside the geographically defined market; and (2) all banks are competing with each other.

Cohen and Mazzeo (2003) bring this structural methodology to banking data. More formally, they let $\Pi_i(I; X_k)$ be the expected long-run profits for bank i (or branch i) that chooses to be active in a certain market j. I is the number of banks active in market j (where for brevity subscript j is dropped), and X_k captures a k-vector of demand and cost shifters. Not operating in a market yields zero profits. The equilibrium condition then requires that

$$\Pi_i(I) \geq 0 > \Pi_i(I+1). \tag{3.15}$$

Entry of one additional bank in the market where I banks are already active implies that competition would become too intense given the market characteristics to generate positive profits. Cohen and Mazzeo (2003), following Bresnahan and Reiss (1991), take the following profit function to capture bank behavior in a symmetric equilibrium in market j:

$$\Pi_j = (\text{Variable Profits}_j * \text{Market Size}_j) - \text{Entry Cost}_j \tag{3.16}$$

In this setup, variable profits hinge on the number of banks in the market:

$$\Pi_{i,j} = X_k\beta - \mu_I + \varepsilon_j, \tag{3.17}$$

with X_k exogenous market factors, μ_I the effect of I competitors on per-bank profits, and ε_j a market-level error term assumed to follow a normal distribution. Given that banks will not enter when having negative profits, the probability of observing I banks becomes

$$P(\Pi_I \geq 0 \text{ and } \Pi_{I+1} < 0) = \Phi(\overline{\Pi}_I) - \Phi(\overline{\Pi}_{I+1}), \tag{3.18}$$

with Φ the cumulative normal density function and $\overline{\Pi}_I = X_k\beta - \mu_I$. The parameters β and μ_I are estimated with an ordered probit model.

Cohen and Mazzeo (2004) extend this basic framework to accommodate for differentiation among different types of competitors—multimarket bank, single-market bank and thrifts. They do this by allowing for a separate profit function for competitors of each type in each market. Suppose there are two types of banks, A and B. An additional market participant of type A will always decrease profits in the market, but this decrease is assumed to be larger for type A than for type B banks. They exploit data from 1,884 non-MSA areas as of June 2000. Population, per capita income, the number of farms and nonfarms capture market size. Cohen and Mazzeo focus on the cross-type effects measuring how banks of one type affect the profits of other-type banks. They find that the effects of same-type banks on these banks' profits are greater than the impact of the other-type institutions. This result suggests that differentiation between bank types is an important feature of banking markets. Moreover, multimarket banks and single-market banks affect each other more than thrifts do.

3.3. Evidence

The previous section showed that the competition literature has made substantial progress by modeling market structure as endogenous. Furthermore,
methodologies have been developed to exploit the rich heterogeneity and
different dimensions of the available data sets. However, "it can be argued
that the standard competitive paradigm is not appropriate for the banking
industry" (Vives 1991, 2001; Allen, Gersbach, Krahnen, and Santomero
2001; Carletti (2008)). Hence, to capture the "special nature of banking
competition," we review the available empirical evidence and structure our
discussion within a framework that finds its roots within the different theories explaining the existence of financial intermediation. We start discussing
the impact of market structure on loan and deposit conditions and then turn
to the question of whether market structure determines market presence.

3.3.1. Market Structure and Conduct

3.3.1.1. Loan Markets

3.3.1.1.1. *Local Markets*   There is ample empirical work starting from
the SCP paradigm investigating the impact of bank market concentration on
bank loan rates (for a review, see, e.g., Gilbert and Zaretsky 2003). Table 3.2
displays the results of selected studies that regress bank loan rates on an
HHI of market concentration (we do not report any studies that employ
number of competitors as a measure; these studies typically find no impact
on the loan rate). Studies employ both U.S. and international data.

Though mostly positive, the magnitude of the impact of the concentration
index on loan rates varies widely. To benchmark the results we calculate
the impact of a change in the HHI of 0.10, which according to widely
accepted cutoffs could mark the transition from a competitive market (HHI
<0.10) to a concentrated market (HHI >0.18). Illustrating the wide range of
results we note that recent studies, for example, indicate that a ΔHHI $= 0.1$
increases the loan rate by between 21*** to 55*** bp in the United States
(Cyrnak and Hannan 1999) and 59*** bp in Italy (Sapienza 2002), but only
3 bp in Norway (Kim, Kristiansen, and Vale 2005) and −4 to 5*** bp
in Belgium (Degryse and Ongena 2005). However, it remains difficult to
compare results across specifications, banking markets, periods, and HHI
measures that are alternatively based on loans, deposits, or branches, and
vary widely (across studies) in geographical span (Morgan 2002). Indeed, a
serious related problem of interpretation is that local market concentration
is often negatively correlated with market size.

Table 3.2. Empirical Work Investigating the Impact of Market Concentration on Loan Rates And Credit Availability

Paper	Data Source and Years / No. Observations in Regressions / Observation Type	Concentration in Bank Markets / Geographic Span: Average Population/Area / Average HHI	Loan Rate or Credit Measure / Impact of Concentration / Impact of ΔHHI = 0.1, in Basis Points
Hannan (1991)	STB ±8,250 U.S. firms	Bank Deposits 4,725 HHI: 0.14	Loan Rate Mostly Positive −6 to 61***
Petersen and Rajan (1995)	NSSBF 1987 ±1,400 U.S. Small Firms	Bank Deposits ±2,250,000[a] HHI: 0.17[a]	Most Recent Loan Rate (Prime Rate on Right Hand Side) Mostly Negative, Especially for Young Firms 0 Years: −170**, 10 Years: −3, Years: 46[a]
Hannan (1997)	FRB Survey 1993 1,994/7,078 U.S. Banks	Bank Deposits ± 2,500,000[a] HHI: 0.14	Small Business Floating Loan Rate Positive 31*** (Unsecured), 12*** (Secured)
Cavalluzzo et al. (2002)	NSSBF 1993 ±2,600 U.S. Small Firms	Bank Deposits ±2,500,000[a] HHI: 0.14	Most Recent Interest Rate on Line of Credit No Effect, but Positive for Hispanics All: −8, Hispanic: 124**
Cyrnak and Hannan (1999)	FRB Survey 1996 511/2,059 U.S. Banks	Bank Deposits ±2,750,000[a] HHI: 0.16	Small Business Floating Loan Rate Positive 55*** (Unsecured), 21*** (Secured)[1]
Claeys and Vander Vennet (2005)	Bankscope 1994–01 2,279 Banks 36 European Countries	Bank Loans 30,000,000[a] HHI: 0.10	Bank Net Interest Margin Positive (West)/Often Negative (East) West: 14*** to 23***; East: -110*** to 190***
Corvoisier and Gropp (2001, 2002)	ECB 2001 ±240 E.U. Countries-Years	Bank loans 30,000,000[a] HHI: 0.13	Country-specific loan rate margin Positive 10 to 20**c and 50***d

(continued)

45

Table 3.2. (Continued)

Paper	Data Source and Years No. Observations in Regressions Observation Type	Concentration in Bank Markets Geographic Span: Average Population/Area Average HHI	Loan Rate or Credit Measure Impact of Concentration Impact of ΔHHI = 0.1, in Basis Points
Fischer and Pfeil (2004)	Survey 1992–95[s] 5,500 German Banks	Bank Branches NA HHI: ±0.20 (West)/±0.30 (East)	Bank Interest Margins Positive 20*
Sapienza (2002)	Credit Register 107,501 Italian Firms	Bank Loans 600,000[a] HHI: 0.06	Loan Rate—Prime Rate Positive 59***
Montoriol Garriga (2006c)	SABI 1990–04 603,350 Spanish Firms	Bank Branches 850,000 HHI: 0.13	Firm Financial Expenses Over Debt Positive 20*** to 30***
Degryse and Ongena (2005)	One Bank 15,044 Belgian Small Firms	Bank Branches 8,632 HHI: 0.17	Loan Rate Mostly Positive −4 to 5***
Kim et al. (2005)	Central Bank of Norway 1,241 Norwegian Firms	Bank Business Credit 250,000[a] HHI: 0.19	Credit Line Rate—3 Month Money Market Rate Insignificantly Positive 3[b]
Petersen and Rajan (1994)	NSSBF ±1,400 U.S. Small Firms	Bank Deposits ±2,250,000[a] HHI: 0.17[a]	% Total Debt/Assets Positive 36***
Petersen and Rajan (1995)	NSSBF 1987 ±1,400 U.S. Small Firms	Bank Deposits ±2,250,000[a] HHI: 0.17[a]	% Trade Credit Paid before Due Date Positive, Especially for Young Firms 140*** to 280***[f], ≤10 yrs: 175** to 740,[g] >10 yrs: 150* to 0[g]
Cavalluzzo et al. (2002)	NSSBF 1993 ±2,600 U.S. Small Firms	Bank Deposits ±2,500,000[a] HHI: 0.14	Various Credit Availability Measures No Effect Overall but Significant Positive Effects for African Americans and Females

Zarutskie (2004)	SICTF 1987–98 ±250,000 U.S. Firms-Years	Bank Deposits ±2,250,000[a] HHI: 0.19	% Outside Debt/Assets Positive 19 to 77***
Scott and Dunkelberg (2001), Scott (2003)	CBSB 1995 ±2,000 U.S. Small Firms	Bank Deposits ±2,500,000[a] HHI: 0.19	No Credit Denial Positive + to + + +[e]
Shikimi (2005)	JADE 2000–02 28,622 Japanese Small Firms	Credit NA CR3: 0.44	% Debt/Assets No Effect 0
Angelini et al. (1998)	Survey 1995 2,232 Italian Small Firms	Bank Loan Median: <10,000 HHI: 0.42	Perceived Access to Credit No Effect 0

The table lists the main findings of selected empirical work investigating the impact of bank market concentration (third column) on bank loan rates (fourth column in the upper panel) or measures of bank credit availability (fourth column in the lower panel). The papers are listed according to country size and sample period (the most recent samples are ranked last). The measure of concentration in all studies is either the three-bank concentration ratio (CR3) or the Herfindahl-Hirschman Index (HHI), which can be calculated by squaring the market share of each bank competing in the market and then summing the resulting numbers (0 < HHI < 1). CBSB, Credit, Banks and Small Business Survey collected by the National Federation of Independent Business; ECB, European Central Ban; FRB, Federal Reserve Board of Governors of the Federal Reserve System; JADE, Japanese Accounts and Data on Enterprises; NSSBF, National Survey of Small Business Finance; SABI (Bureau van Dijk), Spanish company data set; SICTF, Statistics of Income Corporate Tax Files; STB, Federal Reserve's Survey of the Terms of Bank Lending to Business. 0, Included in the specifications but not significant.

[a] Our calculations or estimates.

[b] For HHI increasing from 0.09 to 0.19.

[c] Their models 2 and 5.

[d] Coefficients in regressions for short-term loans in their models 3, 5, and 6.

[e] Based on their COMPETITION variable, not on the HHICTY.

[f] Linear approximation using their table IV coefficients and assuming that the mean HHI below 0.1 equals 0.05 and above 0.18 equals 0.59.

[g] Linear approximation assuming that the mean HHI below 0.1 equals 0.05 and above 0.18 equals 0.59, based on means and medians in their table V.

*** Significant at 1%, ** at 5%, * at 10%.

+ + + Positive and significant at 1%, + + at 5%, + at 10%.

↔↔↔ Negative and significant at 1%, ↔↔ at 5%, ↔ at 10%.

Source: Updated from Degryse and Ongena (2008).

In their seminal paper, Petersen and Rajan (1995) investigate the effects of competition between banks not only on the loan rate but also on the availability of bank credit to firms. Petersen and Rajan model how especially firms with uncertain future cash flows are negatively affected by competition between banks. Banks may be unwilling to invest in relationships by incurring initial loan losses that may never be recouped in the future (as firms can later on obtain a low loan rate in a competitive banking or financial market).

Petersen and Rajan provide evidence on the impact of concentration both on loan rates and availability of credit. They document that young firms—having uncertain future cash flows—in more concentrated banking markets obtain substantially lower loan rates than firms in more competitive banking markets. The loan rates decreases by more than 150** bp for de novo firms, if the HHI increases by 0.1. They also document somewhat easier access to bank credit in more concentrated markets (lower part of table 3.2, fourth column), but even for young firms the effects seem modest economically speaking and statistically not always significant. An increase of 0.1 in the HHI roughly augments the percentage trade credit paid before the due date by between 1.5*** and 3*** percent across all firms and by around 2* to 8 percent for young firms. The effect of concentration on credit availability may further depend on how the bank–firm transactions are mediated, as in De Mello (2007) and Montoriol Garriga (2006b).[13]

The effects of banking competition on the firms' capital structure decisions seem even more subdued. For example, Petersen and Rajan (1994) document that a ΔHHI of 0.1 increases firm percent total debt/assets by only 0.36 percent, while a paper by Zarutskie (2004) shows an increase in percent outside debt/assets by only between 0.19 and 0.77*** percent. Similarly, Cavalluzzo, Cavalluzzo, and Wolken (2002) find no significant aggregate effect of an increase in HHI on a variety of credit availability measures (though they do find significant positive effects for small firms owned by African Americans or females), while Angelini, Di Salvo, and Ferri (1998) record no economically significant effect on perceived access to credit for a sample of small Italian firms.

3.3.1.1.2. *Multimarket*   The presence of banks operating in several geographical areas or several industries—multimarket banks—may impact local loan rate conditions. The influence on the local loan rates depends on whether the multimarket banks apply uniform or discriminatory pricing

---

13. Carbó Valverde, Rodriguez Fernández, and Udell (2006) compare the "performance" of the HHI and Lerner index for the Petersen and Rajan (1995) credit availability hypothesis.

across local markets and on the structure of each local banking market (including the importance of the multimarket banks present in that market).

Radecki (1998), for example, reports that most banks set uniform rates on auto loans and home equity loans *within* a U.S. state. Loan rates, however, can differ *across* states. Berger, Rosen, and Udell (2002) address the issue of whether in the U.S. large regional or nationwide banks compete in different ways than do small, local institutions. Their study is motivated by the observation that U.S. banking consolidation over the period 1984–98 had only a minor impact on "local" HHI but a major effect on bank size because many "market-extension" M&As (mergers and acquisitions), that is, mergers between banks operating in different local markets, took place. Berger et al. (2002) document that loan rates to SMEs (small- and medium-sized enterprises) are lower in markets with a large bank presence. They find that interest rate spreads charged in markets with a large bank presence are 35* bp lower than in other markets; on the other hand, the probability these SMEs obtain a loan may also be lower (Craig and Hardee 2007).

A key paper by Sapienza (2002) investigates the impact of Italian bank M&As on interest rates to continuing borrowers. She actually compares the impact of "in-market" versus "out-of-market" bank mergers on loan rates. Interestingly enough, she finds that "in-market" mergers decrease loan rates but only if the acquired bank has a sufficiently low local market share. The decrease in loan rates is much less important for "out-of-market" mergers.

Panetta, Schivardi, and Shum (2004) study the link between firm risk, measured by bank credit ratings, and interest rates. They find that the risk-rate schedule becomes steeper after bank mergers (i.e., the merged bank prices risk sharper) and attribute this result to the informational benefits arising from bank mergers. Important in this context is their finding that the risk-rate schedules are even steeper for "out-of-market" than for "in-market" mergers, suggesting that "out-of-market" mergers even yield more informational benefits to the banks than "in-market" mergers. Finally, a paper by Berger, Hasan, and Klapper (2004b) reports cross-country evidence on the importance of small, domestic, community banks for local economic activity in general. They find that higher shares of community banks in local bank markets are associated with more overall bank lending, faster GDP growth, and higher SME employment.

3.3.1.2. Deposit Markets

3.3.1.2.1. *Local Market*   There is also a long line of research, at least going back to Berger and Hannan (1989), investigating the impact of bank market concentration on bank deposit rates. Table 3.3 summarizes the findings of this literature. Studies employ both the three-bank concentration

Table 3.3. Empirical Work Investigating the Impact of Market Concentration on Deposit Rates

Paper	Data Source and Years No. Observations in Regressions Observation Type	Concentration in Markets Geographic Span: Average Population/Area Average CR3 or HHI	Deposit Rate Measure Impact of Concentration on the Deposit Rate Impact of ΔCR3 = 0.3 or ΔHHI = 0.1,[b] in BP
Berger and Hannan (1989)	FRB Survey 1985 4,047 U.S. Banks	Bank Deposits 2,000,000[a] CR3: NA	Bank Rates −18*** (Demand), −12*** To −1 (Time), −19*** (Savings)
Calem and Carlino (1991)	FRB Survey 1985 444/466 U.S. Banks	Bank Deposits 2,000,000[a] CR3: 0.45	Bank Rates −17*** (Time), −5 (Savings)
Neumark and Sharpe (1992)	FRB Survey 1983–87 49 Months, 255 Banks U.S. Banks-Years	Bank Deposits 2,000,000[a] HHI: 0.08	Bank Deposit Rates −26*** (Time), −27*** (Savings)
Sharpe (1997)	FRB Survey 1983–87 49 Months, 222 Banks U.S. Banks-Years	Bank Deposits 2,000,000[a] HHI: 0.08	Bank Deposit Rates Restricted Market: −19*** (Time), −20*** (Savings) Liberalized Market: −7*** (Time), −4 (Savings)
Neuberger and Zimmerman (1990)	California 1984–87 3,415 Californian NOW Accounts	Bank Deposits NA CR3: 0.63	NOW Account Rate −5***
Hannan (1997)	FRB Survey 1993 ±330 U.S. Banks	Bank Deposits 2,500,000[a] HHI: 0.14	Bank Rates −5 (Demand), −5 (Time), −6* (Savings)[1]
Radecki (1998)	FRB Survey 1996 197 U.S. Banks	Bank Deposits MSA = 2,650,000; State = 10,240,000 HHI: MSA = 0.17; State = 0.11	Bank Rates MSA = Mixed; State = Negative MSA2 = 10* (Demand), 3 (Time), 5 (Savings) State[3] = −4 (Demand), −6 (Time), −33*** (Savings)

			Bank Rates
Hannan and Prager (2004)	Reports of C&I 1996/1999 6,141/5,209 U.S. Banks-Years	Bank Deposits 96 = 1,034,000; 99 = 1,092,000; HHI: 1996 = 0.23; 1999 = 0.22	$96^1 = -4^{***}$ (Demand), -3^{***} (Time), -1 (Savings) $99^1 = -4^*$ (Demand), -7^{***} (Time), -4^{***} (Savings)
Heitfield and Prager (2004)	Reports C&I 1988/1992/1996/1999 ±11,500/10,250/8,250/7,250 U.S. Banks-Years	Bank Deposits ±1,000,000 HHI: ±0.22	Bank Rates 1999 Local = -1^{***} (Demand), -0 (Savings) 1999 State = -23^* (Demand), -8^{***} (Savings)
Rosen (2003)	Reports C&I 1988–00 89,166 U.S. Banks-Years	Bank Deposits ±1,000,000 HHI: 0.35	Bank Rates Urban: -8^{***} (Demand), -7^{***} (Savings) Rural: -1 (Demand), 1 (Savings)
Corvoisier and Gropp (2002)	ECB 2001 246 E.U. Country-Years	Bank Deposits 30,000,000[a] HHI: 0.13	Country-Specific Deposit Rate Margins[c] -70^{***} (Demand), 50^{***} (Time), 140^{***} (Savings)[6]
Fischer and Pfeil (2004)	Survey 1992–95[d] 5,943/5,873 German Banks	Bank Branches NA HHI: ±0.20 (West)/±0.30 (East)	Bank Interest Margins 9 (Time), -2^{**} (Savings)

The table lists the main findings of empirical work investigating the impact of bank market concentration on bank deposit rates. The papers are listed according to country size and sample period (the most recent samples are ranked last). The measure of concentration in all studies is either the three-bank concentration ratio (CR3) or the Herfindahl-Hirschman Index (HHI), which can be calculated by squaring the market share of each bank competing in the market and then summing the resulting numbers ($0 < \text{HHI} < 1$). C&I, condition and income; ECB, European Central Ban; FRB, Federal Reserve Board of Governors of the Federal Reserve System; MSA, metropolitan statistical area.

[a] Our calculations.

[b] Assuming equal market shares for the three largest banks and market shares of the other atomistic banks that can be disregarded, an increase in the CR3 from 0.1 to 0.4 increases the HHI from 0.003 to 0.053, while an increase in the CR3 from 0.3 to 0.6 increases the HHI from 0.03 to 0.12.

[c] The margin in their paper is the money market rate minus the deposit rate. For consistency, we multiply all results by (-1).

[d] Source: Fischer (2001). Superscript numbers refer to their models 1, 2, 3, or 6.

*** Significant at 1%, ** at 5%, * at 10%.

Source: Updated from Degryse and Ongena (2008).

51

ratio (CR3) and the HHI as concentration measures. Overall, most papers find a negative impact of an increase in concentration on time and savings deposit rates, but as with the loan rate studies, the effects vary across samples and specifications. We take a change in CR3 by 0.3 to be approximately comparable to a change in HHI by 0.1. The effect of the changes in either the CR3 or HHI on U.S. time and savings deposits rates ranges then from -26^{***} to -1 and from -27^{***} to $+5$ bp, respectively. Rates on demand deposits seem less affected by market concentration with estimates varying from -18^{***} to $+10^{*}$ bp. But there is evidence of more downward price rigidity and upward price flexibility in demand deposit rates than in time deposit rates especially in more concentrated markets (Neumark and Sharpe 1992).

More recent studies typically find smaller negative effects for all deposit products, possibly reflecting the widening geographical scope of banking competition (Radecki 1998) and the ensuing difficulties delineating the relevant local market (Heitfield 1999; Biehl 2002). Geographical markets in the United States for demand deposits may be currently "smaller than statewide" but not necessarily "local" (Heitfield and Prager 2004), suggesting both local and statewide measures of concentration and multimarket contact variables should be included in the analysis. Heitfield and Prager (2004) find that the coefficients on "state" concentration measures became larger in absolute value over time than the coefficients on the "local" measures in particular for demand deposits. In 1999, for example, a 0.1 change in the local HHI affected the NOW deposit rate by only -1^{*} bp while a similar change in the state HHI decreased the rate by 23^{***} bp. Finally, Rosen (2007) finds that in addition to multimarket bank presence, market size structure also has an impact on deposit rates.

A paper by Corvoisier and Gropp (2002) studies European national banking markets, in geographical and economic span often comparable to U.S. states. They find a substantial effect of -70^{***} bp on demand deposit rates (corresponding an increase in HHI of 0.1), but a surprising increase of $+50^{***}$ and $+140^{***}$ bp for time and savings deposits rates. Corvoisier and Gropp argue that local markets are more relevant for demand deposits, whereas customers may shop around for time and savings deposits. Shopping around would imply an increase in contestability, breaking the expected link between HHI and this deposit rate. Demand deposit rates are often posted within a national market after being determined at the banks' headquarters where competition (or lack thereof) may be perceived to be nationwide. On the other hand, for the time and savings deposit markets the coefficient on HHI may actually pick up bank efficiency (even though various bank cost measures are included) or the effect of bank mergers caused by an unobservable increase in contestability. In any case, this study again underlines the methodological difficulties in interpreting the reduced form coefficients in interest rate-market concentration studies.

3.3.1.2.2. *Multimarket*   A number of papers explore the impact of multimarket banks on deposit pricing. Radecki (1998) provides evidence of uniform pricing across branches of banks operating throughout an entire U.S. state or large regions of a state. He interprets this finding as evidence in favor of an increase of the geographic reach of deposit markets over time. Heitfield (1999) shows, however, that uniform pricing is practiced only by multimarket banks that operate statewide, and not by single-market banks that operate in one MSA only. Hence, "charging the same deposit rate" may result from a deliberate decision of uniform pricing and not mechanically from a geographical expansion of market boundaries. Heitfield and Prager (2004) further fine-tune the previous findings by exploring heterogeneity in the pricing of several deposit products. They report that the geographic scope of the markets for NOW accounts remains local, but that the scope of money market deposit accounts and savings accounts markets has broadened over time.

Hannan and Prager (2004) explore the competitive impact of multimarket banks on local deposit conditions, using U.S. data for 1996 and 1999. They document that multimarket banks offer lower deposit rates than single-market banks operating in the same market. Moreover, a greater presence of multimarket banks relaxes competition as single-market banks offer lower deposit rates. On the other hand, Calem and Nakamura (1998) argue that multimarket banks mitigate localized market power in rural areas,[14] but that multimarket branching reduces competition in already competitive (urban) markets. Work by Barros (1999) reasons that the presence of banks across markets may lead to local interest rate dispersion, without implying different conduct of banks. Collusive behavior among banks could impact the degree of price dispersion. His empirical findings for Portugal provide strong support for Nash behavior, but given the small sample size, collusion cannot be rejected. Using a similar setup, collusive behavior among Spanish banks in the loan market in the early 1990s can not be rejected (Jaumandreu and Lorences 2002).

What about the impact of M&As? Focarelli and Panetta (2003) document that "in-market" mergers hurt depositors in the short run due to lower deposit

---

14. Rosen (2003) finds that having more large banks in a market generally increases deposit rates at all banks but also increases their sensitivity to changes in the concentration ratio.

rates—a drop of 17*** bp. The short-run impact of "out-of-market" mergers, however, is negligible. In the long run, depositors gain from both "in-market" and "out-of-market" mergers as deposit rates increase with 14*** and 12*** bp, respectively, compared to the premerger level. Hence, in the long-run efficiency gains seem to dominate over the market power effect of bank mergers, leading to more favorable deposit rates for consumers.

3.3.1.3. Interplay between Markets

The links between the different banking markets have also been empirically investigated.[15] Park and Pennacchi (2003), for example, discuss the impact of the entry by large multimarket banks on competition in *both* loan and deposit markets. Park and Pennacchi (2003) posit that multimarket banks may enjoy a funding advantage in the wholesale market. As a result, they establish that a higher presence of the multimarket banks promotes competition in loan markets, but harms competition in deposit markets if these multimarket banks have funding advantages. Hence, their paper nicely shows that the impact of "size structure" could be asymmetric across markets.

3.3.2. Market Structure and Strategy: Product Differentiation and Network Effects

Empirical work measuring product differentiation and network effects in banking is still rather limited, despite the fact that theoretical models are already highly developed and rich in testable hypotheses (see Carletti (2008)). Within the area of product differentiation, we can distinguish between studies dealing with *vertical* and *horizontal* differentiation.

Kim et al. (2005), for example, study whether banks can pursue strategies in order to vertically differentiate their products and services. If customers are willing to pay for banks enjoying a higher reputation, then banks may invest in variables increasing their reputation. They consider a bank's capital ratio, its ability to avoid loan losses, bank size, and branch networks as possible strategies. The empirical question addressed is whether borrowers are actually willing to pay for "quality" characteristics. If so, a strategy of vertical differentiation would allow banks to charge higher loan rates and to soften competition.

Softening of competition by way of vertical product differentiation may, however, induce market discipline. If borrowers pay a premium for

---

15. Kashyap, Rajan, and Stein (2002), e.g., link lending and deposit taking at the bank level, while Berg and Kim (1998) connect behavior in retail and corporate banking markets.

borrowing from banks providing certification (low loan-loss provisions) or from solvent banks with few problems in meeting future refinancing needs, banks face market discipline induced by borrowers. This asset side market discipline effect is different from the conventional one on the liability side (uninsured deposit and money market funding), which has been extensively studied in the banking literature. A possible disciplinary effect from borrowers may reinforce the market disciplinary effect stemming from the liability side and make banks less financially fragile.[16]

Using panel data of Norwegian banks over the period 1993–98, Kim et al. (2005) find empirical support for the ability to avoid loan losses, measured by the ratio of loss provisions. A doubling of the loss provisions relative to the mean implies a reduction in the interest rate spread of about 56*** bp. Other evidence for willingness to pay for bank reputation is provided in Billett et al. (1995). They find that announcements of banks loans granted by lenders with higher credit ratings are associated with larger abnormal returns on the borrowing firm shares.

Another element leading to vertical differentiation stems from network effects (see Carletti (2008)). For example, depositors exhibit a higher willingness to pay for banks with a larger ATM network. The size of this network also hinges on the degree in which depositors can use rivals' ATMs. The ATM market has exhibited a varying degree of compatibility between networks. Over time, networks in several countries moved from incompatibility toward compatibility. However, as documented in Knittel and Stango (2004), new ATM charges to rivals' clients reintroduces some incompatibility. We expect that such rival charges have a larger impact on depositors of banks owning few ATMs.

Knittel and Stango (2004) evaluate the effect of the introduction of such surcharge fees on deposit account prices, measured as the ratio of annual income associated to deposit accounts over deposit account balances. Indeed, they find that (1) a doubling of the number of ATMs in the local market increases bank's deposit account prices by 5–10 percent, and (2) incompatibility strengthens the link between own ATMs and deposit account prices and weakens the link between rival's ATMs and deposit account prices.

ATMs also have aspects of horizontal differentiation, as customers prefer banks with conveniently located ATMs. Banks also compete for clients by

---

16. See, e.g., Calomiris and Kahn (1991), for a theoretical model explaining how depositors can discipline bank managers. Martinez Peria and Schmukler (2001) provide empirical evidence of depositors disciplining banks' risk taking.

establishing branches and locating them optimally. Optimal location allows the banks to increase market share and to avoid perfect competition as clients may have preferences over locations. In other words, branching provides local market power.

Some papers start from an equilibrium situation, taking branching decisions as exogenously given, and address whether there is evidence for localized competition. Barros (1999), for example, documents for Portugal that the volume of deposits banks attract hinges on the network of branches. He also finds indirect evidence for the importance of transportation costs: urban markets have higher transportation costs than rural markets. Degryse and Ongena (2005) find evidence of spatial price discrimination in Belgium: borrowers that are located close to the loan-granting branch and far from competing branches pay significantly higher loan rates.

Other papers also endogenize bank branching decisions. When deciding on the location of their branches, banks take into account all existing networks and their expectations of rivals' future location and network choices. The papers endogenizing branching decisions incorporate features of both horizontal and vertical product differentiation, as *all* consumers may have a preference for larger networks but clients may disagree on the optimal location of specific branches. Using panel data from Norwegian banks, Kim and Vale (2001) report that a bank-specific branch network positively affects market shares in loan markets but does not affect the total size of loan markets.[17] And Berger and Dick (2007) find that even entrants can attain a significant market presence if they offer large branch networks, thus reducing the disadvantage of entering later. On the other hand, Kim et al. (2005) find no evidence for the size of bank branch network as a quality variable for borrowers in the Norwegian banking market.

Product differentiation also dictates in how far different types of financial institutions are perceived as substitutes. As indicated in the methodology section, Cohen and Mazzeo (2004) present results for thrifts, multimarket banks, and single-market banks operating in the United States. They find that competition is more intense between financial institutions of the same type than between institutions of differing types. This suggests that there is substantial differentiation between types of financial institutions.

---

17. This finding corroborates those by Jayaratne and Strahan (1996), who document only weak evidence that bank lending increased following interstate branch reform in the United States.

4

The Lender–Borrower Relationship

4.1. Introduction

4.1.1. Definitions

The lender–borrower relationship, henceforth "bank relationship," can be defined in many ways. Ongena and Smith (2000a), for example, delineate a bank relationship to be "the connection between a bank and customer that goes beyond the execution of simple, anonymous, financial transactions," while Boot (2000, p.10) defines relationship banking as "the provision of financial services by a financial intermediary that (1) invests in obtaining customer-specific information, that is often proprietary in nature; and that (2) evaluates the profitability of these investments through multiple inter-actions with the same customer over time and across products" (see also Berger and Udell 2002, who provide a similar definition of relationship banking).

Given such a wealth of definitions, there is no need for a new one.[1] Rather, after a close but concise reading of the theoretical arguments,

---

1. There is also no need for another rehash of earlier theory and evidence. Consequently, this chapter broadly takes off in reviewing the empirical literature where Berger and Udell (2002), Boot (2000), Ongena and Smith (2000a), and Degryse and Ongena (2008) concluded their surveys. Other reviews on various aspects of bank relationships include Berlin (1996), Bornheim and Herbeck (1998), Degryse and Ongena (2002), Eber (1996), Elyasiani and Goldberg (2004), Holland (1994), Ongena (1999), Rivaud-Danset (1996), Samolyk (1997), and Ziane (2003).

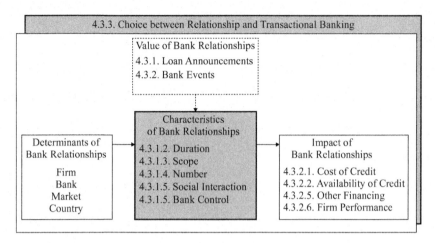

Figure 4.1.   Discussion of bank–firm relationships throughout this chapter.

this chapter reviews selected empirical methodologies and comprehensively summarizes existing empirical evidence, to arrive at some pointed conclusions about the value, characteristics, determinants, and impact of bank–firm lending relationships. Figure 4.1 provides a graphical road map to the discussion of bank relationships in this and preceding chapters.

While this chapter focuses on the firm–bank relationship, we are well aware that relationship lending is just one the many ways in which banks interact with firms seeking funds and other banking products. Berger and Udell (2006), for example, distinguish between eight different lending technologies. And while there is tentative evidence that credit scoring and transactional lending in general has become more important over the last decades (e.g., DeYoung, Frame, Glennon, McMillen, and Nigro 2007; Cerqueiro, Degryse, and Ongena 2007), relationship banking may remain a key modus operandi. Commentators recently even started to blame the deep agency problems in the originate-and-distribute lending model involving the securitization of many loans originated by the banks—and one of the most advanced types of transactional banking—as a root cause of the 2007 banking crisis (e.g., Mishkin 2008; see also chapter 11). Relationship banking may therefore even regain some of its former luster over the next few years.

4.1.2. Asymmetric Information

Asymmetric information, a phenomenon intrinsic to credit markets in general and banking markets in particular, makes bank credit unique. Repeated exchanges of information tie bank and borrower into a relationship and generate informational capital that is bank specific (i.e., such information cannot be communicated credibly to others). This informational capital is likely to vary across the different segments in the credit market and depends, for example, on the banks' ability to gather private information as well as the possibilities of firms to communicate this information in a credible way with other external financiers. The informational advantage bank's are able to extract therefore hinges on the borrowers' relative ability to signal their quality to outside lenders, and the expectations on how flexible borrowers will be in the future. A number of recent studies examine how the character of the information flows between lenders and borrowers and the ensuing relationships influence the way in which banks compete.

Fama (1985) already alludes to the importance of the bank relationship in financial intermediation, as a relationship may affect a firm's ability to raise capital both from within the bank and through other nonbank sources. His reasoning is as follows. Bank loans are typically short term. Each time a bank renews a short-term loan contract, the renewal acts as an accreditation of the ability for the firm to meet the bank obligation. This renewal further creates two positive externalities as (1) it enables other providers of financing to avoid duplicating the evaluation process of the bank, and (2) it provides accreditation to the public that the firm will be able to produce enough cash flows in the future to meet its fixed obligation. Hence, periodic evaluation and subsequent loan renewals are one important characteristic of a developing firm–bank relationship. The previously discussed evidence in James (1987) and Lummer and McConnell (1989), for example, indeed suggest that bank loan announcements and renewals contain value about the future prospects of the firm.

4.1.3. Theory

Haubrich (1989) partly establishes the link between the existence of financial intermediaries and the occurrence of long-term relationships. In particular, Haubrich (1989) extends the Diamond (1984) model and assumes that frequent loan renewal and observation of repayment make the cost for a bank of maintaining long-term relationships to be lower than repeated direct monitoring. As a result in his model, informational asymmetries cause financial intermediaries to arise that choose for long-term relationships with borrowers. Two points need to be noted though. Haubrich (1989) assumes the existence of relationships, and in his model, borrowers cannot switch.

In contrast to Haubrich (1989), Fischer (1990), Sharpe (1990), Rajan (1992), and von Thadden (2004) assume that financial intermediaries exist, but derive that, because of informational asymmetries, relationships arise endogenously even in competitive loan markets. Sharpe (1990), for example, argues that long-term bank relationships arise in a competitive loan market because an incumbent bank has the ability to observe first-period loan repayments. As a result, the incumbent bank can offer only above-cost loans to its best customers and prevent customers from receiving competitive financing elsewhere. The incumbent bank gains this monopoly power through its informational advantage over competitors. A high-quality firm that tries to switch to a competing uninformed bank gets pooled with low-quality firms and is offered an even worse, breakeven interest rate. As a result, there is actually no switching in the analysis of Sharpe (1990), a technical incompleteness that is resolved in a mixed strategy equilibrium in Fischer (1990), Rajan (1992), and von Thadden (2004).

4.1.4. Switching Costs

This discussion should make clear that relationship capital may affect the way banks allocate credit across groups of borrowers. Banks can extract higher profits from captured and locked-in (opaque) borrowers than from borrowers that have ready access to other financing alternatives. A switch between banks may entail not only the observable direct (transactional) cost of closing an account with one bank and opening a new one elsewhere, but also the unobservable, but perhaps more significant, cost associated with the foregone capitalized value of the (previously established) long-term customer–bank relationship.[2]

---

2. The vast theoretical literature on switching costs is summarized in Klemperer (1995). This literature deals with the main issues of industrial organization, e.g., entry deterrence and the command over supranormal rents. Shapiro and Varian (1998) provide numerous examples of the impact of switching costs on market behavior. Selten (1965) and von Weizsäcker (1984) are early contributions to this literature. Klemperer (1985) examines a two-period differentiated-product duopoly in which customers are partially "locked-in" by switching costs they face in the second period. Lock-in results in higher prices in both periods compared to the non-switching-cost case. Klemperer (1987) introduces switching costs in order to explain the emphasis placed on market share as a goal of corporate strategy. Beggs and Klemperer (1992) show how switching costs make the market more attractive to a new entrant and Klemperer (1987) examines how the threat of new entry affects the incumbent's behavior, thereby providing an explanation for limit pricing. Chen and Rosenthal (1996) consider a stochastic game with slowly changing customer loyalties resulting in Markov perfect equilibrium. Padilla (1992) develops a model resulting in ex

Both firms and banks can try to preserve the benefits and rents embedded in long-term relationships (and the buildup of the relationship capital flowing from it) by reinforcing existing switching costs. Banks, for example, can start charging account closure fees to increase transactional switching costs or invest in information gathering to increase informational switching costs. Or even when operating under an information sharing regime, banks could grant most of their current borrowers the same (top) credit rating (Ioannidou and Ongena 2007), in order to confuse the competing banks that would have access to this information.

By now, it should be clear that the banking sector may well be a major place in the economy where switching costs continue to play a substantial role. Switching costs may exert important real consequences, not only on the specific captive enterprises, but also on the efficient allocation of credit in the economy as a whole. Indeed, switching costs limit substitution, the key for the efficient functioning of the price system in this part of the economy. Since (short-term) bank financing constitutes an important source of funding for both individuals and SMEs (small- and medium-sized enterprises), the actual allocation of bank credit can have important real consequences for an economy.

4.1.5. Relevance and Outline of This Chapter

To conclude, lending relationships between banks and firms and the resultant switching costs are a natural topic for financial economists. If banks exist as institutions primarily to help in solving informational asymmetries pervasive in credit markets, relationships with borrowing firms may arise endogenously not just as a natural corollary but also the primary conduit through which informational problems emanate. Hence, assessing the value and characteristics of relationships (duration, scope, and number, e.g.) is necessary from a bank-theoretic perspective, not only to understand why banks exist but also to assess whether banks are special.

But knowledge about bank relationships is also interesting for a much wider audience of economists, as bank relationships constitute a singularly

---

ante identical firms having ex post asymmetric market shares and Padilla (1995) shows that in an infinite-horizon model with stationary Markovian strategies, the intensity of competition is assuaged. Caminal and Matutes (1990) consider a model with endogenous switching costs and show that in the second period of the game firms discriminate against newcomers. Cabral and Greenstein (1990) claim that there may be economic merit to ignoring switching costs because the increased competitiveness in response to bidding parity can outweigh the costs of switching between suppliers.

observable and measurable phenomenon intimately tied to an important
market imperfection (i.e., the omnipresent information asymmetry in credit
markets). Hence, lessons learned studying bank relationships also have a
lot of relevance for our understanding of other markets where informational
problems may give rise to intense relationships, for example, labor markets
or insurance markets.

Before weaving together the disparate strings of results emanating from
a recently burgeoning empirical literature, we review key econometric
methodologies that can be used to assess the duration, the number, and
the type of relationships (but delay a discussion of endogeneity issues and
instrumental variables estimation to section 4.2.2).

4.2. Methodology

4.2.1. Duration Analysis

This section develops the econometric methodology employed in analyzing
the duration of (bank) relationships (see, e.g., Heckman and Singer 1984b;
Kiefer 1988).[3] We begin by introducing terminology common to duration
analysis and then describe the hazard function estimators. Let T represent
the duration of time that passes before the occurrence of a certain random
event. In the econometrics literature, the passage of time is often referred
to as a "spell," while the event itself is called a "switch."[4] A simple way to
describe the behavior of a spell is through its survivor function:

$$S(t) = P(T \geq t), \tag{4.1}$$

which yields the probability that the spell T lasts at least to time t. The
survivor function equals one minus the cumulative distribution function
of T.

The behavior of a spell can also be described through the use of the hazard
function. The hazard function determines the probability that a switch will
occur, conditional on the spell surviving through time t, and is defined by

$$\lambda(t) = \lim_{\Delta t \to 0} \frac{P(t \leq T < t + \Delta t | T \geq t)}{\Delta t} = \frac{-d \log S(t)}{dt} = \frac{f(t)}{S(t)}, \tag{4.2}$$

---

3. Our discussion is based partly on Ongena and Smith (2001).

4. Admittedly, this generic terminology is potentially confusing as we also refer to "switching costs," etc., in a more specific banking context.

where $f(t)$ is the density function associated with the distribution of spells. Neither the survivor function nor the hazard function provides additional information that could not be derived directly from $f(t)$. Instead, these functions present economically interesting ways of examining the distribution of spells.

The hazard function does provide a suitable method for summarizing the relationship between spell length and the likelihood of switching. When $\lambda(t)$ is increasing in t, the hazard function is said to exhibit positive duration dependence, because the probability of ending the spell increases as the spell lengthens. Similarly, negative duration dependence occurs when $\lambda(t)$ is decreasing in t, and constant duration dependence indicates the lack of a relation between $\lambda(t)$ and t.

When estimating hazard functions, it is econometrically convenient to assume a proportional hazard specification, such that

$$\lambda(t, X(t), \beta) = \lim_{\Delta t \to 0} \frac{P(t \leq T < t + \Delta T | T \geq t, X(t), \beta)}{\Delta T} = \lambda_0(t) \exp(\beta' X_t),$$

(4.3)

where X_t is a set of observable, possibly time-varying explanatory variables, β is a vector of unknown parameters associated with the explanatory variables, $\lambda_0(t)$ is the baseline hazard function, and $\exp(\beta' X_t)$ is chosen because it is nonnegative and yields an appealing interpretation for the coefficients, β. The logarithm of $\lambda(t, X(t), \beta)$ is linear in X_t. Therefore, β reflects the partial impact of each variable in X on the log of the estimated hazard rate.

The baseline hazard $\lambda_0(t)$ determines the shape of the hazard function with respect to time. Equation 4.3 can be estimated without specifying a functional form for the baseline hazard. The Cox (1972) partial likelihood model bases estimation of β on the ordering of the duration spells. Because it specifies no shape for $\lambda_0(t)$, we refer to the Cox (1972) partial likelihood model as "semiparametric."

Two commonly used parametric specifications for the baseline hazard are the Weibull and the exponential distributions. The Weibull specification assumes:

$$\lambda_0(t) = \lambda \alpha t^{\alpha-1},$$

(4.4)

and allows for duration dependence. When $\alpha > 1 (\alpha < 1)$, the distribution exhibits positive (negative) duration dependence, implying that the hazard increases (decreases) in time. The exponential distribution, which exhibits constant duration dependence, is nested within the Weibull as the case

$\alpha = 1$. To estimate hazard functions using the Cox (1972) partial likelihood model, Weibull, exponential or other specifications one uses maximum likelihood methods.

Explanatory variables can vary through time. To obtain interpretable estimates from the proportional hazard models, it is required that the variables be either "defined" or "ancillary" with respect to the duration of a spell (see Kalbfleisch and Prentice 1980). A defined variable follows a deterministic path. Age is an example of a defined variable because its path is set in advance of the relationship and varies deterministically with relationship duration. An ancillary variable has a stochastic path, but the path cannot be influenced by the duration of the spell. One can also assume that the conditional likelihood of ending a spell depend only on the value of an ancillary variable at time t, and not on past or future realizations of the variable.

Censoring is a crucial issue to be addressed when estimating a duration model. Not knowing when a relationship starts, or when it ends, or both, means we are unable to observe the true duration of the relationship for these observations. With no adjustment to account for censoring, maximum likelihood estimation of the proportional hazard models produces biased and inconsistent estimates of model parameters. Figure 4.2 provides an example of fixed and variable, left and right censoring.

Accounting for right-censored observations can be accomplished by expressing the log-likelihood function as a weighted average of the sample density of completed duration spells and the survivor function of

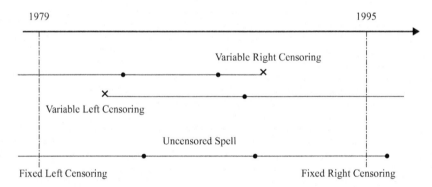

Figure 4.2. Fixed and variable left and right censoring of bank–firm relationship spells, from Ongena and Smith (2001). The fixed left and right censoring is the result of the sample beginning in 1979 and end in 1995. The variable left and right censoring is the result of firms listing and delisting on the Oslo Stock Exchange, which collects the bank–firm relationship information. •, spell end; x, a listing or delisting of the firm.

uncompleted spells (see Kiefer 1988). Controlling for left censoring is less straightforward and in economic duration analysis often ignored. However, Heckman and Singer (1984a) argue that the biases induced by left censoring can be as severe as those created by right censoring. To analyze the sensitivity of results to left censoring, an estimation strategy proposed by Heckman and Singer (1984a) yields consistent, albeit inefficient, estimates of duration under left censoring.

Finally, to graph a survivor function, one can use the Kaplan and Meier (1958) estimator,

$$\hat{S}(k) = \prod_{i=0}^{1}(1 - \hat{\lambda}(i)), \qquad (4.5)$$

which is the estimated probability that a relationship survives beyond year k. Without a correction for right censoring, $\hat{\lambda}(i)$ is the number of firms leaving the data set during year i, divided by the total number of firms remaining in the data set at the beginning of year i. With a correction for censoring, $\hat{\lambda}(i)$ is the number of firms observed to terminate a relationship in year i, divided by the number of surviving firms.

4.2.2. Tobit and Count Models

Suppose we observe the number of bank relationships a firm has, and want to estimate how this choice is determined by a set of firm-specific variables. For example, in Ongena and Smith (2000b), the number of $y_i = 1, 2, \ldots, 70$ [*sic*], is the discrete, integer choices made by each firm.

Using a discretely valued dependent variable creates several problems. First, estimation using ordinary least squares (OLS) will produce biased estimates of the slope coefficient and standard errors, and fitted values will not necessarily lie on the integer interval $[1, 70]$.[5] Moreover, OLS does not account for the fact that the dependent variable is truncated below at one.

A truncated linear model (Tobit) deals with the latter issue, while count regressions, that is, Poisson and negative binomial models, that explicitly model the choice in terms of a discrete random variable address the first issue. While count models can also account truncation, we will limit ourselves to the nontruncated application.

---

5. See Maddala (1983) or Cameron and Trivedi (1986) for an elaboration on how ordinary least squares produces biased estimates when using a discretely-valued dependent variable.

Suppose there is an underlying latent variable y^*,

$$y^* = x\beta + u, \quad u|x \sim N(0, \sigma^2), \tag{4.6}$$

but that we can only observe y:

$$y = \max(1, y^*) \tag{4.7}$$

The Tobit model will use maximum likelihood to estimate both β and σ. Given its nonlinear character, the estimated coefficients are not immediately interpretable, however. Indeed, the marginal effect of x on y (as we will typically not be interested in y^*) can be derived from

$$E(y|x) = \Phi\left(\frac{x\beta}{\sigma}\right) x\beta + \phi\left(\frac{x\beta}{\sigma}\right) \sigma. \tag{4.8}$$

The partial derivative of this expression equals

$$\frac{\partial E(y|x)}{\partial x_j} = \beta_j \Phi\left(\frac{x\beta}{\sigma}\right). \tag{4.9}$$

Consequently, the effect is also determined by the value of x at which this expression is evaluated. The effect of x on $E(y)$ and $P(y > 1)$ has to be similar in sign for the Tobit to be appropriate (and errors need to be homoskedastic and normally distributed).

To deal with discreteness we can use a Poisson model. For a random variable $y = 1, 2, \ldots,$

$$P(y|\mu) = \left(\frac{e^{-\mu}\mu^y}{y!}\right). \tag{4.10}$$

μ is the mean and variance of y. As μ increases, the probability of a zero count decreases and the Poisson distribution approximates a normal distribution.

In practice, the Poisson model rarely fits due to overdispersion, that is, unobserved heterogeneity among the observations:

$$P(y|\mu) = \left(\frac{e^{-\mu \exp(\varepsilon)}(\mu \exp(\varepsilon))^y}{y!}\right), \tag{4.11}$$

with

$$\exp(\varepsilon) \sim \Gamma(1, \alpha). \tag{4.12}$$

α is an additional parameter, "the rate of overdispersion," which role becomes clear when calculating

$$\frac{\text{var}(y)}{E(y)} = 1 + \alpha E(y). \tag{4.13}$$

If there is overdispersion, estimates of the Poisson model are inefficient with standard errors that are biased downward. Accordingly, it is important to test for overdispersion. Because the negative binomial reduces to the Poisson when the parameter that reflects the unobserved heterogeneity among observations is equal to 0, we can test for overdispersion (Cameron and Trivedi 1990; Greene 1997, p. 937).

4.2.3. Nested Multinomial Logit

Suppose we want to investigate the choice of a bank by a firm ready to engage in a cross-border relationship and that banks can be differentiated by nationality (home, host, or third country, vis-à-vis the firm's country) and by reach (global, regional, or local, in terms of geographical footprint of the bank).[6] Assume that in the first stage, firms pick bank nationality as a function of host nation characteristics, geographic, cultural, and financial differences between the home and host nations, and attributes of the multinational corporations.[7] In the second stage, firms select bank reach conditional on the nationality choice and attributes of the corporation. Some of the explanatory variables may actually be included in part to control for factors that affect the willingness and ability of banks to supply services in the relevant nations.

Such a model of the choice of bank nationality and reach can be estimated using the nested multinomial logit methodology proposed by McFadden (1978). Let Y_i^N be a discrete-valued dependent variable that takes on the

---

6. Our discussion is based partly on Berger, Dai, Ongena, and Smith (2003).

7. Berger et al. (2003) argue that firms may base their nationality decision on the relative attractiveness of the concierge effect, which tends to push a firm toward a host nation bank, vis-à-vis the "home cooking" effect, which tends to push a firm toward a home nation bank. Firms may choose third-nation banks when the concierge and home cooking effects are both relatively weak.

value of 0, 1, or 2, depending on whether firm i chooses a host, home, or third-nation bank, respectively. Assume that the discrete value Y_i^N is the observed outcome from a continuously valued, latent variable Y_i^{N*} that reflects the net benefits flowing to a firm from selecting a host, home, or third-nation bank. The first stage of the model is then

$$Y_i^{N*} = f \text{ (Host Nation Characteristics, Differences between Home and}$$
$$\text{Host Nations, Corporate Attributes).} \tag{4.14}$$

In the second stage, the firm chooses bank reach conditional on the nationality choice and attributes of the corporation. Assume that firms base their bank reach decisions on the tradeoff between having access at the corporate level to the broad product ranges and expertise associated with banks with extensive reach versus the benefits from relationship-oriented services and country-specific knowledge associated with banks with relatively short reach. We assume the existence of a latent variable $Y_i^{R|N*}$ that reflects the flow of benefits to firm i from choosing a global, regional, or local bank (assigned the values of 0, 1, or 2, respectively), conditional on the nationality chosen in the first stage,

$$Y_i^{R|N*} = h_N \text{ (Corporate Attributes)}, N = (0, 1, 2). \tag{4.15}$$

The set of corporate attributes can actually differ across nationality choice. Following McFadden (1978), assume that Y_i^{N*} and $Y_i^{R|N*}$ are linear in their regressors and that the regressions errors follow a generalized extreme-value distribution. This assumption implies that one can write the joint probability of observing a firm choosing nationality N and reach R as

$\Pr(N, R)$

$$= \frac{\exp\left(\alpha_1 ' Z_N^{\text{Host Nation}} + \alpha_2 ' Z_N^{\text{Differences between Home and Host Nation}} + \beta_N ' Z_{N,R}^{\text{Corporate}}\right)}{\sum\limits_{N=0}^{2} \sum\limits_{R=0}^{2} \exp\left(\alpha_1 ' Z_N^{\text{Host Nation}} + \alpha_2 ' Z_N^{\text{Differences between Home and Host Nation}} + \beta_N ' Z_{N,R}^{\text{Corporate}}\right)},$$
$$\tag{4.16}$$

the conditional probability of choosing R given N as

$$\Pr(R|N) = \frac{\exp\left(\beta_N ' Z_{N,R}^{\text{Corporate}}\right)}{\sum\limits_{R=0}^{2} \exp\left(\beta_N ' Z_{N,R}^{\text{Corporate}}\right)}, \tag{4.17}$$

and the unconditional probability of choosing N as:

$\Pr(N, R)$

$$= \frac{\exp\left(\alpha_1 {}' Z_N^{\text{Host Nation}} + \alpha_2 {}' Z_N^{\text{Differences between Home and Host Nation}}\right) \sum\limits_{R=0}^{2} \exp\left(\beta_N {}' Z_{N,R}^{\text{Corporate}}\right)}{\sum\limits_{N=0}^{2} \exp\left(\alpha_1 {}' Z_N^{\text{Host Nation}} + \alpha_2 {}' Z_N^{\text{Differences between Home and Host Nation}}\right) \sum\limits_{R=0}^{2} \exp\left(\beta_N {}' Z_{N,R}^{\text{Corporate}}\right)},$$

(4.18)

Define what McFadden (1978) terms to be the "inclusive value":

$$I_N = \ln\left(\sum\limits_{R=0}^{2} \exp\left(\beta_N {}' Z_{N,R}^{\text{Corporate}}\right)\right)$$

(4.19)

Then equation 4.18 can be expressed as

$\Pr(N, R)$

$$= \frac{\exp\left(\alpha_1 {}' Z_N^{\text{Host Nation}} + \alpha_2 {}' Z_N^{\text{Differences between Home and Host Nation}} + \rho I_N\right)}{\sum\limits_{N=0}^{2} \exp\left(\alpha_1 {}' Z_N^{\text{Host Nation}} + \alpha_2 {}' Z_N^{\text{Differences between Home and Host Nation}} + \rho I_N\right)},$$

(4.20)

The parameters β_N, α, and ρ are estimated by working backward in the decision tree, applying multinomial logit at each stage. First, the β_N are estimated at each nationality node (N = home, host, and third) by regressing the conditional bank reach observations $Y_i^{R|N}$ on corporate characteristics. Then, estimated values of β_N are used to construct inclusive values for each nationality node using equation 4.19. These inclusive values summarize the impact of corporate characteristics on the reach decision, conditional on a given choice of nationality. In the second step, α and ρ are estimated by regressing the bank nationality observations Y_i^N on host nation characteristics, differences between home and host nation characteristics, and the inclusive values.

One can also impute partial derivative estimates of the unconditional impact of the explanatory variables on bank reach. The unconditional probability of choosing a bank of a given reach, $P(R)$, can be expressed as

$$P(R) = \sum\limits_{N=0}^{2} P(R|N) \cdot P(N).$$

(4.21)

Partial derivatives can then be computed using the chain rule:

$$\frac{\partial P(R)}{\partial Z} = \sum_{N=0}^{2} \left[\frac{\partial P(R|N)}{\partial Z} \cdot P(N) + P(R|N) \cdot \frac{\partial P(N)}{\partial Z} \right] \qquad (4.22)$$

One can obtain estimates by replacing the right-hand side of equation 4.22 with the estimates of $\partial P(R|N)/\partial Z$ and $\partial P(N)/\partial Z$ from equation 4.17 and equation 4.20, respectively, and fitted values of $P(N)$ and $P(R|N)$. Standard errors for the imputed estimates are calculated in a similar fashion. Note that equation 4.22 reflects the effects of all three sets of explanatory variables on bank reach through their effects on the choice of bank nationality, as well as the direct effects of the corporate attributes.

4.2.4. Heteroskedastic Regression

Suppose we want to investigate the determinants of the degree of discretion used by a bank (loan officer) in setting loan conditions. Such an investigation could reveal the drivers of the choice the bank makes between offering relationship versus transactional oriented banking.

In order to identify the determinants of the dispersion of loan rates, for example, one can employ a regression model with multiplicative heteroskedasticity introduced by Harvey (1976).[8] The heteroskedastic version extends the linear regression model by also parametrizing the unexplained variance as function of exogenous covariates.

It is as if the heteroskedastic regression model comprises two equations—one to model the mean of the dependent variable, and one for the residual variance. In this application the mean equation captures the loan-pricing model while the variance equation (and its variables) determines the precision of the loan-pricing model. Hence, in the example, a higher precision implies the stricter application of rules, possibly as a result of a focus on transactional banking, while a lower precision could indicate the presence of extensive discretion granted to loan officers under a relationship banking strategy.

A conventional formulation of the heteroskedastic model is given by

$$y_i = X_i' \beta + u_i \qquad (4.23)$$

---

8. Our discussion is based partly on Cerqueiro et al. (2007).

and

$$Log\sigma_i^2 = Z_i'\gamma, \qquad (4.24)$$

with the identifying assumptions

$$E[u_i|X_i] = 0 \qquad (4.25)$$

and

$$Var[u_i|Z_i] = \sigma_i^2 = \exp\{Z_i'\gamma\}. \qquad (4.26)$$

y_i is the dependent variable, X_i a vector of explanatory variables in the mean equation, u_i a disturbance term, σ_i^2 the residual variance, and Z_i a vector of explanatory variables in the variance equation.

Under the normality assumption, the conditional distribution of y_i converges in distribution to the following normal distribution:

$$y_i|X_i, Z_i \xrightarrow{d} N(X_i'\beta, \exp\{Z_i'\gamma\}) \qquad (4.27)$$

As a result, we obtain maximum-likelihood estimates in the heteroskedastic regression model by maximizing the following log-likelihood function with respect to β and γ:

$$Log\,L = \frac{n}{2}\log(2\pi) - \frac{1}{2}\sum_{i=1}^n Z_i'\gamma - \frac{1}{2}\sum_{i=1}^n \exp(-Z_i'\gamma)(y_i - X_i'\beta)^2 \qquad (4.28)$$

From a theoretical perspective, the maximum likelihood estimators for the parameters in the mean and variance equations are, in expectation, uncorrelated (see Harvey 1976).

An alternative estimation procedure is to estimate the parameters in the mean equation by OLS and to use the squared errors as raw estimates of the individual variances. Then, one obtains estimates of the parameters in the variance equation by regressing the log of squared errors on the set of covariates in the vector Z. Despite being computationally simpler, there is a dramatic loss of efficiency in this two-step procedure (Harvey 1976). For that reason, our estimates are usually obtained via maximum likelihood.

The interpretation of the parameters of interest (γ) is crucial for the intended analysis here. Pick one variable in Z, say Z_k, and the respective parameter, γ_k. A positive γ_k indicates that the precision of the loan-pricing model decreases in Z_k. One can interpret such a result as evidence of a positive correlation between the variable Z_k and the weight of "discretion" in the loan-rate-setting process.

Cerqueiro et al. (2007) apply this methodology to banking and focus on the impact of a set of variables on loan rate dispersion as measured on the coefficients γ in equation 4.26. They find that larger loans, incorporated firms, firms without tax problems, firms with longer relationships, and younger firms exhibit a lower variance. These findings are economically significant. For example, an increase in loan amount from \$25,000 (the 25th percentile) to \$550,000 (the 75th percentile) implies a nearly sixfold increase in the fit of the mean equation, showing that residual variance becomes less important.

4.3. Evidence

4.3.1. Determinants of Characteristics of Bank Relationships

We first complete our discussion on the value of bank relationships by reviewing empirical work on the switching probabilities and costs underlying or resulting from relationship formation. Next, we review empirical evidence pertaining to the determinants of relationship characteristics such as the duration, scope, and number of relationships and subsequently summarize the many findings on the impact of bank relationships on the cost/availability of credit and firm performance (figure 4.1 provides the graphical road map for this part, as well).

4.3.1.1. Switching Probabilities and Costs

4.3.1.1.1. *Importance*   Some empirical studies investigate the effect of switching costs on prices and market power. Ausubel (1991), for example, shows that switching costs may explain the high interest rates on credit card balances, while Stango (1998), using variables related to switching, finds that switching costs are an important influence on pricing in that market. Sharpe (1997) finds that (banking) retail deposit rates drop when there are fewer noncommitted customers, that is, when the impact of switching costs is expected to be high. Dahlby and West (1986) support the effect of costly search on price dispersion in the liability insurance and document a similar result for the auto insurance.

Although the aforementioned empirical studies do point to the importance of switching costs in the determination of conduct and how it may be affected by various firms' policies, we generally lack information on the magnitude and significance of switching costs. Whether switching costs are an important empirical phenomenon probably depends on the specific environment, industry, product type, and time period. One possible reason for the lack of empirical documentation on the magnitude and significance of switching costs is that the necessary micro data on individual-level transitions are rarely, if ever, available to researchers, and this may be especially true for banking data. Hence, the estimation of switching costs, which are unobservable, cannot practically be accomplished using discrete choice models, as in Anderson, de Palma, and Thisse (1989) and Berry, Levinsohn, and Pakes (1995), for example. In the context of estimating switching costs, the unobservables are individual customers' purchase decision histories. More specifically, one usually lacks information on the identity of customers' previous suppliers (but see Ioannidou and Ongena 2007).

4.3.1.1.2. *Magnitude* The only structural model amenable for econometric estimation pertaining to the magnitude and significance of switching costs in the provision of bank loans is the one introduced by Kim, Kliger, and Vale (2003).[9]

In their model Kim et al. (2003) provide a setup that feeds on highly aggregated (conventionally available) data, lacking information on customer-specific transition history. They jointly estimate a first-order condition, demand and supply equations in a Bertrand oligopoly to extract information on the magnitude and significance of switching costs from highly aggregated data that do not contain customer-specific information. Their point estimate of switching cost obtained from panel data for Norwegian bank loans is 4.12 percent, suggesting that switching costs are quite substantial in this market (amounting to roughly one-third of the average interest rate on loans for the period of analysis). Their results also suggest that switching costs are even larger for smaller, retail customers.

In addition, Kim et al. (2003) are able to extract several counterfactuals of interest from their model such as the duration of the relationships and the value of lock-in for the banks. The range of customer–bank duration relationship is estimated to be between 11.3 and 16.7 years, with an average of 13.6 years, if markets are defined by branch-network size, or between 7.5 and 19.4 years, with an average of 13.5 years, if the definition is according

---

9. Another model by Shy (2002) generates a formula according to which switching costs are calculated.

to loan size. The interesting point though is the general pattern that the duration of relationship is smaller for the large banks (7.5 years for those with loans >12 billion Norwegian krones), consistent with Berg and Kim (1998).

The duration of relationship estimated is very much in line with recent literature on relationship lending within a bank-based system using detailed (survey) microdata. Ongena and Smith (2001) use panel data of connections between firms listed on the Oslo Stock Exchange and their banks, for the 1979–95 period (see also Ongena and Smith 1998). After correcting for censoring bias, the estimated mean duration of firm–bank relationship varies between 15 and 18 years. This is broadly in line with other studies using European and American survey data. Angelini, Di Salvo, and Ferri (1998), for example, report a mean duration of 14 years for Italy, and Harhoff and Körting (1998b) 13 years for Germany. On the other hand, Cole (1998) and Petersen and Rajan (1994) report between 7 and 11 years for the United States, while Degryse and Van Cayseele (2000) find the mean relationship length to be only 8 years in Belgium (table 4.1).

The estimated parameters Kim et al. (2003) also suggest that the contribution of the previous period's market share to the current one, is 0.2 when considering the entire sample. This means that about 20 percent of the average bank's market share is due to its bank–borrower relationship in the previous period. This however, can be as low as 17 percent and 0.2 percent for the very large banks when the market is defined by the branch network size and by the loan size, respectively. When smaller banks are also included, it is 32 percent and 42 percent, respectively. Again, this points to the higher mobility of (larger) customers working with larger banks where output is characterized by a higher proportion of wholesale loans.

4.3.1.1.3. *Value for the Bank*   An interesting and important issue is that of the proportion of the marginal value of a locked-in customer to the marginal increase of the bank's present value which is due to an additional locked-in customer. Based on the total sample, the marginal value of lock-in for a bank is 0.16; that is, 16 percent of the customer's added value is attributed to the lock-in phenomenon generated by switching costs.

It is also worth noting that the contribution of locked-in customers to banks' value decrease as the size of bank increases. Specifically, the contribution of locked-in customers to banks' value ranges from a low of 13 percent for the very large banks to 30 percent for the group including also the smaller ones when the market is defined according to branch-network

Table 4.1. Duration of Bank Relationships

Paper	Country	Year(s)	Sample Size	Average (Median) Firm Size	Average (Median) Duration, in Years
Bodenhorn (2003)	United States	1855	2,616	Small Firms	4.1
Petersen and Rajan (1995)	United States	1987	3,404	Employees: 26 (5)	10.8
Blackwell and Winters (1997)	United States	1988	174	Book Assets: 13.5	9.01
Cole (1998)	United States	1993	5,356	Book Assets: 1.63	7.03
Brick and Palia (2007)	United States	1993	766	Sales: 11.1 (5)	8.5 (6)
Scott (2004)	United States	2001	1,380	Employees: 16.6 (6)	4.5 (4.5)
Gopalan et al. (2007)	United States	1990–06	13,788	Total Assets: 4,245	4[a]
Horiuchi, Packer, and Fukuda (1988)	Japan	1962–72	479	Largest Firms	(21)
		1972–83	668		(30)
Gan (2007)	Japan	1984–93	11,393	All Publicly Listed Firms	6.85 (7)
Uchida, Udell, and Watanabe (2006a)	Japan	2002	1,863	SMEs	31.9
Elsas and Krahnen (1998)	Germany	1992–96	125/year	Sales: (30–150)	22.2
Harhoff and Körting (1998b)	Germany	1997	994	Employees: ± 40 (10)	±12
Lehmann and Neuberger (2001)	Germany	1997	357	SMEs	4.8[a]
Lehmann, Neuberger, and Rathke (2004)	Germany	1997	357	SMEs	4.8[a]
Ziane (2003)	France	2001	244	Employees: 32 (22)	14.4 (10)
Angelini et al. (1998)	Italy	1995	1,858	Employees: 10.3	14.0
Guiso (2003), Herrera and Minetti (2007)	Italy	1997	4,267	Employees: 67.7	16.1
Castelli, Dwyer, and Hasan (2006)	Italy	1998–00	10,764	Employees: 80 (30)a	17.6 (15)
Hernandez-Canovas and Martinez-Solano (2006)	Spain	1999	153	Sales: 10.0 (4.1)	16.8 (15)

(continued)

Table 4.1. *(Continued)*

Paper	Country	Year(s)	Sample Size	Average (Median) Firm Size		Average (Median) Duration, in Years
Sjögren (1994)	Sweden	1916–47	50	Largest Firms		>20 (5–29)
Zineldin (1995)	Sweden	1994	179	Employees: (< 49)		(>5)
Alem (2003)	Argentina	1998–99	4,158	80% Corporations		8
Bebczuk (2004)	Argentina	1999	143	Sales: 3.9		19.6
Degryse and Van Cayseele (2000)	Belgium	1997	17,776 loans	Employees: (1)		7.82
de Bodt, Lobez, and Statnik (2005)	Belgium	2001	296	TotalAssets: 0.03		11.7 (15)[a]
Farinha and Santos (2002)	Portugal	1980–96	1,471	Employees: 46.0		(4.7)
Thomsen (1999)	Denmark	1900–95	948	Assets: 125		15.5
Ongena and Smith (2001)	Norway	1979–95	111/year	Market Equity: 150		(15.8–18.1)
Kim et al. (2003)	Norway	1988–96	139 to 177/year	All Firms		8.9–13.6
Menkhoff and Suwanaporn (2007), Menkhoff, Neuberger, and Suwanaporn (2006)	Thailand	1992–96	555	Assets: 880 (10)		7.96

The table lists the reported duration of bank relationships. The papers are listed according to country size and sample period (the most recent samples are ranked last). The second column reports the country affiliation of the related firms, and the third column the sample year(s). Sample size is the number of firms (unless indicated otherwise). The average (median) firm size column lists both the size measure and the average (median) size of the firms in millions of U.S. dollars or number of employees. The final column provides the average (median) duration of firm–bank relationships in years.

[a] Our calculations.

Source: Updated from Degryse and Ongena (2008).

76

size. It is more pronounced when considering loan size as the definition of the market, where locked-in customers contribute only 1 percent in the case of the large banks, and 32 percent in the case of the smaller banks. Once more, these results emanate from the higher proportion of mobile wholesale customers of larger banks. It is noted that on the average (for either definition of the market) the locked-in customers contribute 23 percent to banks' value.

It is worth at this stage to highlight the facts emanating from studies concerning banking relationships. As can be expected, both partners to a lending relationship derive positive value from this engagement. As we saw in section 2.3, firms derive accreditation and the economic value emanating from it, as highlighted in the work by James (1987), who finds that bank loan announcements are associated with positive and statistically significant stock price reactions (shown to equal 193*** bp in a 2-day window), while announcements of privately placed and public issues of debt experience zero or negative stock price reactions.

The positive stock-price reaction supports the Fama (1985) argument that a bank loan provides accreditation for a firm's ability to generate a certain level of cash flows in the future. This contribution to borrowers is accompanied by gains to the bank emanating from borrowers' captivity generated by high switching costs. Significant switching costs confer positive marginal value to the bank from a borrower's lock-in and can contribute to 23 percent of the bank's value.

4.3.1.2. Duration

To understand the variation in the duration of bank–firm relationships across countries (table 4.1), recent papers have started to explore the impact of characteristics specific to relationships, firms, banks, and markets on the duration of bank–firm relationships (employing only within-country data so far). Tables 4.2 and 4.3 summarize the findings.

Take duration itself. Both Ongena and Smith (2001) and Farinha and Santos (2002) find that the estimated hazard functions display positive duration dependence, indicating that the likelihood a firm replaces a relationship increases in duration or alternatively, and as symbolized in table 4.3, that the continuation of a relationship is negatively affected by duration itself. The number of bank relationships the firm maintains also negatively influences the length of a relationship. Hence, both duration and the number of (other) bank relationships decrease borrowers' reticence to drop a relationship. An increase in duration may result in fiercer holdup making switching more attractive. Alternatively, relationship continuation and/or multiplicity

Table 4.2.   Determinants of the Duration of Bank Relationships: United States and Japan

	Paper	BMPRS	SCS	BDSS	GUY	UUW
	Country	United States	United States	United States	United States	Japan
	Sample Years	1993	1993	86–01	90–06	2002
	No. Observations	1,131	935	401,699	<12,287	1,863
	Model	IV	Logit	Logit	Logit[a]	IV
Type	Dependent	Length	Drop	Choose[b]	New	Length
Loan	Amount				+++	
	Lag Excess Yield				↔↔	
	Lag Excess Amount				+++	
	Purpose: Repayment				+	
	Purpose: Takeover				0	
	Asset Backed				0	
	Maturity				↔↔	
Relation	Duration		0		↔↔↔[c]	
	Number				0/+++[c]	
	Scope		+++	+++		
	Trust		+++			
Firm	Age	+++				+++
	(Age)^2					↔↔
	Size	+	0	+++	+++	+++
	Growth		0		0	
	Cash Flow					+++
	Profitability			+++		+++
	Leverage	0			↔	↔↔↔
	Audit/Certified					0
	In Compustat				+++	
Bank	Age	+++				
	Size	↔↔↔	0		↔↔↔	0
	No. Branches	+++				0
	Profitability		↔↔↔			
	Merged				↔↔↔	
Market	Local Banks			+++		
	Concentration	+	0			0

The table summarizes the results from studies on the determinants of the duration of bank relationships. Positive signs indicate that an increase in the indicated variable corresponds to a significantly longer duration of the bank relationships. The papers are listed from left to right according to country size and sample period (the most recent samples are ranked most to the right). The first column lists the variable names. The other columns contain the results from the respective papers. The paper citations on the first row are abbreviated to conserve space: BMPRS, Berger et al. (2005b); SCS, Saparito; Chen, and Sapienza (2004); BDSS, Bharath et al. (2007); GUY, Gopalan et al. (2007); UUW, Uchida et al. (2006a). The fifth row lists whether the employed empirical model is an instrumental variable (IV) or logit model. The sixth row indicates the specific dependent variable used in the paper. Other rows list the sign and significance levels of the coefficients on the independent variables as reported in the paper. Significance levels are based on all reported exercises and the authors' assessment.

[a] Multiple specifications are combined to conserve space.

[b] The signs of the independent variables are reversed to facilitate comparisons. T: target banks.

[c] Time between deals and syndicated loans. 0: Included in the specifications but not significant.

+++ Positive and significant at 1%, ++ at 5%, + at 10%.

↔↔↔ Negative and significant at 1%, ↔↔ at 5%, ↔ at 10%.

Source: Updated from Degryse and Ongena (2008).

Table 4.3. Determinants of the Duration of Bank Relationships: European Countries

		S	HM	FS	DMM	HK	HPW	T	OS	KOS
	Paper	S	HM	FS	DMM	HK	HPW	T	OS	KOS
	Country	IT	IT	PT	BE	DE	UK	DK	NO	NO
	Sample Years	89–95	2001	80–96	97–03	1997	1996	00–95	79–95	79–00
	No. Observations	50,000	3,494	1,471	600,000	1,228	±120	948	383	598
	Model	Probit	OLS	TVD	Logit	Logit	Logit	Logit	D	TVD
Type	Dependent	Drop	Length[a]	Hazard	Drop	Drop	Drop	Drop	Hazard	Hazard
Relation	Duration			↔↔↔				+/↔↔↔	↔↔↔	↔↔↔
	Switches			↔↔↔						
	Number				↔↔↔				↔↔↔	↔
Firm	Age	0	+++	0	+++	0	↔	++	+	
	(Age)²		↔↔							
	Size	↔↔↔	0	↔↔↔	+++	0	0	++	+++	+++
	Growth			↔↔↔			0		↔	
	Cash Flow		+++	++						
	Intangibles			0		↔	↔			
	Profitability	+++		0	+++		0		↔↔	0
	Fixed Assets		+++							
	Constrained					↔	↔↔↔			
	Leverage	↔↔↔		0	+++		++		↔↔↔	
	Bank Debt			↔↔↔						
	Urban					0				
	Audit/Certified		↔↔↔							
	Major Owner		↔↔↔							
Bank	Age			0						
	Size			0	+++	0		++	++	
	No. Branches		↔↔							
	Growth			0						
	Liquidity			0	+++					
	Profitability	T: +++	0	0	↔↔↔					
	Efficiency	T:↔↔↔			+++		++			
	Risk	T:↔↔↔			↔↔↔				0	
	Merged	T:↔↔↔			T:↔↔↔				0	T:↔↔↔
	State									+
Market	Local Banks			0						
	Concentration		++	0		0				

The table summarizes the results from studies on the determinants of the duration of bank relationships. Positive signs indicate that an increase in the indicated variable corresponds to a significantly longer duration of the bank relationships. The papers are listed from left to right according to the average number of bank relationships (as reported in Ongena and Smith 2000b) and sample period (the most recent samples are ranked most to the right). The first column lists the variable names. The other columns contain the results from the respective papers. The paper citations on the first row are abbreviated to conserve space: S, Sapienza (2002); HM, Herrera and Minetti (2007); FS, Farinha and Santos (2002); DMM, Degryse et al. (2006); HK, Harhoff and Körting (1998b); HPW, Howorth, Peel, and Wilson (2003); T, Thomsen (1999); OS, Ongena and Smith (2001); KOS, Karceski, Ongena, and Smith (2005). The second row lists country codes: IT, Italy; PT, Portugal; BE, Belgium; DE, Germany; DK Denmark; NO, Norway. The fifth row lists whether the employed empirical Model is an ordinary least squares (OLS), logit, probit, duration (D), or time-varying duration (TVD) model. The sixth row indicates the specific dependent variable used in the paper. Other rows list the sign and significance levels of the coefficients on the independent variables as reported in the paper. Significance levels are based on all reported exercises and our assessment. T, target banks; 0, included in the specifications but not significant.

[a] The signs of the independent variables are reversed to facilitate comparisons.

+++ Positive and significant at 1%, ++ at 5%, + at 10%.

↔↔↔ Negative and significant at 1%, ↔↔ at 5%, ↔ at 10%.

Source: Updated from Degryse and Ongena (2008).

may impart a good repayment record to competing banks thereby lowering borrowers' switching costs.

Most studies find that young, small, high-growth, intangible, constrained, or highly leveraged firms switch bank faster ceteris paribus. But there are some notable exceptions. Interestingly enough, the direction in which particular firm variables affect switching rates changes sign going "north to south" in Europe (table 4.3), not unlike the increase that is observed in the number and duration of relationships. For example, small firms severe relationships more easily than large firms in Norway, Denmark, and Belgium, at the same rate in the United Kingdom and Germany, but at a slower rate in Portugal and Italy. Hence, in Norway small firms may churn bilateral relationships, while in Italy small firms cherish their multiple relationships. On the other hand, in Norway large firms nurture a few steady relationships, while in Italy large firms continue to juggle, and drop, (too) many relationships.

A few studies also include bank and market characteristics. Larger and to a lesser extent, more liquid and efficient banks seem to retain borrowers longer (Gopalan, Udell, and Yerramilli 2007). Berger, Miller, Petersen, Rajan, and Stein (2005b) show it is the number of branches that matters for borrower retention, not bank asset size. The latter variable is actually negatively related to duration. Borrowers of target banks in a merger are often dropped. Market characteristics seem mostly to have no effect on the drop rate.

4.3.1.3. Scope

The number of lending and nonlending "products" that a bank "cross-sells" to a firm may be a second defining characteristic of a bank relationship. Conceptually, scope of a bank relationship is different from the concentration of borrowing (see section 4.3.1.4) or bank orientation (see section 4.3.3). In practice, empirical measures such as "Hausbank" status (as in Elsas and Krahnen 1998; Machauer and Weber 1998) may capture elements of all three dimensions.

Take the plain vanilla checking account as a banking product. By observing the parties and amounts involved in the many checking account transactions that take place, a bank may obtain an informational advantage vis-à-vis its competing banks (Nakamura 1993b), Vale (1993). Indeed, recent evidence confirms that observing these accounts is a valuable source of private information for the bank. On the basis of account information, the bank can lend to sounder businesses or react more swiftly when their outlook deteriorates (Mester, Nakamura, and Renault 2007), especially when dealing with small businesses (Norden and Weber 2007).

Only few studies have directly investigated the determinants of the scope of bank relationships (an exception is Liberti 2004). Most studies explore relationship scope within the wider context of the transactional versus relationship banking question that these studies address. Consequently, we return to the empirical work that is in part dealing with scope in section 4.3.3.

4.3.1.4. Number (and Concentration)

In addition to duration and scope, a third key characteristic of any bank relationship is the number of bank relationships the firm maintains and the resulting concentration of borrowing (and other products obtained) at the bank. For example, a firm has a relationship with a bank for 10 years and US$100,000 in credit and five other products outstanding. It is clear that this relationship with the bank is very different depending on the other bank relationships the firm maintains. Contrast the "no other banks" case with the situation in which the firm is also serviced by, for example, three other banks with a total of US$500,000 (and 15 other products) outstanding.

Table 4.4 assimilates estimates of the average and median number of bank relationships per firm across of variety of countries and data sets. We list details on the country of origin (alphabetized in the table), sample period, sample size, and average size of the firm (by sales or assets) within each sample. The data set in Ongena and Smith (2000b) covers 20 European countries, while Qian and Strahan (2007) employed data for a couple of dozen of countries where syndicated loans are situated.

There is large variation across data sets in the average number of bank relationships per bank, though multiple-bank relationships are a common feature to nearly all of the data sets. The first thing to note from the table is that multiple bank relationships are common across almost all the data sets. Small firms tend to maintain fewer bank relationships than large firms. For example, U.S. studies using the NSSBF (National Survey of Small Business Finance) data estimate the mean of two banks per firm and a median of one, while for the large U.S. firms in Houston and James (1996) the mean is five. The correspondence between firm size and number of relationships has been further documented for France by Dietsch (2003), for Italy by Guiso (2003), for Germany by Hommel and Schneider (2003), and for Thailand by Menkhoff and Suwanaporn (2007), for example.

There is also appears a strong country effect. Firms in the United Kingdom, Norway, and Sweden maintain relatively few bank relationships—fewer than three on average—while firms in Italy, Portugal, and Spain, for

Table 4.4.   Number of Bank Relationships

Country	Reference	Sample Year Start	End	Number of Observations	Number of Banks Mean	Median	Sales or Assets (A) Mean	Median
Argentina	Qian and Strahan (2007)	1994	2003	129		4		
Argentina	Streb, Bolzico, Henke, Rutman, and Escudero (2002)	1999	1999	16,095	3	2		
Argentina	Alem (2003)	1998	1999	1,364	2	1		
Australia	Qian and Strahan (2007)	1994	2003	677		3		
Austria	Ongena and Smith (2000b)	1996	1996	37	5		1,500	
Austria	Qian and Strahan (2007)	1994	2003	8		2		
Bangladesh	Qian and Strahan (2007)	1994	2003	4		1		
Belgium	Ongena and Smith (2000b)	1996	1996	10	11		3,500	
Belgium	Qian and Strahan (2007)	1994	2003	50		9		
Belgium	Soenen and Aggarwal (1989)	1987	1987	100	7	3		
Belgium	Degryse, Masschelein, and Mitchell (2004)	2002	2002	117,509	1	1		1
Belgium (F)	de Bodt et al. (2005)	2001	2001	296	3	2		
Brazil	Qian and Strahan (2007)	1994	2003	144		3		
Brazil	Castelar Pinheiro and Moura (2003)	2000	2000	178,832	2	1		
Canada	Anvari and Gopal (1983)	1981	1981	121	1	1		15
Chile	Qian and Strahan (2007)	1994	2003	70		6		
Chile	Repetto, Rodriguez, and Valdes (2002)	1990	1998	21,000	3	2	113	49
China	Qian and Strahan (2007)	1994	2003	230		3		
Colombia	Qian and Strahan (2007)	1994	2003	33		4		
Czech Rep.	Ongena and Smith (2000b)	1996	1996	59	5		50	
Denmark	Ongena and Smith (2000b)	1996	1996	51	4		750	
Denmark	Qian and Strahan (2007)	1994	2003	12		1		
Egypt	Qian and Strahan (2007)	1994	2003	9		5		
Finland	Qian and Strahan (2007)	1994	2003	60		6		
Finland	Ongena and Smith (2000b)	1996	1996	89	4			
France	Proust and Cadillat (1996)	1992	1995		13			
France	Ongena and Smith (2000b)	1996	1996	25	11			
France	Qian and Strahan (2007)	1994	2003	534		7		
France	Lefilliatre (2002)	1999	1999	415	6	5	750	
France	Refait (2003)	1993	1997	565	5	4		
France	Lefilliatre (2002)	1999	1999	2,428	3	2	250	
France	Ziane (2003)	2001	2001	244	2	2	32	22
France	Dietsch (2003)	1993	2000	2,530,353		2		
France	Proust and Cadillat (1996)	1992	1995		1			
France	Lefilliatre (2002)	1999	1999					
Germany	Ongena and Smith (2000b)	1996	1996	67	8		3,500	
Germany	Qian and Strahan (2007)	1994	2003	447		8		
Germany	Elsas and Krahnen (1998)	1992	1996	125	6	5		
Germany	Fischer (2000)	1997	1997	270		4		
Germany	Hommel and Schneider (2003)	2002	2002	390	3			
Germany	Harhoff and Körting (1998a)	1997	1997	994	2	1	40	10
Ghana	Qian and Strahan (2007)	1994	2003	22		5		
Greece	Ongena and Smith (2000b)	1996	1996	41	7		750	
Greece	Qian and Strahan (2007)	1994	2003	77		6		
Guatemala	Qian and Strahan (2007)	1994	2003	1		2		

Table 4.4. (*Continued*)

Country	Reference	Sample Year Start	End	Number of Observations	Number of Banks Mean	Median	Sales or Assets (A) Mean	Median
Hong Kong	Qian and Strahan (2007)	1994	2003	881		1		
Hungary	Ongena and Smith (2000b)	1996	1996	44	4		175	
Hungary	Qian and Strahan (2007)	1994	2003	36		3		
India	Berger, Klapper, Martinez Peria, and Zaida (2006)	2001	2001	3,423	3	1		
India	Qian and Strahan (2007)	1994	2003	234		2		
Indonesia	Qian and Strahan (2007)	1994	2003	581		5		
Indonesia	Jiangli et al. (2008)	1996	1998	320	2	1		
Ireland	Qian and Strahan (2007)	1994	2003	40		9		
Ireland	Ongena and Smith (2000b)	1996	1996	67	3		750	
Israel	Qian and Strahan (2007)	1994	2003	16		3		
Italy	Cesarini (1994)	1993	1993	263,376	33		large	
Italy	D'Auria et al. (1999)	1994	1994	177	30			
Italy	Detragiache, Garella, and Guiso (1997)	1989	1993	4,000	16	13	926	193
Italy	D'Auria et al. (1999)	1994	1994	572	16			
Italy	Ongena and Smith (2000b)	1996	1996	70	15		1,500	
Italy	Rossignoli and Chesini (1995)	1993	1993	1,527	15			
Italy	Pagano, Panetta, and Zingales (1998)	1982	1992	19,274	14	11	737	258
Italy	D'Auria et al. (1999)	1994	1994	1,473	11			
Italy	Tirri (2007)	1997	2004	25,000	10[a]	10[a]	A: 14	A: 14
Italy	Volpin (2001)	1993	1998	560	9	7		
Italy	Guiso (2003)	1997	1997	4,267	6		68	
Italy	Castelli et al. (2006)	1998	2000	10,764	5	4	80	30
Italy	Qian and Strahan (2007)	1994	2003	131		5		
Italy	Angelini et al. (1998)	1995	1995	1,858	2		10	
Italy	Cesarini (1994)	1993	1993	263,376	2		Small	
Ivory Coast	Qian and Strahan (2007)	1994	2003	3		9		
Japan	Hwan Shin et al. (2003)	1999	1999	570	15	12		
Japan	Tsuruta (2003)	2002	2002	25,000	9	8	450	
Japan	Horiuchi (1993)	1990	1990	309	8		450	
Japan	Sterken and Tokutsu (2003)	1982	1999	20,740	8	6		
Japan	Tsuruta (2003)	2002	2002	25,000	6	5	200	
Japan	Qian and Strahan (2007)	1994	2003	1,023		5		
Japan	Tsuruta (2003)	2002	2002	25,000	4	4	60	
Japan	Horiuchi (1993)	1990	1990	126	3		150	
Japan	Tsuruta (2003)	2002	2002	25,000	3	3	10	
Japan	Horiuchi (1994)	1992	1992	189	3	3	15	
Japan	Horiuchi (1994)	1992	1992	175	3	3	5	
Luxembourg	Ongena and Smith (2000b)	1996	1996	8	5		375	
Malaysia	Qian and Strahan (2007)	1994	2003	482		2		
Mexico	Qian and Strahan (2007)	1994	2003	256		6		
Morocco	Qian and Strahan (2007)	1994	2003	4		8		
Mozambique	Qian and Strahan (2007)	1994	2003	1		11		
Netherlands	Soenen and Aggarwal (1989)	1987	1987	85	7	3		
Netherlands	Qian and Strahan (2007)	1994	2003	371		6		
Netherlands	Ongena and Smith (2000b)	1996	1996	49	4		1,500	

(*continued*)

Table 4.4.   (*Continued*)

Country	Reference	Sample Year Start	End	Number of Observations	Number of Banks Mean	Median	Sales or Assets (A) Mean	Median
New Zealand	Qian and Strahan (2007)	1994	2003	108		3		
Nigeria	Qian and Strahan (2007)	1994	2003	5		12		
Norway	Ongena and Smith (2000b)	1996	1996	41	2		750	
Norway	Qian and Strahan (2007)	1994	2003	70		2		
Norway	Ongena and Smith (2001)	1979	1995	1,500	1	1	A: 150	
Pakistan	Qian and Strahan (2007)	1994	2003	38		3		
Panama	Qian and Strahan (2007)	1994	2003	10		10		
Peru	Qian and Strahan (2007)	1994	2003	26		6		
Philippines	Qian and Strahan (2007)	1994	2003	131		1		
Philippines	Jiangli et al. (2008)	1996	1998	171	3	2		
Poland	Qian and Strahan (2007)	1994	2003	39		6		
Poland	Ongena and Smith (2000b)	1996	1996	13	3			
Portugal	Qian and Strahan (2007)	1994	2003	24		17		
Portugal	Ongena and Smith (2000b)	1996	1996	43	12		750	
Portugal	Farinha and Santos (2002)	1980	1996	54,182	2	1	27	
Senegal	Qian and Strahan (2007)	1994	2003	4		5		
Singapore	Qian and Strahan (2007)	1994	2003	301		2		
Slovenia	Qian and Strahan (2007)	1994	2003	4		2		
South Africa	Qian and Strahan (2007)	1994	2003	50		10		
South Korea	Bae, Kang, and Lim (2002)	1996	1997	486	6	6	A: 404	
South Korea	Ferri, Kang, and Kim (2002)	1995	1999	15,305	3			
South Korea	Qian and Strahan (2007)	1994	2003	612		2		
South Korea	Jiangli et al. (2008)	1996	1998	557	6	4		
Spain	Ongena and Smith (2000b)	1996	1996	68	10		1,500	
Spain	Hernandez-Canovas and Martinez-Solano (2006)	1999	1999	153	3	2		
Spain	Qian and Strahan (2007)	1994	2003	449		2		
Sri Lanka	Qian and Strahan (2007)	1994	2003	1		1		
Sweden	Qian and Strahan (2007)	1994	2003	85		5		
Sweden	Ongena and Smith (2000b)	1996	1996	50	3		1,500	
Sweden	Berglöf and Sjögren (1998)	1984	1993	90		1		
Sweden	Zineldin (1995)	1994	1994	179		1		25
Switzerland	Qian and Strahan (2007)	1994	2003	85		9		
Switzerland	Ongena and Smith (2000b)	1996	1996	39	4		3,500	
Switzerland	Neuberger, Pedergnana, and Räthke-Döppner (2008)	1996	1996	1,703	2	2		
Switzerland	Neuberger, Räthke, and Schacht (2006)	2002	2002	305,807	2	2		4
Switzerland	Neuberger et al. (2008)	2002	2002	1,700	2	2		
Taiwan	Shen and Wang (2003)	1991	2000	349	8	9		
Taiwan	Yu and Hsieh (2003)	1990	2002	3,759	8	7		
Taiwan	Yu, Pennathur, and Hsieh (2007)	1991	2000	579	6	4		
Thailand	Menkhoff and Suwanaporn (2007)	1992	1996	557	4			
Thailand	Qian and Strahan (2007)	1994	2003	401		3		
Thailand	Jiangli et al. (2008)	1996	1998	396	3	2		
Tunisia	Qian and Strahan (2007)	1994	2003	3		5		
Turkey	Qian and Strahan (2007)	1994	2003	50		5		

Table 4.4. (*Continued*)

| Country | Reference | Sample Year | | Number of Observations | Number of Banks | | Sales or Assets (A) | |
		Start	End		Mean	Median	Mean	Median
United States	Petersen and Rajan (1995)	1987	1987	3,404	1	1	26	5
United States	Brick and Palia (2007)	1993	1998	1,125	1	1		
United States	Houston and James (1996)	1980	1990	750			5	
United Kingdom	Soenen and Aggarwal (1989)	1987	1987	70	30	8		
United Kingdom	Qian and Strahan (2007)	1994	2003	1,961		4		
United Kingdom	Ongena and Smith (2000b)	1996	1996	142	3		1,500	
Uruguay	Qian and Strahan (2007)	1994	2003	1		1		
Venezuela	Qian and Strahan (2007)	1994	2003	47		4		
Zambia	Qian and Strahan (2007)	1994	2003	9		4		
Zimbabwe	Qian and Strahan (2007)	1994	2003	3		1		

The table lists the reported number of bank relationships. The papers are listed alphabetically according to country name and the reported mean/median number of banks (high to low). Number of observations is the number of firms (unless indicated otherwise). The sixth and seventh columns list the mean and median number of banks the firms engage. The last two columns report the average and median firm size by sales or assets (book or market, indicated by A).

a Our calculations.

example, maintain on average 10 or more bank relationships.[10] Ongena and Smith (2000b) show that the relative rankings in table 4.4 of the European countries holds after controlling for firm size (along with other firm characteristics). Thus, although firm size is important in describing the number of bank relationships per firm, the size of firms within a country alone does not explain the variation in the average number of bank relationships across countries.

4.3.1.4.1. *Micro Factors*   Theory offers many, often complementary, insights on the choice of bilateral versus multilateral credit relationships, and on the optimal number of relationships in case multiple liens are maintained. Multiple bank relationships may reduce the holdup problem of relationship lending (Rajan 1992; von Thadden 1992), but it can lead to coordination failure in case of default (Bolton and Scharfstein 1996; Hart 1995; Dewatripont and Maskin 1995).[11] Bolton and Scharfstein (1996), for example, show that multiple bank lending lowers the liquidation value

---

10. For some countries, e.g., Belgium, there is a large discrepancy between the number of domestic cash management relationships (around 10, as reported in Ongena and Smith 2000b) and the number of banks from which the firms contemporaneously obtains loans as recorded in the credit register (one or two, as in, e.g., Degryse, Masschelein, and Mitchell 2006). Differences in relationship definition and sample characteristics (firm size, e.g.) may partly explain the difference.

11. Our discussion is based partly on Ongena et al. (2007b). See also Gangopadhyay and Mukhopadhyay (2002), Du (2003), or Povel (2004), e.g., for related arguments.

of the firm and only the firms of the highest credit quality tend to borrow from multiple creditors. Bris and Welch (2005), on the other hand, argue that higher quality firms choose fewer creditors signaling their confidence of not going bankrupt given that concentration enhances their creditors' bargaining power. Bhattacharya and Chiesa (1995), Yosha (1995), and von Rheinbaben and Ruckes (2004) draw attention to the confidentiality in a bilateral bank–firm relationship, potentially attracting R&D intensive and high-quality firms to opt for such a financing arrangement.

Other studies emphasize the banks' side as well when exploring the optimality of the number of relationships. Detragiache et al. (2000), for example, explain multiple relationships as the need for diversification of bank liquidity risk by firms. Carletti (2004) explores how the number of bank relationships affects banks' monitoring incentives, and Carletti, Cerasi, and Daltung (2007) analyze banks' incentives to finance a firm together with other banks when they have limited lending abilities and monitoring is important (see also Fluet and Garella 2007).

We tabulate the results from many studies regressing a bilateral/multilateral relationship dummy or the number of relationships as the dependent variable on a variety of relation, loan, firm, bank, and/or market characteristics. We split the studies in European (table 4.5) and other countries (table 4.6). Specifications differ rather dramatically, but quite a few results seem robust across the many studies we list. Not surprisingly, older and larger firms have more bank relationships ceteris paribus. Less profitable, distressed, low-cash-flow, intangible, and leveraged firms also maintain more relationships. These findings broadly fit models, for example, in which firms signal their low quality through a multilateral financing arrangement, either because multiple creditors have less bargaining power in bankruptcy (Bris and Welch (2005) or because multilateral borrowing ensures the firms' low quality is revealed resulting in accommodation by their product market competitors (Yosha 1995). Of course, these findings could also be due to the lack of willingness of the banks to bear all the risk of such borrowers (e.g., D'Auria, Foglia, and Reedtz 1999).

Characteristics of the banks enjoying the bank–firm relationship are also often included in the regressions. An engagement with an older, larger, state, or foreign bank is more likely to be part of a multilateral arrangement, potentially to reduce the holdup problem of repeated borrowing from this type of bank (Rajan 1992; von Thadden 1992).

4.3.1.4.2. *Macro Factors* As already mentioned, one unexpected aspect in this line of empirical investigation is the strong country effect, comprehensively documented in Ongena and Smith (2000b) and Qian and

Table 4.5. Determinants of the Number of Bank Relationships: In-Country Studies Using European Data

		DGG	V	CM	T	Z	DG	DMM	HK	MW
	Papers	DGG	V	CM	T	Z	DG	DMM	HK	MW
	Country	Italy	Italy	Italy	Italy	France	France	Belgium	Germany	Germany
	Sample Year(s)	1994	1993–98	1997	1997–04	2001	1993–00	2000	1997	1992–96
	No. Observations	1,754	560	393	>25,000	244	NA	123,413	1,228	723
	Average (Median) Firm Size	Small	S: 1,700	S: 18	A: ±14 (14)[a]	E: 32 (22)	NA	Small	E: ±40 (10)	S: (30–150)
Type	Dependent Variable	%	No.	No.	% >2	No.	%	No.	No.	No.
Relation	Duration					++				+++
	Scope					↔↔				↔↔↔↔
Firm	Age	0		+++	0	0			+++	
	(Age)²				0					
	Size	+++	+++	+++	+	++	+++	+++	+++	+++
	(Size)²				↔↔↔					0
	Profitability	↔↔↔			↔↔	↔↔↔	↔↔↔↔	+++	↔↔↔	
	(Profitability)²	0			+++		↔↔↔↔	↔↔↔↔		
	Cash Flow				0		+++		++	0
	Risk or Distress				0		+			
	Sales Growth				↔↔↔		+++			
	Intangibles	0		++	0		+++		0	
	Tangibles/Bank Debt				↔↔↔↔		+++	+++		
	Leverage	+++	+++	++	+	++		+++		
	Bank Debt	+++	+++	+++						
	Other/All Debt								0	
	Listed		↔↔↔							
	Owner Income Rights		+++						↔↔↔	
	Urban									

(continued)

87

Table 4.5. *(Continued)*

	DGG	V	CM	T	Z	DG	DMM	HK	MW
Papers	DGG	V	CM	T	Z	DG	DMM	HK	MW
Country	Italy	Italy	Italy	Italy	France	France	Belgium	Germany	Germany
Sample Year(s)	1994	1993–98	1997	1997–04	2001	1993–00	2000	1997	1992–96
No. Observations	1,754	560	393	>25,000	244	NA	123,413	1,228	723
Average (Median) Firm Size	Small	S: 1,700	S: 18	A: ±14 (14)[a]	E: 32 (22)	NA	Small	E: ±40 (10)	S: (30–150)
Type — Dependent Variable	%	No.	%	% >2	No.	%	No.	No.	No.
Bank — Size	++							+++	
Growth	0								
Liquidity	↔↔↔	+++							
Bad Loans	↔	++							
Market — Concentration				+++	++			0	
(Concentration)²				↔↔↔	↔↔↔				
No. of Branches				0	0				
Past No. of Branches				↔↔↔	+++				
Current Δ No. of Branches				0	++				
No. of Savings Banks				++	0				
No. of COOP Banks				++	0				
Urban				0					

The table summarizes the results from in-country studies on the determinants of the number of bank relationships. Positive signs indicate that an increase in the indicated variable corresponds to a significantly higher number of bank relationships. The papers are listed from left to right according to the average number of bank relationships (as reported in Ongena and Smith 2000b) and sample period (the most recent samples are ranked most to the right). The first column lists the variable names. The other columns contain the results from the respective papers. The paper citations on the first row are abbreviated to conserve space (using author and journal initials and years): DGG, Detragiache et al. (2000); V, Volpin (2001); CM, Cosci and Meliciani (2002); T, Tirri (2007); Z, Ziane (2003); DG, Dietsch and Golitin-Boubakari (2002); DMM, Degryse et al. (2006); HK, Harhoff and Körting (1998a); MW, Machauer and Weber (2000). The fifth row reports the average (median) firm size as either assets (A) or sales (S) of the firms in millions of U.S. dollars in the last year of the sample or as the number of employees (E). The sixth row indicates the specific dependent variable used in the paper: % (>2), probability of multiple (more than two) bank relationships; No., number of bank relationships. Other rows list the sign and significance levels of the coefficients on the independent variables as reported in the paper. Significance levels are based on all reported exercises and our assessment. 0, Included in the specifications but not significant.

+++ Positive and significant at 1%, ++ at 5%, + at 10%.

↔↔↔ Negative and significant at 1%, ↔↔ at 5%, ↔ at 10%.

[a] Our calculations.

Table 4.6.   Determinants of the Number of Bank Relationships: Other In-Country Studies

Panel A	Papers	NPR	NPR	RS	HSF	ST	UUW	BKSZ	YH
	Country	CH	CH	United States	United States	JP	JP	IN	TW
	Sample Year(s)	1996	2002	88–03?	1998	82–99	02	01	90–02
	Number of Observations	1,703	1,700	218	1,117	20,740	1,863	3,423	3,397
	Average (Median) Firm Size	E:4	E:4	S:6,327		NA	E:75	Small	A: ±250
Type	Dependent Variable	No. and %	No. and %	%	%	%	No.	%	%
Relation	Duration				+				
	Scope					++	++		
Loan	Collateral	+++	+++	0					
	Purpose			0					
	Type			0					
Firm	Age						↔/++	0	0
	Size	+++	+++	++		0	++	↔↔↔↔↔ ↔↔↔↔↔	+++
	Profitability			0		0	0	0	0
	Cash Flow					0	0		
	Growth			0	↔↔↔↔ ↔	↔↔↔			↔↔↔↔
	Tobin's Q			0					
	Distress			0					
	Intangibles					++			+++
	Leverage			++			++		
	Bank Debt					++			+++
	Other/All Debt				0/++	↔↔↔		+++	+++
	Listed							+++	
	Incorporated	++							

(continued)

Table 4.6. (*Continued*)

Panel A	Papers	NPR	NPR	RS	HSF	ST	UUW	BKSZ	YH
	Country	CH	CH	United States	United States	JP	JP	IN	TW
	Sample Year(s)	1996	2002	88–03?	1998	82–99	02	01	90–02
	Number of Observations	1,703	1,700	218	1,117	20,740	1,863	3,423	3,397
	Average (Median) Firm Size	E:4	E:4	S:6,327		NA	E:75	Small	A: ±250
Type	Dependent Variable	No. and %	No. and %	%	%	%	No.	%	%
	Owner Income Rights				0				+++
	Owner Manager				+				
	Other Owner Specs.				0				
	Business Group						0		
	Audit							+++ +++	
	International	0	0						
Bank	Age	++					0	+++	+++
	Size	+	0					+++ +++	+++
	Government-Owned							+++ +++	+++
	Foreign-Owned							+++ +++	
Market	Concentration	+	0				0	↔	
	Branch Density		0				0	0	
	Population Density						0	0	

90

Panel B	Paper		JUY		
		ID	KR	PH	TH
	Country				
	Sample Year(s)	1996–98	1996–98	1996–98	1996–98
	No. Observations	320	557	171	396
	Average (Median) Firm Size				
Type	Dependent Variable	No.	No.	No.	No.
Firm	Size	+++	+++	+++	+
	Capacity Utilization	↔	0	0	0
	Growth	0	0	++	0
	Leverage	++	+++	0	+
	International	0	0	0	0

The table summarizes the results from in-country studies on the determinants of the number of bank relationships. Positive signs indicate that an increase in the indicated variable corresponds to a significantly higher number of bank relationships. The papers are listed from left to right according to country size and sample period (the most recent samples are ranked most to the right). The first column lists the variable names. The other columns contain the results from the respective papers. The paper citations on the first row are abbreviated to conserve space (using author initials): NPR, Neuberger et al. (2008); RS, Roberts and Siddiqi (2004); HSF, Han; Storey; and Fraser (2006); ST, Sterken and Tokutsu (2003); UUW, Uchida et al. (2006a); BKSZ, Berger et al. (2006); YH, Yu and Hsieh (2003); JUY, Jiangli et al. (2008). The second row lists country codes (CH, Switzerland; JP, Japan; TW, Taiwan; IN, India; ID, Indonesia; KR, South Korea; PH, Philippines; TH, Thailand). The fifth row reports the average (median) firm size as either sales (S) of the firms in millions of U.S. dollars in the last year of the sample or as the number of employees (E). The sixth row indicates the specific dependent variable used in the paper: %, probability of multiple bank relationships; No., number of bank relationships. Other rows list the sign and significance levels of the coefficients on the independent variables as reported in the paper. Significance levels are based on all reported exercises and our assessment. 0, Included in the specifications but not significant.

+++ Positive and significant at 1%, ++ at 5%, + at 10%.

↔↔↔ Negative and significant at 1%, ↔↔ at 5%, ↔ at 10%.

Strahan (2007), but reflected in the many single country data sets reported in table 4.5. Table 4.7 summarizes the findings of the three cross-country studies we are aware of that regress the number of relationships on country characteristics. Firms located countries with a French or German legal origin, with a lower degree of judicial efficiency or shareholder protection, have more bank relationships, results not incompatible with, for example, the diversification motive in Detragiache et al. (2000).

One interesting question that has received only recently some attention is whether and how the number of bank relationships varies over time or the business cycle, and how large firms may move between market and bank finance depending upon the business cycle (see Kashyap, Stein, and Wilcox 1993). The few studies that do have access to the necessary data come to interesting conclusions. The number of relationships seem overall quite stable, especially for small firms (Proust and Cadillat 1996), without any clear trend (the number trends down in Hommel and Schneider 2003), up in Dietsch (2003). On the other hand, there seems some tantalizing evidence of variation, at a business cycle frequency, in the number of relationships maintained by large firms (Lefilliatre 2002; Sterken and Tokutsu 2003; D'Auria et al. 1999). More research on this front could be fruitful.

4.3.1.4.3. *Number versus Concentration* Most of the literature addressing multiple banking thus far assumes equal financing shares. However, "unequal," "asymmetric," or "concentrated" bank borrowing is widespread, as firms often borrow extensively from one relationship lender and smaller amounts from multiple arm's length lenders. Creditor concentration may play a pivotal role in balancing the holdup problem of relationship lending with the coordination failure of multiple bank lending (Elsas, Heinemann, and Tyrell 2004; Hubert and Schafer 2002), but only a few recent papers study creditor concentration. Table 4.8 summarizes their findings.

Guiso and Minetti (2005), for example, argue that banks prevent unsound firms from defaulting for the purpose of seizing their assets during the restructuring process. As a result, firms with more valuable and redeployable assets tend to spread their borrowing more unevenly to prevent this behavior by the relationship lender during restructuring (because with higher asymmetry less informed banks would have no incentives to continue the project).

Ongena et al. (2007b) find that higher quality firms with more redeployable assets tend to concentrate their borrowing (for contradictory findings, see Guiso and Minetti 2005). Ongena et al. (2007b) also find that the degree of creditor concentration is positively related to the regional market concentration of bank lending (showing that firms are geographically limited in their funding choices) and increases when the relationship lender is more

Table 4.7.   The Number of Bank Relationships: Cross-Country Studies

Type	Paper	OS	V	MSW	QS
	Country	21 European	16 European	3 European	60 Countries
	Sample Years	1996	1996	2001	1994–03
	No. Observations	1,010 firms	16 countries	305 firms	11,083
	Firm Sales	750	750	Around 2	
	Dependent Variable	No.	No.	%	Ln(No.)
Loan	Line of Credit	0			+++
	Size				+++
Relation	Scope	0		++	
	Distance			+++	
Firm	Size	+++		++	
	Age			++	
	R&D Investment			$\leftrightarrow$	
Bank	Size			+++	
Market	Concentration Measure	$\leftrightarrow\leftrightarrow$	0	$\leftrightarrow\leftrightarrow\leftrightarrow$	
	Competition Measure			+++	
	Bank Fragility	$\leftrightarrow\leftrightarrow\leftrightarrow$	0		
	(Bank Fragility)^2	+++	0		
Country	Economic Development			+++	$\leftrightarrow$
	Equity Market	$\leftrightarrow$	0	$\leftrightarrow\leftrightarrow\leftrightarrow$	
	Bond Market	+++	0		
	Banking Sector			++	0
	Judicial Efficiency	$\leftrightarrow\leftrightarrow\leftrightarrow$	$\leftrightarrow\leftrightarrow$	$\leftrightarrow\leftrightarrow\leftrightarrow$	
	Creditor Protection	$\leftrightarrow\leftrightarrow\leftrightarrow$	0		0
	Shareholder Protection		$\leftrightarrow\leftrightarrow$		
	Ownership Protection				0
	French Legal Origin				+
	German Legal Origin				+
	Scandinavian Legal Origin				0
	Socialist Legal Origin				0
	Legal Formalism				0
	Lack of Corruption				+

The table summarizes the results from cross-country studies on the determinants of the number of bank relationships. Positive signs indicate that an increase in the indicated variable corresponds to a significantly higher number of bank relationships. The papers are listed from left to right according to publication date. The first column lists the variable names. The other columns contain the results from the respective papers. The paper citations on the first row are abbreviated to conserve space (using author initials): OS, Ongena and Smith (2000b); V, Volpin (2001); MSW, Mercieca, Schaeck, and Wolfe (2008); QS, Qian and Strahan (2007). The second row lists the number and type of countries. The fifth row reports the average firm sales in millions of U.S. dollars in the last year of the sample or as the number of employees (E). The sixth row indicates the specific dependent variable used in the paper: %, probability of multiple bank relationships; No., number of bank relationships. Other rows list the sign and significance levels of the coefficients on the independent variables as reported in the paper. Significance levels are based on all reported exercises and our assessment. 0, Included in the specifications but not significant.

+++ Positive and significant at 1%, ++ at 5%, + at 10%.

$\leftrightarrow\leftrightarrow\leftrightarrow$ Negative and significant at 1%, $\leftrightarrow\leftrightarrow$ at 5%, $\leftrightarrow$ at 10%.

Table 4.8.   Determinants of the Concentration of Bank Relationships: In-Country Studies

		GM		OTW		R			
Papers		GM		OTW		R			
Country		United States		Germany		France			
Sample Year(s)		1993–98		1993–03		1993–97			
Number of Observations		3,628		±17,000		565			
Average (Median) Firm Size		E: 30		A: 44 (7)		S: 40 (10)			
Dependent Variable		%	1 − HHI	%	1 − HHI	%	1 − HHI	No.	>1 Main
Type									
Relation	Duration	↔↔↔↔						0	
Firm	Size	+++		+++	+++	+++	+++	+++	+++
	Profitability			0	0	0/+++	0	0/0	0/+
	Growth					0	↔↔↔↔/0	0/+	0
	Investments					0		0	
	Cash Flow/Liquidity	↔↔↔↔		+++	↔↔↔↔	↔↔		↔↔↔↔	↔↔↔↔
	Risk or Distress	+++		+++	+++				
	Intangibles	+++						0	0
	Leverage	+++		+++	+++	0		+++	+++
	Trade Credit					+++	+++	↔↔↔↔	↔↔↔↔
	Public Debt	0				+++	+++	↔↔↔↔	↔↔↔↔
	Owner Share	0							
	Urban	↔↔↔		↔↔					
	Geographical Scope	++		++					

The table summarizes the results from in-country studies on the determinants of the number and concentration of bank relationships. Positive signs indicate that an increase in the indicated variable corresponds to a significantly higher number or lower concentration of bank relationships. The papers are listed from left to right according to country size. The first column lists the variable names. The other columns contain the results from the respective papers. The paper citations on the first row are abbreviated to conserve space (using author and journal initials and years); GM, Guiso and Minetti (2005); OTW, Ongena et al. (2007b); R, Refait (2003). The fifth row reports the average (median) firm size as either sales (S) of the firms in millions of U.S. dollars in the last year of the sample or as the number of employees (E). The sixth row indicates the specific dependent variable used in the paper: %, probability of multiple bank relationships; 1 − HHI, is one minus the Herfindahl-Hirschman Index of loan shares; No., number of bank relationships; >1 main, probability the number of main bank relationships exceeds 1. Other rows list the sign and significance levels of the coefficients on the independent variables as reported in the paper. Significance levels are based on all reported exercises and our assessment. 0, included in the specifications but not significant.

+++ Positive and significant at 1%, ++ at 5%, + at 10%.

↔↔↔↔ Negative and significant at 1%, ↔↔↔ at 5%, ↔↔ at 10%.

profitable. Overall, these results indicate the importance of firm, bank, and market characteristics in the determination of the concentration of financing.

4.3.1.5. Intensity, Social Interaction, and Bank Control

Besides duration, scope, and number (concentration), it is also possible to reflect on and measure the intensity (Binks and Ennew 1997; Bodenhorn 2003) and social interaction (Lehmann and Neuberger 2001) embedded in a bank–firm relationship. These elements also play a role in determining bank geography and organization, issues we discuss in section 5.2.

Bank control is another dimension of the bank–firm relationship that is widely discussed. Banks can own equity in the firm. Even a small stake may be relevant to limit rent extraction, for example, as in Mahrt-Smith (2006). Banks may also dispatch (receive) board members, the so-called "bankers on boards."

We summarize the results of a few studies on the determinants of bankers on boards in table 4.9. Large and tangible firms may have more bankers on their boards. Especially firm distress decreases the likelihood U.S. firm boards contain bankers, as board membership may undercut the bank's claim vis-à-vis other creditors in case of default. On the other hand, in some countries, such as Japan, banks may actually send board members over to help turn around badly performing firms (Miarka 1999).

Finally, one can also study the determinants and choice of domestic versus cross-border bank–firm relationships. We delay a discussion of a paper by Berger et al. (2003) dealing with the choice of this particular characteristic of the relationship to section 5.2.3.2 (see also Berger and Smith 2003).

4.3.1.6. Relationships in Deposit and Interbank Markets

There are only a few studies on the magnitude and determinants of customer switching cost in bank deposit markets. Shy (2002), for example, calculates depositor switching costs for four banks in Finland in 1997. He finds that costs are approximately 0, 10, and 11 percent of the value of deposits for the smallest to largest commercial bank and up to 20 percent for a large Finnish bank providing many government services.

Kiser (2002) focuses on the length of household deposit relationships with their banks and on the determinants of their switching costs. She uses U.S. survey data for 1999. Median U.S. household tenure at is equals 10 years. The geographical stability of the household and the quality of the customer service offered at the bank are key factors in determining whether or not customers stay with the bank. Switching costs seem nonmonotonic

Table 4.9.   Determinants of Bank Control

Paper	Byrd and Mizruchi (2005)	Kroszner and Strahan (2001)	Santos and Rumble (2006)	Morck and Nakamura (1999)	Kaplan and Minton (1994)	Gorton and Schmid (2000)
Country	United States	United States	United States	Japan	Japan	Germany
Sample Years	1980–91	1992	2000	1981–87	1980–88	1975 + 1986
Number of Observations	456	430	27,051	2,371	933	138
Firm size	Large	Large	Large	Large	Large	Large
Measure	Presence and Number of bankers on board	Presence of a banker on board	Presence of a banker on board	Probability of a banker appointment	Probability of a banker appointment	Fraction of board seats held by banks
Relation						
Firm Scope				+		
Size	0	+++	++			↔↔
Growth	0					
Profitability			+	↔↔	0	
Stock return				↔↔↔	↔↔	
Risk	↔↔	+/↔↔↔			↔↔↔↔	
Cash Flow	0					
Intangibility	0	↔↔↔↔		↔↔		
Debt		0	+	0		
Bank Debt		↔↔↔		+++	+++	
Short-Term Debt	0					
Bank Debt by Largest Lender					+	
Group Member					0	
Concentration of Ownership or Control Rights					0	0
Board size	↔ +++					
Bank Equity Control Rights			+			+++
Voting Rights						++

The table summarizes the results from studies on the determinants of bank control. Positive signs indicate that an increase in the indicated variable corresponds to significantly more control. The papers are listed from left to right according to country size and sample period (the most recent samples are ranked most to the right). The first column lists the variable names. The other columns contain the results from the respective papers. The fifth row reports the average firm assets in millions of U.S. dollars in the last year of the sample or as the number of employees (E). The sixth row indicates the specific dependent variable used in the paper. Other rows list the sign and significance levels of the coefficients on the independent variables as reported in the paper. Significance levels are based on all reported exercises and our assessment. 0, included in the specifications but not significant.

++ Positive and significant at 1%, ++ at 5%, + at 10%.

↔↔↔ Negative and significant at 1%, ↔↔ at 5%, ↔ at 10%.

Source: Updated from Degryse, Ongena, and Tümer-Alkan (2007).

in income: higher income as well as more educated households and lower income as well as minority households switch less often. Hence, the opportunity cost of time for the first group and the information available to households in the other group may play a role in determining household switching.

While the existence and importance of relationships between borrowers/depositors and banks has been widely documented and discussed by bankers and academics alike, recent preliminary evidence by Cocco, Gomes, and Martins (2003) shows that even in the anonymous and highly liquid interbank market, relationships between banks may play a role in overcoming informational problems and in the provision of insurance. Especially smaller, less profitable, risky banks that are subject to frequent liquidity shocks seem to rely on relationships.

Interesting questions arise also about how switching costs in one market may be linked to behavior in another market. Switching costs in deposit markets may have consequences for behavior in loan markets. Berlin and Mester (1999), for example, tie bank funding to orientation (relationship vs. transactional banking). In particular Berlin and Mester show that banks with better access to rate inelastic core deposits engage in more loan rate smoothing (relationship lending) than banks that lack such access. In other words, banks enjoying market power in core deposits can insulate their borrowers from adverse credit shocks by loan rate smoothing.

4.3.2. Impact of Bank Relationships

4.3.2.1. Impact on the Cost of Credit

Are relationships a source of bank rents? If yes, how do banks extract rents? Do relationship banks simply charge higher loan rates, have lower costs, or also impose more stringent loan conditions? Are banks applying the "bargain then rip-off" strategy; that is, are they first competing fiercely for new customers and then charge above marginal cost prices (e.g., Sharpe 1990)? To commence answering these questions, many studies have run reduced-form regressions of the cost of credit for the borrowing firms on duration and/or number of bank–firm relationships (studies typically control for a variety of firm, bank, and market characteristics). The typical equation that has been estimated looks as follows:

$$Cost\ of\ Credit_{it} = \alpha + \beta\ Relationship\ intensity\ measures + \gamma Controls + \varepsilon_{it}.$$
(4.29)

The estimated coefficient $\hat{\beta}$ measures the impact of relationship intensity indicators—such as the duration and the number of relationships—on the cost of credit. Some studies also include proxies for the scope of the relationship such as the number of other bank products the borrower obtains from the relationship bank.

Table 4.10A lays out the many findings.[12] The results seem rather mixed. Most U.S. studies document loan rates actually decrease by around 3** to 9** bp per relationship year, while many European studies find that loan rates are either unaffected or increase by around 1*** to 10*** bp per year (though there may even be regional variation within countries in this respect). The impact of the number of relationships on the loan rate seems equally mixed. Most U.S. studies find loan rates increase by 10*** to 30*** bp per additional bank, while many European studies (again with a few exceptions) report that loan rates are either unaffected or decrease by around 1*** to 10*** bp per extra bank. A few U.S. studies find no or a small negative effect of scope and the same seems true in Europe with a few exceptions (that document large positive or negative coefficients).

Overall it seems that only European banks extract rents from their relationship borrowers (i.e., those with long relationships and few banks) through higher loan rates, while U.S. banks actually charge lower rates. What could account for these remarkably divergent results? We offer a number of tentative explanations. First, the set and definition of control variables that are included differ from study to study. However, the overlap seems large enough to make results comparable. Second, the definition of what constitutes a bank–firm relationship diverges across studies. For example, in some cases frequent past borrowing defines a relationship, in other cases firms or banks assess and report whether or not a relationship existed.

Third, the cost of credit, the dependent variable, differs across studies. Often the level of loan rates or spreads are used, in some cases reference interest rates are included on the right hand side as explanatory variables. Following Berger and Udell (1995) some studies consider only lines of credit, while others include all type of corporate loans. However, a priori it may seem unclear why holdup problems on relationship customers should apply to one class of loans only. Loan fees, on the other hand, are potentially a thornier problem. Fees are not relevant in most European studies. For example, there are no fees on lines of credit in Italy or small loans in

---

12. There is only indirect evidence of the impact of relationship duration on the deposit rate. Sharpe (1997), e.g., shows that the amount of household migration, in most cases probably resulting in the severance of a deposit relationship, has a positive effect on the level of deposit interest rates. The magnitude of this effect in some cases depends on the degree of market concentration.

Table 4.10. Duration, Scope and Number of Bank Relationships and the Cost of Credit, Collateral, Availability of Credit and Maturity

Panel A Cost of Credit	Paper	Source Year	Observations Firm Size	Cost of Credit, in Basis Points	Duration Δ = 1 year	Scope Δ = 1	Number Δ = 1 bank
United States	Bodenhorn (2003)	1 Bank 1855	2,616 s	Loan Rate – A1 Commercial Paper	–2.9**		
	Petersen and Rajan (1994)	NSSBF 1987	1,389 s	Most Recent Loan Rate (Prime on RHS)	3.7	0.8^c	32.1***
	Berger and Udell (1995)	NSSBF 1987	371 s	Line of Credit – Prime Rate	–9.2**		
	Uzzi (1999)	NSSBF 1987	2,226 s	Most Recent Loan Rate (Prime on RHS)	–1.3**	–4.2**	
	Blackwell and Winters (1997)	6 Banks 1988	174 s	Revolver – Prime Rate	–0.9	0.0	
	Berger et al. (2002)	NSSBF 1993	520 s	Line of Credit – Prime Rate	–5.3**		
	Brick and Palia (2007)	NSSBF 1993	766 s	Line of Credit – Prime Rate	–2.4**		–18.8
	Hao (2003)	LPC 1988–99	948 l	Facility Coupon + Fees – LIBOR			8.0***g
	Bharath et al. (2007)	LPC 1986–01	9,709 l	Facility Coupon + Fees – LIBOR		–6.6***a	
	Agarwal and Hauswald (2007)	1 Bank 2002	33,346	Bank Offers E-Loan Bank Offers In-Person Loan	–68** –34***	–42.1*** –30.0***	
	Gopalan et al. (2007)	LPC 90–06	12,235 l	Loan Yield	0		
Japan	Weinstein and Yafeh (1998)	JDB 1977–86	6,836 l	Nonbond Interest Expenses – Debt		53***	
	Miarka (1999)	1985–98	1,288 s m	Interest Rate on Borrowing		–22.2***	18***
	Shikimi (2005)	JADA 00–02	78,695	Loan Rate – Prime Rate			
	Kano, Uchida, Udell, and Watanabe (2006)	SFE 2002	1,960	Maximum Loan Rate < 1 Year	No/–3.5****h	No/4***a,h	

(continued)

99

Table 4.10. (Continued)

Panel A Cost of Credit	Paper	Source Year	Observations Firm Size	Cost of Credit, in Basis Points	Duration Δ = 1 year	Scope Δ = 1	Number Δ = 1 bank
Germany	Harhoff and Körting (1998b)	Survey 1997	994 s	Line of Credit	1.7		−0.2
	Elsas and Krahmen (1998)	5 Banks 1996	353 m l	Line of Credit – FIBOR	0.3	−4.8	
	Machauer and Weber (1998)	5 Banks 1996	353 m l	Line of Credit – Interbank Overnight	−0.3	1.3	0.0
	Ewert, Schenk, and Szczesny (2000)	5 Banks 1996	682 m l	Line of Credit – FIBOR	0.7***	−22.1	0.6
	Lehmann and Neuberger (2001)	Survey 1997	318 s m	Loan Rate – Refinancing Rate	1.8[a]	−5.6	
	Lehmann et al. (2004)	Survey 1997	W: 267 s m E: 67 s m	Loan Rate – Refinancing Rate	w: 1.6 e: −0.5	w: −2.0 e: 20.3	
France	Ziane (2003)	Survey 2001	244 s	Credit Interest Rate	−20.2	20.1*	51.4
Italy	Conigliani, Ferri, and Generale (1997)	CCR 1992	33,808 m	Loan Interest Rate	−14.1****e		−2***
	Ferri and Messori (2000)	CCR 1992	33,808 m	Loan Interest Rate	nw: −19.1* ne: −13.5NA so: 9.6NA		nw: −0.3 ne: 0.7NA so: −13.6*a
	D'Auria et al. (1999)	CCR 1987–94	120,000 l	Loan Interest Rate – Treasury Bill Rate	2.5***		−1.3***
	Angelini et al. (1998)	Survey 1995	2,232 s	Line of Credit	ccb: −1.8 oth: 6.4***		−10.0***
	Cosci and Meliciani (2002)	1 Bank 1997	393 s	Interest Payments – Total Debt	43***		−0.2
	Pozzolo (2004)	CCR 1992–96	52,359	Loan Interest Rate			
Spain	Hernández-Cánovas and Martínez-Solano (2006)	Survey 99–00	184 s	Average Cost of Bank Finance – Interbank	5*	8.5	60*
	Montoriol Garriga (2006c)	SABI 90–05	510,840	Average Cost of Capital			3**

	Paper	Source Year	Observations Firm Size	No Collateral, in %	Duration Δ = 1 year	Scope Δ = 1	Number Δ = 1 bank
Canada	Mallett and Sen (2001)	CFIB 1997	2,409 s	Loan Interest Rate	0	0	
Argentina	Streb et al. (2002)	CDSF 1999	8,548	Highest Overdraft Interest Rate		−69.0***	6.9***
Belgium	Degryse and Van Cayseele (2000)	1 Bank 1997	17,429 s	Loan Yield Till Next Revision	7.5***	−39.3***	
	Degryse and Ongena (2005)	1 Bank 1997	15,044 s	Loan Yield Till Next Revision	11.0***	−40.7***	
Chile	Repetto et al. (2002)	SBIF 1990–98	20,000	Interest Rate Paid	−65.1**e	−26.5	−47.0**
Finland	Peltoniemi (2007)	1 Bank 95–01	279 s	Effective Loan Rate	−12***	6.6b	
		1 Nonbank	576 s		−2*		
Thailand	Menkhoff and Suwanaporn (2007)	9 Banks 92–96	416 l	Loan Rate – Min. Overdraft Rate	−0.9	−22.0**	−6.5**
Bolivia	Ioannidou and Ongena (2007)	CIRC 99–03	33,084 s m	Loan Rate	>30**	−16.5	−39.6*
57 Countries	Qian and Strahan (2007)	LPC 1980–04	3,608 l	Drawn All-in Spread		−28.7***a	

Panel B Collateral	Paper	Source Year	Observations Firm Size	No Collateral, in %	Duration Δ = 1 year	Scope Δ = 1	Number Δ = 1 bank
United States	Bodenhorn (2003)	1 Bank 1855	2,616 s	No Guarantors	2.6**		
	Berger and Udell (1995)	NSSBF 1987	371 s	No Collateral	12.1**		
	Chakraborty and Hu (2006)	NSSBF 1993	983 s	No Collateral L/C	2*a	−7.4al	−1.2a
			649 s	No Collateral Non-L/C	−1a	3**al	−1.4a
	Hao (2003)	LPC 1988–99	948 l	Not Secured			1g
	Roberts and Siddiqi (2004)	LPC 1988–03?	218 l	No Collateral			−0.0a
Japan	Kano et al. (2006)	SFE 2002	1,960	No Collateral	−*	−**	

(continued)

Table 4.10. (*Continued*)

Panel B Collateral	Paper	Source Year	Observations Firm Size	No Collateral, in %	Duration Δ = 1 year	Scope Δ = 1	Number Δ = 1 bank
Germany	Harhoff and Körting (1998b)	Survey 1997	994 s	No Collateral	7.0**		−10.0**
	Machauer and Weber (1998)	5 Banks 1996	353 m l	Unsecured % of Credit Line	−0.1*	−9.4***	0.6**
	Elsas and Krahnen (2002)	5 Banks 1996	472 m l	No Collateral		−17.6**	
	Lehmann and Neuberger (2001)	Survey 1997	318 s m	No Collateral	−0.8[a]	−4.1***	
	Lehmann et al. (2004)	Survey 1997	W: 267 s m E: 67 s m	No Collateral	w:−1.6*** e:5.2**	w:−15*** e:−12.9**	
France	Ziane (2003)	Survey 2001	244 s	No Collateral	8.3	−2.8*	−2.3**
Italy	Pozzolo (2004)	CCR 1992–96	52,359	No Real Guarantees	−17***		5***
				No Personal Guarantees	14***		1***
Belgium	Degryse and Van Cayseele (2000)	1 Bank 1997	17,429 s	No Collateral	4.2*	−64.5***	
Finland	Peltoniemi (2004)	1 Bank 95–01	562 s	No Collateral	−2[a]	50***[b]	
Thailand	Menkhoff et al. (2006)	9 Banks 92–96	4161	No Collateral	1	−33**	23**
Bolivia	Ioannidou and Ongena (2007)	CIRC 99–03	33,084 s m	Uncollateralized % of Loan	16		

Panel C Credit Availability	Paper	Source Year	Observations Firm Size	Availability of Credit, in %	Duration Δ = 1 year	Scope Δ = 1	Number Δ = 1 bank
United States	Bodenhorn (2007)	1 Bank 1855	2,616 s	Loan Amount	+***	+***	
	Petersen and Rajan (1994)	NSSBF 1987	1,389 s	% Trade Credit Paid on Time	2.3**		−1.9**

Country	Study	Data	N	Measure			
	Uzzi (1999)	NSSBF 1987	2,226 s	Credit Accessed	−0.1	0.5	
	Cole (1998)	NSSBF 1993	2,007 s	Extension of Credit	5.0***	−22.0^c	−12.0***
	Cole, Goldberg, and White (2004)	NSSBF 1993	585 s	Extension of Credit by Small Banks	−0.0	5.9**c	−1.1
	Scott and Dunkelberg (2003)	CBSB 1995	520 s	Single Credit Search	21.5***		−25.7***
	Gopalan et al. (2007)	LPC 90–06	17,1211	Loan Amount	+*		
	Agarwal and Hauswald (2007)	1 Bank 2002	33,346	Bank Offers E-Loan	0	0	
				Bank Offers In-Person Loan	+***	+*	
Japan	Shikimi (2005)	JADA 00–02	78,695	Debt/Assets			18***
	Kano et al. (2006)	SFE 2002	1,960	No Loan Denial	0.0	0.0/++**h	
Germany	Lehmann and Neuberger (2001)	Survey 1997	318 s m	Credit Approval	0.1***a	0.9***	
France	Dietsch (2003)	1993–00	2,530,353	Loans/Turnover	2.7**a	10.1**	1.5**a
Italy	Angelini et al. (1998)	Survey 1995	2,232 s	No Rationing	7.0**		−6.4**
	Cosci and Meliciani (2002)	1 Bank 1997	393 s	1 − [Credit Used/Credit Offered]			23.3**
	Guiso (2003)	SMF 1997	3,236 s	No Loan Denial	0.8	−0.1	0.0
	Tirri (2007)	CCR 97–04	±25,000	Credit Drawn/Granted > 1			−***
Argentina	Streb et al. (2002)	CDSF 1999	8,548	Unused Credit Line Ratio		21.4	−2.7***
Belgium	de Bodt et al. (2005)	Survey^f 2001	296 s	No Rationing	20.0**a		−22.0**
Chile	Repetto et al. (2002)	SBIF 1990–98	±20,000	Debt/Capital	1.7**	−45.4**	11.9**
Thailand	Menkhoff and Suwanaporn (2007)	9 Banks 92–96	416^l	Ratio L/C/(Liabilities + L/C)	0.3	9.6***	0.0
	Bebczuk (2004)	UIA 1999	139	Probability of Obtaining Credit	No		
Bolivia	Ioannidou and Ongena (2007)	CIRC 99–03	33,084 s m	Loan Amount	+		

(continued)

Table 4.10. (Continued)

Panel D Maturity	Paper	Source Year	Observations Firm Size	Loan Maturity, in months	Duration Δ = 1 year	Scope Δ = 1	Number Δ = 1 bank
United States	Bodenhorn (2007)	1 Bank 1855	2,616 s	Loan Maturity	0.8***	0.8***i	
	Ortiz-Molina and Penas (2008)	NSSBF 1993	995 s	Length of Commitment	−0.3*	−0.7	0.0
Bolivia	Ioannidou and Ongena (2007)	CIRC 99–03	33,084 s m	Loan Maturity	−1.8**		

The table reports the coefficients from studies on the impact of the duration, scope, and number of bank relationships on the cost of credit (Panel A), collateral (Panel C), and maturity (Panel D). The papers are listed according to country size and sample period (the most recent samples are ranked last). The first column lists the country affiliation of the related firms and the second column provides the paper citation. The third column reports the data source and year(s), the fourth column the number of observations and an indicative firm size (small, medium, and/or large). The fifth column gives a precise definition of the dependent variable, and the next three columns indicate the impact on the dependent variable of an increase in duration (by one year), scope (from 0 to 1), and number (by one relationship) of bank relationships. Coefficients and significance levels are based on the reported base specification. All coefficients for logged duration or number measures are averaged over the [1, 4] interval, and the impact is calculated at the mean of the dependent variable. CBSB, Credit, Banks, and Small Business Survey collected by the National Federation of Independent Business; ccb, credit granted by chartered community banks to CCB members; CCR, Central Credit Register; CDSF, Center of Debtors of the Financial System at the Central Bank of Argentina; CFIB, Canadian Federation of Independent Business; CIRC, Central de Información de Riesgos Crediticios; FIBOR, Frankfurt Interbank Offered Rate; JADE, Japanese Accounts and Data on Enterprises; JDB, Japan Development Bank; l, large; L/C, line of credit; LPC, Loan Pricing Corporation Dealscan database; m, medium; NSSBF, National Survey of Small Business Finances; ne, northeast; nw, northwest; oth, all other credit; RHS, right hand side; s, small; SABI, Spanish company data set; SBIC, small business investment companies; SBIF, Chilean Supervisory Agency of Banks and Financial Institutions; SFE, Survey of the Financial Environment; SMF, Survey of Manufacturing Firms; so, South.

a Our calculations.
b For a doubling from 10 to 20 bank services taken.
c Checking account at the bank.
d Based on a dummy.
e Based on contract length.
f French-speaking part.
g Number of lenders in facility.
h Result only for small banks/firms without audits and low banking market competition.
i For an increase from 0 to 12 loans.
*** Significant at 1%, ** at 5%, * at 10%.

Source: Updated from Degryse and Ongena (2008).

Belgium. But fees may play a role in the United States, though the data in most studies are not rich enough to adjust for it (Hao 2003).

Fourth, the composition of the pool of borrowers may change over (relationship) time as banks get to know their customers better and favor certain types. Controls in cross-sectional studies may fail to capture these dynamic effects and differences in the average (median) duration across studies therefore may complicate comparisons.

4.3.2.2. Impact on Collateral, Loan Size, Credit Availability, and Maturity

Most studies implicitly assume the loan collateral decision to be taken either independently or sequentially after the loan granting decision but before the determination of the loan rate. Under these assumptions most studies find that relationship borrowers pledge less collateral; that is, an increase in the duration of the relationship increases the probability that no collateral is pledged while the number of relationships decreases that probability (table 4.10B). Not surprisingly, increasing the scope of the relationship increases collateral pledging, presumably to cover the increase in products and bank exposure.

Similarly most studies find that relationship borrowers (longer duration, wider scope, fewer banks) have better access to credit (table 4.10C). But these results may need further qualification, as Houston and James (1996), for example, find that single relationship but high-growth firms actually use less bank debt than multiple relationship high-growth firms, potentially to help mitigate holdup.

Finally, Ortiz-Molina and Penas (2008) study the effects of relationship characteristics on loan maturity,[13] that is, the length of the bank commitment (table 4.10D). They find that only relationship duration is at best marginally significant and negatively affects loan maturity (a result also present in Ioannidou and Ongena 2007), while the scope and number of relationships seem to have no effect.

4.3.2.3. Jointness

Brick and Palia (2007) revisit the U.S. NSSBF data but relax the independence assumption. They examine the joint impact of duration and number of relationships on loan rate, fees, and collateral (we list their paper in table 4.10A). Technically, they run the following system of two equations,

---

13. See also Berger, Espinosa-Vega, Frame, and Miller (2005a) for the role of risk and asymmetric information in debt maturity.

encompassing previous studies and endogenizing some of the variables that were treated as exogenous in previous studies:

$$Loan\ rate = \alpha_{LR} + \beta_{LR}\ Relationship\ intensity\ measures + \gamma_{LR}\ Collateral$$

$$+ \Omega_{LR}X + \lambda_{LR}Z_{LR} + \varepsilon,$$

$$Collateral = \alpha_c + \beta_c\ Relationship\ intensity\ measures + \gamma_c\ Loan\ rates$$

$$+ \Omega_c X + \lambda_c Z_c + \varepsilon_c, \tag{4.30}$$

where X represents the set of common control variables and Z the vector of specific instruments for each endogenous variable. They discuss different specifications where the loan rate either includes fees or not and where a distinction is made between firm collateral and personal collateral.

Brick and Palia (2007) find that endogenizing collateral and fees not necessarily weakens any significant negative impact of duration on the loan rate, though the effect does not survive in any of their robustness exercises[14] and introduces a negative, though not always statistically significant, impact of the number of banks on the loan rate.

Hence, joint estimation makes the U.S. results somewhat more comparable to the European findings estimated under the independence assumption. However, not only fees but also collateral may play a smaller role in a few European samples, making the modeling of fee and collateral decisions potentially less influential for those studies. For example, in Degryse and Van Cayseele (2000), only 26 percent of loans are collateralized, while in Berger and Udell (1995) 53 percent are.

However, the point raised by Brick and Palia (2007) is more general, we think, once also the cross-selling of loans and other commercial bank products are considered (see also Jiangli, Unal, and Yom 2008). A number of recent papers find indeed evidence of relationship tie-in pricing between investment and commercial bank services (Drucker and Puri 2005; Bharath, Dahiya, Saunders, and Srinivasan 2007) and document the importance of cross-selling efforts toward larger firms at the level of the relationship manager (Liberti 2004).

To conclude, estimating the impact of relationship characteristics on the loan rate (or any other loan contract term) fielding a single equation could be problematic, in particular, when loan fees, collateral requirements, and cross-selling opportunities are important.

---

14. An earlier version of Brick and Palia's paper (Brick, Kane and Palia 2005) that included the 1998 NSSBF in the sample showed that the effect of duration on loan rates was actually eliminated because of the joint estimation.

A recent paper by Ioannidou and Ongena (2007) aims to address these concerns raised so far by matching the 1,062 loans of borrowers who are changing banks, that is, switching loans, in their Bolivian sample with any of the other 33,084 new loans that share a large number of bank, borrower, loan, and relationship characteristics. Switching loans carry an 80 bp lower loan rate (and a larger size and longer maturity), but after an initial grace period the new inside bank inexorably starts to hike the loan rate (and to somewhat tighten up the other loan conditions). Banks seemingly apply the "bargain then rip-off" strategy in their sample.

Kim et al. (2007) make a related point, by developing a theoretical model that predicts that the banks' interest rate markups follow a life-cycle pattern over the borrowing firms' age. Due to endogenous bank monitoring by competing banks, borrowing firms initially face a low markup, thereafter an increasing markup due to informational lock-in, until the markup falls again for older and opaque firms when lock-in is resolved. Kim et al. (2007) study a large sample of small Norwegian unlisted firms and a new measure of asymmetric information. They find that firms with significant asymmetric information problems have a more pronounced life-cycle pattern of interest rate markups. Specifically, for the most transparent firms, the flight to captivity during the firms' young age increases their loan markup by 35 bp, for the opaque firms by 93 bp. For the transparent firms who can fly captivity and switch, markup decreases by 52 bp, more than wiping out the initial increase when they entered captivity. For the most opaque firms, on the other hand, the markup continues to grow.[15] These results are in line with those in Ioannidou and Ongena (2007), even though they emphasize relationship duration and not firm age.

4.3.2.4. Impact of Other Relationship Characteristics

While many papers have included duration, scope, and/or the number (concentration) of bank relationships in regressions explaining the cost and availability of credit, a few recent studies also include other measures of the intensity and strength of the bank—firm engagement.

A study by Lehmann and Neuberger (2001), for example, considers four measures of social interaction between bank and firm that captures the experience, obligation, information, and stability of the bank–firm relationship. They find that the availability of credit increases but that the cost is unaffected by more social interaction. This result seems broadly consistent with

---

15. Kim et al. (2007) control for collateral, concentration measure, and bankruptcy probability.

Table 4.11. Impact of Social Interaction on Credit Conditions

Paper Country	Source, Year Sample, Firm Size	Measure of Social Interaction (low to high)	Impact on Credit	
			Cost	Availability

Scott (2003), Scott and
    Dunkelberg (2003)
United States
	CBSB 1995
	±2,000 small
		Account manager turnover
		    (high to low)
		Quality of social contact
				+++
				
				+++

Harhoff and Körting (1998b)
Germany
	Survey 1997
	994 small
		Respondent in firm thinks firm
		    and most important (credit)
		    institution trust each other
		    very much
			↔↔	+

Lehmann and Neuberger
    (2001)
 	
Germany
	1997
	318 SMEs
		Four measures of social
		    interaction (capturing
		    experience, obligation,
		    information, and stability)
			0	++

Hernandez-Canovas and
    Martinez-Solano (2006)
Spain
	Survey 1999
	153 Small
		Trust placed by the loan officer
		    in the firm's managers
			0	+++

Coleman, Esho, and Sharpe
    (2004)
Australia
	SDC 95–99
	3,694 large
		Monitoring Effort:
		    Input: Salary Expense
		    Output: Loan Performance
			+++
			0
				+
				+++

The table summarizes the results from studies on the impact of the degree of social interaction on the cost and availability of bank credit. Positive signs indicate that more social interaction corresponds to a significantly higher interest rate or to higher credit availability. The papers are listed according to country size and sample period (the most recent samples are ranked last). The first column lists the paper citation on the first row and the country affiliation of the related firms on the second row. The second column reports data source and year (first row) and sample size and an indication of firm size (second row). The third column defines the measure of social interaction. The fourth and fifth columns indicate the sign and significance of the impact on the cost and availability of credit. Significance levels are based on all reported exercises and our assessment. 0, included in the specifications but not significant. CBSB, Credit, Banks and Small Business Survey collected by the National Federation of Independent Business; SDC, Securities Data Corporation; SMEs, small and medium-sized enterprises.
+++ Positive and significant at 1%, ++ at 5%, + at 10%.
↔↔↔ Negative and significant at 1%, ↔↔ at 5%, ↔ at 10%.

the other studies, listed in table 4.11, that investigate the interaction–credit correspondence.

Other papers focus on the connection between control by the bank of the firm and credit (table 4.12). Bank control is measured, for example, by having a representative on the board of the firm or not. The effect of bank control on credit availability is again mostly positive, while the cost of credit seems lower when bank control is stronger.

4.3.2.5. Impact on Other Financing

Bank relationships may also affect the conditions of other financing. Prior and concurrent bank credit may, for example, reduce underwriter fees

Table 4.12.   Impact of Bank Control on Credit Conditions

Paper Country	Source, Year Sample, Firm Size	Measure of Bank Control (Low to High)	Impact on Credit	
			Cost	Availability
Ciamarra (2006) United States	S&P Firms 02 and 04 403 listed	Bankers on Board	↔ ↔	+++
Agarwal and Elston (2001) Germany	Bonn 70–86 1,660 Largest	Bank Influence: controlling ownership or board chairmanship	+	↔
Laeven (2001) Russia	WB Survey 1994 161 Large	Firm is majority shareholder in a bank	0	0: % ++: Size
Garcia-Marco and Ocana (1999) Spain	Survey 1991–94 129 Large	Financier has more than 10% of shares (or 80% of shares of largest owner)		++
La Porta, Lopez-de-Silanes, and Zamarripa (2003) Mexico	1995 1,470 Large	(Family members of) shareholders, directors or officers of bank are (officers or directors of) borrowers	↔ ↔ ↔	+++

The table summarizes the results from studies on the impact of the degree of bank control on the cost and availability of bank credit. Positive signs indicate that more bank control corresponds to a significantly higher interest rate or to higher credit availability. The papers are listed according to country size and sample period (the most recent samples are ranked last). The first column lists the paper citation (first row) and the country affiliation of the related firms (second row). The second column reports the on the first row the data source and year and on the second row the sample size and an indication of firm size. The third column defines the measure of bank control. The fourth and fifth indicate the sign and significance of the impact on the cost and availability of credit. Significance levels are based on all reported exercises and our assessment. 0, included in the specifications but not significant. S&P, firms included in the S&P 500 index; WB, World Bank.
+++ Positive and significant at 1%, ++ at 5%, + at 10%.
↔ ↔ ↔ Negative and significant at 1%, ↔ ↔ at 5%, ↔ at 10%.

(Drucker and Puri 2005; James and Wier 1990), lessen IPO underpricing (Slovin and Young 1990; Schenone 2005), and in general improve access to equity markets (Kutsuna, Smith, and Smith 2003). Similarly, public debt may become cheaper if firms have prior bank relationships (Datta, Iskandar-Datta, and Patel 1999), though the effect on public debt yields seems unclear (Roten and Mullineaux 2002). Finally, bank credit may influence the availability of trade credit, as empirically tested in Petersen and Rajan (1994), for example.[16]

4.3.2.6. Impact on Firm Performance
A strong bank relationship may improve firm performance directly through cheaper and better access to bank and other financing, but also indirectly

---

16. Burkart, Ellingsen, and Giannetti (in press) find that U.S. firms that have more trade credit available borrow from a larger set of uninformed banks. This finding challenges the notion that firms using trade credit are unable to access bank credit.

through the widening of contracting flexibility ex ante (Boot and Thakor 1994) or the reduction in the agency problems through enhanced control (Rajan 1992).[17] Close relationships may further enable reputation building as a means for establishing enough credibility to eventually borrow through public debt or equity markets (Diamond 1991). The confidentiality of bank borrowing (Campbell 1979), especially in a bilateral relationship, may limit the leakage of proprietary information, which may enhance the performance of firms engaging in research and development (Bhattacharya and Chiesa 1995).

Table 4.13 summarizes the many studies that investigate the impact of the key characteristics of bank relationships on a variety of firm performance measures, such as profitability, growth, investment, and innovation.[18] With the exception of Degryse and Ongena (2001), Fok, Chang, and Lee (2004), and Montoriol Garriga (2006a), most studies ignore the potential effects of firm performance on the choice of the optimal financing arrangement.

Longer, wider, fewer, and more intense bank–firm credit relationships typically result in better firm performance (even when recognizing the potential two-way causality), but there are limitations and exceptions. Relationship banks may not play any special role in innovation, for example (Italy, Herrera, and Minetti 2007); engaging more banks may decrease investment sensitivity to cash flows when projects are large (United States, Houston and James 2001),[19] and adding extra foreign banks may boost firm return on assets (Taiwan, Fok et al. 2004). On the other hand, stronger bank control through equity ownership,[20] and/or board positions, seems not uniformly to enhance firm performance.

In Japan, for example, banks may have also successfully assisted corporate mergers and investment, for example (Kang, Shivdasani, and Yamada 2000). But their general positive effect on firm performance may have waned since the 1980s (Tsuru 2001) as banks themselves became low performing and firms did not switch.[21] Spiegel and Yamori (2003), for example,

---

17. See also Brito and Mello (1995), who study the impact of financial constraints through firm survival rate and firm rate of growth on firms' ex-post performance.

18. Earlier studies investigated the effects of bank borrowing in general on firm profitability. Calem and Rizzo (1992), e.g., find that hospitals that borrow more from banks are more profitable.

19. See also Elston (1995) and Morgan (2000) who provide further evidence.

20. See also Arping (2002), Agarwal and Elston (2001), and Krahnen and Elsas (2004) who provide further insights on this account.

21. Bank market concentration may matter, e.g., in determining the relationship–performance correspondence (Shen and Huang 2003).

Table 4.13. Impact of Bank Relationships on Firm Performance

Study Country	Source, Year Sample, Firm Size	Measure of Performance	Impact on Firm Performance				
			Duration	Scope	Number	Social Interaction	Control
Byrd and Mizruchi (2005) United States	1980–91 456 Largest	Market Equity/Assets					↔↔
Houston and James (2001) United States	1980–93 250 Large	No Cash Flow Sensitivity for Investment			0/+++ large projects		
Korkeamaki and Rutherford (2006) United States	NSSBF 1998 1,729 Small	Leverage	↔		++		
Agarwal and Hauswald (2007) United States	One Bank 2002 14,613	No Credit Delinquency	+++	+++			
Gopalan et al. (2007) United States	LPC 1990–06 30,582	Capital Expenditures or Leverage	↔↔				
Hoshi, Kashyap, and Scharfstein (1991) Japan	1977–82 145 Listed	No Cash Flow Sensitivity for Investment					↔↔↔↔
Suzuki and Wright (1985) Japan	1974–78 56 Listed	Firm Does Not Default		++			
Weinstein and Yafeh (1998) Japan	JDB 1977–86 6,836 Large	Ordinary Income/Sales		↔↔↔			↔↔↔
Morck, Nakamura, and Shivdasani (2000) Japan	Data 1986 373 Large	Tobin's Q					↔↔↔↔
Morck and Nakamura (1999) Japan	Data 1981–87 2,371 Large	Various					0/↔
Kaplan and Minton (1994) Japan	1980–88 119 Large	Executive Turnover					+++
Gibson (1995) Japan	NN 1992 1,355 Listed	Investment		0/↔ 'weaker' bks			0/↔ 'weaker' bks

(continued)

Table 4.13. (*Continued*)

Study Country	Source, Year Sample, Firm Size	Measure of Performance	Impact on Firm Performance				
			Duration	Scope	Number	Social Interaction	Control
Gibson (1997) Japan	JDB 1995 1,682 Large	Investment		0			0
Hiraki, Ito, and Kuroki (2003) Japan	NLI 1991–98 10,344 Listed	Return on Assets		↔↔↔	+++		
Fohlin (1998) Germany	1903–13 75 Larger	Absence Liquidity Sensitivity of Investment					0
Agarwal and Elston (2001) Germany	Bonn 1970–86 1,660 Largest	Operating Income/Sales					0
Gorton and Schmid (2000) Germany	1975 + 1986 283 + 280	Market-to-Book of Equity					++
Edwards and Nibler (2000) Germany	1992 156 Large	Market-to-Book of Equity					++
Seger (1997) Germany	1990–92 144	ROA, ROE, and Others		↔			0/+
Franks and Mayer (2001) Germany	1980–94 75 Large	Board Turnover at Poorly Performing Firms					+
Lehmann and Weigand (2000) Germany	1991–96 361	Return on Assets					++
Meyer and Prilmeier (2006) Germany	1997–06 92 Large	Abnormal Returns on Sales of Bank Stake					+++
Refait (2002) France	BdF 1994–98 170 Medium	Firm Does Not Default			++		
Braggion (2004) United Kingdom	1895–1900–1904 270 + 430	Growth Book Assets				++ proximity	++
Pawlina and Renneboog (2005) United Kingdom	1992–98 985 Listed	No Liquidity Sensitivity of Investment					+
Foglia, Laviola, and Marullo Reedtz (1998)	CCR 1991–95 576 + 1295	Firm Does Not Default			↔↔		

Country / Study	Data	Measure	Results
Italy			
Herrera and Minetti (2007)	MC 2001 3,494 > 10 employees	Product Innovations Process Innovations	+++ + 0 0
Italy Castelli et al. (2006)	MC 1998–00 10,764 (30) employees	ROA, ROE, Interest over Assets, Sales over Assets	0/+ ↔↔
Italy Carmignani and Omiccioli (2007)	CCR 1997–03 ±42,000	Interest Coverage > 1 for lower	+++
Italy Azofra-Palenzuela, López Iturriaga, and Tejerina-Gaite (2007)	1999–02 142 Listed	Return on Assets	HHI 2 bks : ↔↔ 0.5 bk: ++
Spain Montoriol Garriga (2006a)	SABI 2001/2003 41,593 Small	7 Profitability Measures 4 Growth Measures	+++ ↔↔↔ ↔↔↔↔ ++
Taiwan Fok et al. (2004)	TT 1994–98 Large 534 + 356	Return on Assets (Simultaneous Equations)	↔↔↔↔[b] Dom: ↔↔↔↔ For: +++
Taiwan Shen and Wang (2003)	TT 1991–00 373 Large	Investment	↔
Taiwan Yu et al. (2007)	TT 1991–00 579 Large	Return on Assets	↔↔↔↔
Mexico Maurer and Haber (2004)	1888–13 642	Output per Worker	↔↔↔
Netherlands Van Ees and Garretsen (1994)	JNO 1985–90 456 Listed	Lower Liquidity Sensitivity of Investment	+++
Netherlands Degryse and de Jong (2006)	1993–98 132 Listed	Lower Liquidity Sensitivity of Investment	0 to +++ (low Q firms) 0

(continued)

Table 4.13. (Continued)

Study Country	Source, Year Sample, Firm Size	Measure of Performance	Impact on Firm Performance				
			Duration	Scope	Number	Social Interaction	Control
Van Overfelt, Annaert, De Ceuster, and Deloof (2006) Belgium	RF 1905–09 569 Large	Market-to-book of equity, ROA, Std. Dev. of ROA			↔		++
Fuss and Vermeulen (2006) Belgium	1997–02 1,448 Median/Large	Absence Liquidity Sensitivity of Investment			0		
Farinha and Santos (2006) Portugal	BoP 1985–96 6,485 New	Firm Does Not Default			↔		↔↔↔
Degryse and Ongena (2001) Norway	KH 1979–95 1,897 Listed	Various Profitability (Simultaneous Equations)	++		↔↔↔↔		
Limpaphayom and Polwitoon (2004) Thailand	SET 1990–96 1,340	Tobin's Q Investment		↔↔↔↔ $+++^a$			+++ +++

The table summarizes the results from studies on the impact of the various measures of bank relationships on firm performance. Positive signs indicate that higher levels of the respective measure correspond to better firm performance. The papers are listed according to country size and sample period (the most recent samples are ranked last). The first column lists the paper citation on the first row and the country affiliation of the related firms on the second row. The second column reports the data source and year (first row) and the sample size and an indication of firm size (second row). The third column defines the measure of firm performance. The fourth to eighth column indicate the sign and significance of the impact on firm performance of changes in the duration, scope, number, social interaction and bank control. Significance levels are based on all reported exercises and our assessment. 0, included in the specifications but not significant. BdF, Banque de France; bks, banks; CCR, Central Credit Register; JDB, Japan Development Bank; JNO, Yearbook of Dutch Firms; KH, Kierulfs Handbook; MC, survey by the Italian investment bank Mediocredito Centrale; NLI, Nippon Life Insurance Company; NSSBF, National Survey of Small Business Finances; NN, NIKKEI NEDS Interim; RF, Recueil Financier; ROA, return on assets; ROE, return on equity; SET, Stock Exchange of Thailand; TT, Taiwan Economic Journal and Taiwan Security Exchange Council.

+++ Positive and significant at 1%, ++ at 5%, + at 10%.

↔↔↔ Negative and significant at 1%, ↔↔ at 5%, ↔ at 10%.

[a] Bank loans/firm assets.

[b] Bank loans/total loans.

find that Japanese firm stock returns were dependent on main bank returns even in 1997 after many years of substandard bank performance.

4.3.2.7. Impact on Firm Assistance

Bank relationships may not only matter for firm performance, but may become vital when a firm needs assistance. Table 4.14 abridges the many studies by providing the signs and statistical significance of estimates of the impact of the key relationship characteristics on the 'assistance' provided by banks to firms. The direct and indirect measures of assistance include, for example, loan rate smoothing, liquidity provision, the likelihood of loan renewals during a financial panic, workout success, and eventual firm survival.

A long, wide, bilateral, and control relationship with a bank almost always assist firms in weathering periods of firm-specific or economywide financial distress. Elsas and Krahnen (1998), for example, find that workout incidence increases when firms can rely on a Hausbank. On the other hand, their results also suggest Hausbanks may be willing to assist firms but only up to a certain point of deterioration, a finding seemingly also present in the U.S. data investigated by Rosenfeld (2007). After that point firms in distress may actually face a higher likelihood of liquidation if they have a lot of outstanding bank debt (Rauterkus 2003).

4.3.2.8. Market and Macro Impacts

Existing bank relationships may also have an impact on the behavior of other banks, regarding their entry in new markets, for example (Tschoegl 2001), and may play a role in the transmission of monetary policy. Relationship benefits in Kashyap et al. (1993), for example, make bank loans and public bonds imperfect substitutes for the firms, giving rise to a role for money through a credit channel. On the other hand the breakdown of creditor relationships acts as an amplification mechanism in den Haan, Ramey, and Watson (2003).

4.3.3. Strategy: Bank Orientation and Specialization?

4.3.3.1. Theory

Switching costs, discussed above in 4.1.4, may play a key role in how market structure determines bank strategy and market presence. Theory offers conflicting views on the relation between interbank competition and bank orientation (relationship vs. transactional banking) and specialization (see also Degryse and Ongena 2008). A first set of theories argues that competition and relationships are incompatible. Mayer (1988) and Petersen

Table 4.14. Impact of Bank Relationships on Assistance to the Firm

Study Country	Source, Year Sample, Firm Size	Measure of Assistance	Impact on Firm Assistance				
			Duration	Scope	Number	Social Interaction	Control
Bodenhorn (2003) United States	1 Bank 1855 2,616 Small	Loan Renewal During Financial Panic	++				
Rosenfeld (2007) United States	LPC 1982–05 1,431	Firm Survives	+++[a]				
Garcia-Appendini (2005) United States	SSBF 2000 634 Small	Loan Granted Following Late Trade Credit Payment	+				
Morck and Nakamura (1999) Japan	Data 1981–87 2,371 Large	Various Liquidity					+
Helwege and Packer (2003) Japan	Data 1988–92 172	Likelihood of Reorganization					0
Ewert et al. (2000) Germany	Data 1996	Firm Not Affected by Insolvency/Restructuring		0	0		
Elsas and Krahnen (1998) Germany	5 Banks 1996 353 Larger	Financing Share When Firm Distressed		+++			
Elsas and Krahnen (2002) Germany	5 Banks 1996 62 Larger	Workout Incidence		+++			
Brunner and Krahnen (2008) Germany	6 Banks 1999	Workout Success When Firm Bankrupt		0	↔ ↔		

116

		Measure	Result
Germany Ferri and Messori (2000) Italy	100 Larger Data 1997 33,808	Rate Smoothing in Monetary Contraction	0 ↔↔↔
Carmignani and Omiccioli (2007) Italy	CCR 1997–03 ± 42,000	No Liquidation	↔↔↔ for lower HHI
Ferri et al. (2002) South Korea	KCB 1999 4,590 Small	Credit Available during Financial Crisis	↔↔↔
Maurer and Haber (2004) Mexico	1888–1913 642	Likelihood of Survival	++
Alem (2003) Argentina	Data 1999 4,158 All	Financing Small Firms in Bad Times	+ ↔↔↔
Thomsen (1999) Denmark	Greens 1900–95 138 Largest	Firm Survives	+++

The table summarizes the results from studies on the impact of the various measures of bank relationships on assistance to the firm. Positive signs indicate that higher levels of the respective measure correspond to more assistance. The papers are listed according to country size and sample period (the most recent samples are ranked last). The first column lists the paper citation on the first row and the Country affiliation of the related firms on the second row. The second column reports the data source and year (first row) and the sample size and an indication of firm size (second row). The third column defines the measure of firm assistance. The fourth to eighth column indicate the sign and significance of the Impact on firm assistance of changes in the duration, scope, number, social interaction and bank control. Significance levels are based on all reported exercises and our assessment. 0, included in the specifications but not significant. KCB, Korean Credit Bureau; SSBF, Survey of Small Business Finances.

+++ Positive and significant at 1%, ++ at 5%, + at 10%.

↔↔↔ Negative and significant at 1%, ↔↔ at 5%, ↔ at 10%.

[a] Relationship indicator equals one if any lead lender was a prior lender to the firm. Indicated results are for the firms that are not too distressed.

and Rajan (1995) hypothesize that long-term relationships, allowing firms to intertemporally share risks with their banks, arise only if banks enjoy the possibility to extract profits later on in the relationship, that is, when the flexibility of the borrowing firms to switch banks is limited.

On the other hand, Boot and Thakor (2000) argue that more interbank competition leads to more relationship lending. A bank offering a relationship loan augments a borrower's success probability in their model. Relationship lending then allows extracting higher rents from the borrower. Fiercer interbank competition pushes banks into offering more relationship lending, as this activity permits banks to shield their rents better.[22]

4.3.3.2. Local Markets: Indirect and Direct Evidence

4.3.3.2.1. *United States* Most empirical work so far has investigated the effects of interbank competition on indirect measures of bank orientation. Figure 4.3A summarizes the main empirical findings on competition and bank orientation. In their seminal paper, Petersen and Rajan (1995) find that young firms in more concentrated banking markets (HHI > 0.18) obtain lower loan rates and take more early (trade credit) payment discounts (i.e., have easier access to bank credit) than firms in more competitive banking markets. Banks seemingly smooth loan rates in concentrated markets and as a result provide more financing, in line with the predictions of their theoretical model.[23]

Black and Strahan (2002) revisit the local competition–bank orientation issue exploring an alternative measure of local credit availability. In particular, they investigate the rate of new business incorporations across U.S. states. They find that deregulation of bank branching restrictions positively affects new incorporations and, more important, that in contrast to Petersen and Rajan (1995) deregulation reduces the *negative* effect of

---

22. See also Freixas (2005), Gehrig (1998), and Vesala (2007) for related modeling. Relationship lending is further nonmonotonically related to the degree of concentration in banking markets in Dinç (2000) and Yafeh and Yosha (2001).

23. Recent work by Zarutskie (2006), Bergstresser (2001a, 2001b), and Scott and Dunkelberg (2001) analyzing other U.S. data sets broadly confirms these findings. Closest in spirit to Petersen and Rajan's (1995) study is the paper by Zarutskie (2006). She employs a data set containing almost 200,000 small firm–year observations. She finds that the probability of small firms utilizing bank debt increases when the concentration (in local deposit markets) is high, though the effects seem economically small. Similarly Bergstresser (2001a) finds that in more concentrated markets there are fewer constrained consumer-borrowers, while Bergstresser (2001b) documents that in more concentrated markets banks raise the average share of assets lent. Scott and Dunkelberg (2001) find that more competition not only increases the availability of credit but also decreases the loan rate and improves service performance (including knowledge of business, industry, provision of advice, etc.) by banks.

A: Local Markets

Degree of Competition in the Banking Sector

High ← → Low

Paper	Sample
Local Markets	
Petersen and Rajan (1995)	US NSSBF 1988 3,404 Small Firms
Black and Strahan (2002)	US Dun & Bradstreet 76–94 823 State / Years
Agarwal and Hauswald (2007)	One US Bank 2002 33,346
Fischer (2000)	Germany IfO 1996 403 Firms
Elsas (2005)	Germany IfK-CFS 1992–1996 122 Firms
Degryse and Ongena (2007)	One Belgian bank 1995–1997 13,098 Firms

HHI in Local Market for Deposits (0 ... 1)

Transactional Banking | Relationship Banking: Lower loan rate & more early trade credit discounts taken (= more bank credit available) by young firms

Relationship Banking: Probability of business formation. | Transactional Banking

Number of Bank Branches / Banks (Many ... 1)

Transactional Banking | Relationship Banking: Probability of firm's decision to apply for an in-person loan

HHI in Local Market, by Number of Bank Branches (0 ... 1)

Transactional Banking | Relationship Banking: More information transfer & more credit

Relationship Banking: Higher % of Hausbank status | Transactional Banking | Relationship Banking: Higher % of Hausbank status

Higher % Relationship Banking | Transactional Banking | Higher % Relationship Banking

Figure 4.3. Empirical results of research on the impact of competition on direct and indirect measures of bank orientation: paper and the sample being used, and findings of each paper. (A) Local markets. (B) National markets. Source: Updated from Degryse and Ongena (2007).

B: National Markets

Paper	Sample
National Market(s)	
Farinha and Santos (2002)	Portugal ±2,000 Small Firms 1980–1996
Steinherr and Huveneers (1994)	18 Countries 88 Largest Banks 1985–1990
Weill (2004)	12 Countries 1,746 Banks 1994–1999
Cetorelli and Gambera (2001)	41 Countries 36 Industries 1980–1990
Ongena and Smith (2000b)	18 European Countries 898 Largest Firms 1996

Degree of Competition in the Banking Sector

Arrival of New Banks — Many (High) ← → No (Low)
Multiple bank relationships | Single bank relationships

Share of Foreign Banks — High ← → Low
Transactional Banking | Relationship Banking: Higher equity investment by banks

H-Statistic — High ← → Low
Banks are cost inefficient | Banks are cost efficient

Percentage of Assets by Largest Three Commercial Banks — 0% ← → 100%
"Transactional Banking" | Industries dependent on external finance are hurt less by bank concentration

Multiple bank relationships | Single bank relationships

Figure 4.3.   (*continued*)

120

banking market concentration on new incorporations. They also find that the widespread presence of small banks decreases business formation.[24]

Finally, Agarwal and Hauswald (2007) directly investigate the probability that a firm will apply for an in-person loan from one U.S. bank as a monotonic function of the number of branches and competing banks. They find that an increase in the number of branches and competing banks in the vicinity does not affect this probability (though the number decreases the probability of ultimately obtaining a loan).

4.3.3.2.2. *Other Countries* Papers by Fischer (2000) and Elsas (2005) investigate the local competition–bank orientation correspondence using German data (see also table 4.15). Fischer (2000) focuses on the transfer of information and the availability of credit and finds that both are higher in more concentrated markets. Elsas (2005) studies the determinants of relationship lending as measured by the Hausbank status. He finds that the incidence of Hausbank status is actually the lowest for an intermediate range of market concentration with an HHI of around 0.2, though he notes that most observations of the HHI are also in that low range. Nevertheless, his findings broadly suggest the presence of more relationship banking in more competitive markets.

Degryse and Ongena (2007) employ detailed information on bank–firm relationships and industry classification of more than 13,000 Belgian firms to study the effect of market structure on bank orientation and specialization. They find that bank branches facing stiff local competition engage considerably more in relationship-based lending (the effect is convex in HHI but decreases for most observed values of HHI) and specialize somewhat less in a particular industry. These results may illustrate that competition and relationships are not necessarily inimical.

4.3.3.3. National and Cross-Country Studies

Other papers study the effect of nationwide competition on commitment and relationship banking (figure 4.3B). Farinha and Santos (2002), for example, study the switching from single to multiple bank relationships by new Portuguese firms. They find that the arrival of new banks, potentially leading to less concentrated and more competitive banking markets, increases

---

24. Cetorelli (2001, 2003a, 2003b) and Cetorelli and Strahan (2006) also find that banking market power may represent a financial barrier to entry in product markets. However, Bonaccorsi di Patti and Dell'Ariccia (2004) find opposite results for Italy, while Ergungor (2005) find no evidence that market concentration has an impact on the value of small business loans in the United States.

Table 4.15.   Empirical Findings on Competition and Bank Orientation

Type	Paper	SK	UUW	E	DO
	Country	Japan	Japan	Germany	Belgium
	Sample Years	1995–97	2002	1992–96	1996
	Number of Firms	1,225	1,863	122	13,098
	Firm Size	NA	Employ: 75	Sales: 100	Employees: (1)
Type	Scope Measures	Main Bank	Five Transactions	Hausbank	Main Bank, Relationship
Relation	Duration	+++		0	
	Number	↔↔↔		↔↔	
	Control	++			
Firm	Age	++	+++		
	$(\text{Age})^2$		↔↔↔		
	Size	↔↔↔	+++	+	0
	Profitability	0	0		++
	Risk	↔↔		↔↔	
	Cash Flow		0		
	Growth	0			
	Q	+++			
	Intangibility	+		0	
	Debt		0	0	
	Bond/Total Debt	0			
	Audit		+		
Bank	Branch Size				↔↔↔
	Bank Size		↔↔		
Market	Concentration Index			↔↔↔	↔↔↔
	$(\text{Concentration Index})^2$			++	+++

The table summarizes the results from studies on the determinants of the scope of bank relationships. Positive signs indicate that an increase in the indicated variable corresponds to a significantly wider scope of the bank relationship. The papers are listed from left to right according to country size. The first column lists the variable names. The other columns contain the results from the respective papers. The paper citations on the first row are abbreviated to conserve space: SK, Shin and Kolari (2004); UUW, Uchida et al. (2006a); E, Elsas (2005); DO, Degryse and Ongena (2007). The fifth row reports the average (median) firm size as either sales in millions of U.S. dollars in the last year of the sample or as the number of employees (employ). The sixth row indicates the specific dependent variable used in the paper. Other rows list the sign and significance levels of the coefficients on the independent variables as reported in the paper. Significance levels are based on all reported exercises and our assessment.
+++ Positive and significant at 1%, ++ at 5%, + at 10%.
↔↔↔ Negative and significant at 1%, ↔↔ at 5%, ↔ at 10%. 0: Included in the specifications but not significant.

switching rates. There are also cross-country studies. Steinherr and Huveneers (1994), for example, document a negative correspondence between the share of foreign banks and equity investment by banks in 18 countries, Cetorelli and Gambera (2001) find that industries that rely heavily on external finance grow faster in countries with more concentrated banking systems (than those in countries with competitive systems), while Ongena and Smith (2000b) highlight the positive effect of concentration of the national banking markets on the incidence of single bank relationships. The latter two studies measure concentration by calculating the percentage assets by the largest three commercial banks.

5

Equilibrium and Rationing in the Credit Market

5.1. Introduction

Asymmetric information problems in credit markets gives rise to adverse selection and marketwide credit rationing in Stiglitz and Weiss (1981), for example. A substantial literature has theoretically investigated the conditions under which rationing strictu sensu occurs (Jaffee and Stiglitz 1990; Biais and Gollier 1997), but with a few notable exceptions (e.g., Berger and Udell 1992; Chakravarty and Scott 1999), most of the empirical work (discussed in section 4.3.2.2) focuses on the availability of credit measured by loan amount, for example, for firms with particular and observable characteristics, not on the likelihood otherwise similar firms will be denied credit. This is somewhat surprising as the dynamics of credit rationing per se may be very important for our understanding of the relationship between banks and certain sectors, the economy and society in toto (for an early example of this view, see Braverman and Stiglitz 1989).

However, an interesting part of the empirical literature started to focus recently on location (as one of the determinants) of availability (and also pricing) of bank loans. Though also marketwide, geographical rationing has location as an additional driver.

5.2. Evidence on Location: Conduct and Strategy

5.2.1. Distance versus Borders

We follow Degryse and Ongena (2004, 2008) in distinguishing between "distance" and "borders." They think of distance as pertaining to physical proximity that can be bridged by say car or train travel. By spending distance-related costs, banks or their clients can communicate across the distance and engage in transactions with one another. For given locations of banks and borrowers, distance per se is exogenous and bridging it (i.e., the lender visiting the borrower and/or the borrower visiting the lender) may be adequate in addressing the informational problems for the lender concerning its decision about granting and pricing the loan. Competing banks, therefore, play no (or a rather mechanical) role in theoretical competition models featuring only distance.

Borders, on the other hand, are not merely bridgeable by car or train travel, or even more modern technological ways of interacting. Borders introduce a "discontinuity": they endogenously arise through the actions of the competing lenders, or result as an artifact of differences in legal practice and exogenous regulation (Buch 2002). In this section on location and credit rationing, we discuss only the effects of informational endogenous borders that arise because of adverse selection, relationship formation, or (lack of) information sharing between banks. Chapter 9 on regulation deals with the exogenous borders that can consist of differences in legal, supervisory, and corporate governance practices, and political, language, or cultural barriers but can also be "regulatory borders" that may simply prohibit "foreign" banks from engaging borrowers, setting up branches, and/or acquiring local banks.

We first discuss the empirical findings linking distance/borders to bank conduct (availability and pricing of bank loans, market segmentation), then review empirical work on distance/borders and bank strategy. In our discussion, we aim to highlight the relevance for the availability of bank loans.

5.2.2. Conduct

5.2.2.1. Spatial Rationing

Recent theory highlights the importance of distance for the availability and the pricing of bank loans. Lending conditions may depend on both the distance between the borrower and the lender and the distance between the borrower and the closest competing bank. We discuss spatial rationing in this section and return to spatial pricing in the next section.

Distance may affect the availability of credit. Stein (2002), for example, models the organizational impact of the ease and speed at which different types of information can "travel" within an organization. "Hard" information (e.g., accounting numbers, financial ratio's) can be passed on easily within the organization while "soft" information (e.g., a character assessment, the degree of trust) is much harder to relay. Hence, if the organization employs mostly soft information, a simple and flat structure, and local decision making may be optimal. Recent empirical evidence by Liberti (2004) and Ogura (2006), for example, indeed suggests bank centralization and the intensity of usage of hard information go hand in hand.

The type of information, hard or soft, that is needed and available to arrive at optimal lending decisions also translates into a correspondence between distance and credit rationing. For example, lines embedded in credit cards are extended solely on the basis of a quantitative analysis of hard and easily verifiable information (e.g., age, profession, and address of the applicant). As a result, credit cards are offered by mail and across large distances in the United States (Ausubel 1991).

A lot of small business lending, on the other hand, is still "character" lending. To screen successfully, loan officers need to interact with the borrower, establish trust, and be present in the local community. This is "soft" information and is difficult to convey to others within the organization.[1] As a result small (opaque) firms borrow from close, small banks (Petersen and Rajan 2002; Saunders and Allen 2002), while large banks mainly lend to distant, large firms employing predominantly hard information in the loan decision (Berger et al. 2005b; Cole, Goldberg, and White 2004; Uchida, Udell, and Watanabe 2006a; Strahan 2008). However, the firm size–bank size matching may be not be equally strong in all size classes and may be dependent on bank ownership (Delgado, Salas, and Saurina 2007).[2] Small firms then may be subject to credit rationing when seeking financing across larger distances.

However, from an empirical point of view, the severity of credit rationing affecting small firms is not entirely clear (see table 5.1). For example, the results in Petersen and Rajan (2002) indicate that the effect may be economically rather small in the United States, while findings by Carling and Lundberg (2005) and Uchida et al. (2006a) seemingly indicate the absence of distance related credit rationing in the Swedish and Japanese banking sector.

There are potentially two complementary explanations for these findings. Transportation costs may be fixed per loan, that is, do not vary by

---

1. However, Uchida, Udell, and Yamori (2006b) fail to find evidence on this account using recent Japanese survey data.

2. The same may hold for foreign banks and large firms (Mian 2006; Giannetti and Ongena in press), but the evidence seems mixed (see, e.g., De Haas, Ferreira, and Taci 2007).

Table 5.1. Impact of Physical Distance on the Availability and Cost of Bank Credit

Paper Country	Source, Year Sample, Firm Size	Dependent Variable	Distance to Lender	Distance to Closest Competitor
Petersen and Rajan (2002) U.S.	NSSBF 1993 3,523	Probability of Loan Approval	+ + +	
Korkeamaki and Rutherford (2006) U.S.	NSSBF 1998 1,729 small	Leverage	+ + +	
Agarwal and Hauswald (2006) U.S.	One Bank 02–03 12,823	Probability of Loan Approval	↔ ↔ to 0[c]	0[c] to + + +
Carling and Lundberg (2005) Sweden	One Bank 94–00 54,881	Probability of No Credit Rationing[p]		0
Petersen and Rajan (2002) U.S.	NSSBF 1993 3,523	Loan Rate	−37** bp/proj. mile	
Bharath, Dahiya, Saunders, and Srinivasan (2007) U.S.	LPC 86–01 9,709 l	Loan Rate	−25*** bp/state	
Agarwal and Hauswald (2006) U.S.	One Bank 02–03 12,823	All-in Cost of the Loan (APR)	−15*** to −6[c] bp/mile	4[c] to 13* * * bp/mile
Casolaro and Mistrulli (2007) Italy	CCR 2004:06 > 370,000	Loan Rate	−3** bp/province	
Mallett and Sen (2001) Canada	CFIB 1997 2,409 small	Loan Rate		50 to 75** bp/mile
Degryse and Ongena (2005) Belgium	One Bank 1995 15,044	Loan Rate	−18*** bp/mile	18*** bp/mile

The table summarizes the results from studies on the impact of distance on the availability (upper panel) and cost of bankcredit (lower panel). The papers are listed according to country size and sample period (the most recent samples are ranked last). The first column lists the paper citation on the first row and the country affiliation of the related firms on the second row. The second column reports on the first row the data source and year and on the second row the sample size and an indication of firm size. The third column defines the dependent variable. The fourth and fifth indicate the sign and significance of the impact on the distance to the lender and the distance to the closest competitor on either the availability or cost of credit. Sign, size and significance levels are based on all reported exercises and our assessment. 0, included in the specifications but not significant. CCR, Central Credit Register; CFIB, Canadian Federation of Independent Business; NSSBF, National Survey of Small Business Finances.

*** Significant at 1%, ** significant at 5%, * significant at 10%.
+ + + Positive and significant at 1%, + + at 5%, + at 10%.
↔ ↔ ↔ Negative and significant at 1%, ↔ ↔ at 5%, ↔ at 10%.
[a] Our calculations.
[c] Correcting for a sample selection bias.
[p] Proxied by the Initial Credit Rating.

126

loan size, explaining why larger loans are obtained across larger distances mainly by larger firms. Results in Degryse and Ongena (2005) are suggestive in this regard. Alternatively, the theoretical model and empirical results in Degryse, Laeven, and Ongena (2007) show that the lending bank's geographical reach is determined not only by its own organizational structure but also by organizational choices made by its rivals. In particular, they find that the geographical footprint of the lending bank is smaller when rival banks are large and hierarchically organized. Such rival banks may rely more on hard information. Geographical reach increases when rival banks have inferior communication technology, have a wider span of organization, and are further removed from a decision unit with lending authority.

To conclude, distance may determine the availability of funding, though the severity of credit rationing may depend on the characteristics of the firm, loan, lending bank, and/or competing banks. In the next section, we turn to the effects of distance on the pricing of credit.

5.2.2.2. Spatial Pricing

Distance may determine the pricing of loans because either the transportation costs incurred by the borrower (Lederer and Hurter 1986; Thisse and Vives 1988), the monitoring costs incurred by the lender (Sussman and Zeira 1995), or the quality of information obtained by the lender (Hauswald and Marquez 2006) are distance related. Most theories featuring distance related costs or informational quality generates spatial pricing: loan rates decrease in the distance between the borrower and the lender, but increase in the distance between the borrower and the closest competing bank (these loan rate schedules hold for a given number of banks). The availability of information to the borrowers, experience, and other product characteristics may abate the strength of this distance–loan rate correspondence.

Petersen and Rajan (2002) are among the first to provide evidence of spatial loan pricing (see also table 5.1). They find, for example, that a small business located one mile from the lending bank ceteris paribus pays on average 38*** bp less than a borrower located around the corner from the lending bank. Degryse and Ongena (2005) also include the distance to the closest competitors. They find a somewhat smaller impact of physical distance on the loan rates than Petersen and Rajan (2002). But the impact they measure is still highly statistically significant and economically relevant. The impact on the loan rate of both distance to the lender and distance to the closest competitor is actually similar in absolute magnitude, but of an appropriate opposite sign, which in itself is also evidence suggestive of spatial price discrimination. Loan rates decrease 18*** bp per mile to the lender and similarly increase 18*** bp per mile to the closest (quartile) competitor. They further deduce that, given current transportation costs and the opportunity costs of travel, the average first-time borrower in their sample needs to visit the lender between two and three times to obtain a bank loan.

Spatial price discrimination caused by (borrower) transportation costs, (lender) monitoring costs, or asymmetric information may explain the results in both Petersen and Rajan (2002) and Degryse and Ongena (2005). Transportation cost may provide the most consistent and comprehensive interpretation of all the results documented in Degryse and Ongena (2005). Inferred changes in lending technology may make an interpretation of the results in Petersen and Rajan (2002) more difficult.

Degryse and Ongena (2005) also run through a number of straightforward exercises but cannot find any trace of adverse selection increasing in the (admittedly short) distances to the uninformed lenders. Recent evidence by Agarwal and Hauswald (2006) and Casolaro and Mistrulli (2007) raises the possibility of distance related adverse selection, if one controls for internal firm credit ratings or uses the distance to the bank's headquarters as the proximity measure, respectively (clearly, the former could also be determined by distance).

In either case, the results in Degryse and Ongena (2005) suggest that the distance to the closest competitors may be important for competitive conditions and that the actual location of the bank branches may be relevant when assessing the intensity of competition. Their estimates also indicate that spatial price discrimination targeting borrowers located near the lending bank branch yields average bank rents of around 4 percent (with a maximum of 9 percent) of the bank's marginal cost of funding. Taken at face value, their findings substantiate an important additional source of rents accruing to financial intermediaries, based on location.

5.2.2.3. Borders and Segmentation

Next we turn to the impact of borders on conduct. A recent literature investigates how different types of borders shape lending conditions and result in segmentation of credit markets. National borders that often coincide with many of the exogenous economic borders continue to play an important role across the world. Buch, Driscoll, and Ostergaard (2003), for example, suggests that national borders in Europe still hold back cross-border bank investments. As a result, European banks "overinvest" domestically and it is in particular country-specific credit risk that does not seem fully reflected in the interbank rates.

But other types of borders also result in segmented credit markets. Empirical evidence suggests that "outside" lenders often face difficulties (or hesitate) in extending credit to mainly small local firms (Shaffer 1998; Berger, Klapper, and Udell 2001; Harm 2001; Guiso, Sapienza, and Zingales 2004). This happens in particular when existing relationships between incumbent banks and borrowers are strong (Bergström, Engwall, and Wallerstedt 1994) or when the local judicial enforcement of creditor rights is poor (Fabbri and Padula 2004; Bianco, Jappelli, and Pagano 2005). In all these cases borders will lead to market segmentation and difficulties for cross-border outside banks to engage any local borrowers. In effect, this market segmentation highlights the importance for the outside banks to strive to build an actual physical presence in the targeted market.

5.2.3. Strategy

5.2.3.1. Distance and Branching

Only very few papers study the importance of distance in determining the strategy of banks, that is, in determining their market presence via branching or servicing within certain areas. A recent paper by De Juan (2003) is an exception. She studies how distance between own branches influences bank branching decisions in Spain. She finds that the number of own branches in a particular (sub)market has a positive (but small) effect on the further entry decision of the bank in that market. Hence, her results suggest that branch expansion is partly affected by the proximity of other branches of the same bank (see also Felici and Pagnini 2005; Cerasi, Chizzolini, and Ivaldi 2002).

Results by Berger and DeYoung (2001) may provide a partial explanation for these findings. Berger and DeYoung (2001) document how efficiency of bank branches slips somewhat as the distance between branch and headquarters of the bank increases (see also Bos and Kolari 2005). Hence, in order to guarantee consistency in servicing across bank branches, banks may decide to branch out methodically across certain areas rather than to build isolated outposts.

5.2.3.2. Borders and Entry

Academics and bankers alike have long recognized borders as important factors in impelling bank entry and cross-border bank mergers and acquisitions (M&As). A literature going back to Goldberg and Saunders (1981) and Kindleberger (1983) assert that banks often pursue a "follow-the-customer" strategy when deciding upon cross-border market entry (see also Grosse and Goldberg 1991; Ter Wengel 1995; Brealey and Kaplanis 1996; Buch 2000; Buch and Golder 2002; Boldt-Christmas, Jacobsen, and Tschoegl 2001). Recent evidence however casts some doubt on the "follow-the-customer" strategy as the only game in town (Pozzolo and Focarelli 2005). In particular banks entering the U.S. market have not primarily a follow-the-home-country-customer motive but apparently engage many local borrowers (Seth, Nolle, and Mohanty 1998; Stanley, Roger, and McManis 1993; Buch and Golder 2001).

However banks encounter many difficulties (in countries other than the United States) in successfully pursuing a strategy of engaging local firms by cross-border entry through local branches. DeYoung and Nolle (1996) and Berger, DeYoung, Genay, and Udell (2000), for example, document how most foreign bank affiliates are less efficient than domestic banks, the exceptions being the foreign affiliates of U.S. banks in other countries and most foreign bank affiliates in, for example, Eastern Europe and South America. The latter affiliates are often financially sounder than the domestic banks (Crystal, Dages, and Goldberg 2002).

Why are most foreign bank affiliates less efficient than the local crowd (Berger 2007a)? A paper by Buch (2003a) documents the inefficiencies by foreign bank affiliates are mostly due to the presence of economic borders (language, culture, etc.) and do not seem driven by physical distance.[3] Similarly, Gobbi and Lotti (2004) find that outside banks enter new markets only when the provision of financial services that do not require the intensive use of proprietary information seems profitable in these markets.

But there may be a second reason why banks shy away from following-the-customer, apart from the fear of getting stuck with inefficient branch outposts. Findings by Berger et al. (2003) suggest customers are not that interested in being followed![4] Indeed, they find that foreign affiliates of multinational companies choose host nation banks for cash management

---

3. Magri, Mori, and Rossi (2005) find that physical distance negatively affected foreign bank entry in Italy during the period 1983–1998. However, they interpret distance to proxy for geographical and cultural differences between countries and in addition find that risk differentials between countries positively affected entry.

4. In addition, large banks in particular may face competition for their customers from other large home nation banks (Buch and Lipponer 2005), in which case banks may not enter to avoid one another (e.g., Merrett and Tschoegl 2004).

services more often than home nation or third nation banks. This result is consistent with so-called "concierge" benefits dominating "home cooking" benefits. This is a surprising finding given that these large multinationals might be expected to be prime targets for preferential treatment by their home nation banks. On the other hand, the opening of a foreign affiliate may be a good occasion for a firm to escape a holdup problem at "home." In this way, the establishment of new plants or subsidiaries in foreign countries is an opportunity to add a new (foreign) bank relationship.

Berger et al. (2003) also find that bank reach (global vs. local) is strongly associated with bank nationality. For example, if a host nation bank is the choice of nationality, then the firm is much less likely to choose a global bank. Finally, they also find that bank nationality and bank reach both vary significantly with the legal and financial development of the host nation. For example, firms appear to be much less likely to choose a host nation bank and more likely to choose a global bank when operating in the former socialist nations of Eastern Europe.

Berger et al. (2003) conclude on the basis of this evidence that the extent of future bank globalization may be significantly limited as many corporations continue to prefer local or regional banks for at least some of their services (see also Berger and Smith 2003). Of course, this conclusion is reached within a particular financial architecture, and hence predicated on the continuing (and endogenous) absence of foreign direct investment and possibly more important cross-border mergers taking place (Dermine 2003). The point being that if more foreign direct investment and mergers, in particular, take place, firm preferences may change.

Another reason why foreign bank entry may be constrained is found in Claessens and Van Horen (2007). They document that a combination of the quality in institutions in the source country relative to the bank's competitors' countries and the institutional quality of the host country relative to that of competitor host countries determines the entry decisions of banks. In other words, it is a bank's ability to work within a certain institutional environment relatively better than its competitors, which makes it enter a certain market. In some countries, therefore, the presence of competitors may ultimately discourage any further entry.

5.2.3.3. Borders and Mergers and Acquisitions

Cross-border bank M&As are still a rare species in many parts of the world. Focarelli and Pozzolo (2001), for example, demonstrate that cross-border bank M&As occur relative to within-border M&As less frequently than cross-border M&As in other industries ceteris paribus, while Berger,

Demsetz, and Strahan (1999) show that cross-border bank M&As occur less frequently than domestic bank M&As (see also Danthine, Giavazzi, Vives, and von Thadden 1999). And it is again economic borders,[5] not distance, that make cross-border bank M&As less likely (Buch and DeLong 2004).

Hence, taken together, these studies suggest that not only exogenous economic borders (that also affect other industries) but also endogenous economic borders specific to the banking industry (information asymmetries in assessing target bank portfolios) may make it hard to pull off a successful cross-border bank M&A.

Bank managers are apparently aware of the difficulties awaiting them when engaging in a cross-border M&A and seem to refrain from undertaking many. But also investors recognize the dangers. A recent study by Beitel, Schiereck, and Wahrenburg (2004), for example, documents that the combined cumulative abnormal returns (CARs) for stocks of bidder and target bank in cross-border bank M&As in Europe over the last few decades is actually zero or negative! This finding stands in stark contrast with other industries where the combined CARs of cross-border M&As are typically found to be positive. Hence, investors seemingly evaluate cross-border bank M&As as destroying value. Beitel et al. (2004) results are quite similar to findings in DeLong (2001). She reports that in the United States only the combined CARs of geographically focused bank M&As are positive, although it is not entirely clear what factors are driving this empirical finding.

The evidence presented so far makes not clear whether it are exogenous or endogenous (informational) economic borders that create most problems in making a cross-border bank M&A possible and successful. A recent paper by Campa and Hernando (2004) suggests exogenous borders may play a role. Their study shows that the combined CARs of M&As are typically lower in industries, such as banking, that until recently were under government control or are still (or were) most heavily regulated. CARs of cross-border

---

5. Regulatory borders explicitly prohibiting bank M&As have been removed in Europe. However, national and political interests frequently result in the mobilization of the national antitrust authority or the banking safety apparatus to block cross-border bank M&As. We acknowledge these actions are somewhere in the gray area between explicit prohibition of cross-border bank M&As (regulatory borders) and inherent political and cultural differences, creating difficulties in making a cross-border bank M&A possible and successful (economic borders).

M&As in these industries are actually negative, evidence in line with Beitel et al. (2004). One possible interpretation is that the (lingering) effects of regulation make for harder economic borders.

Bank industry observers sometimes note that, for example, bank organization and corporate governance may be areas shaped in ways that may hinder merger activity. The mutual structure of dominant banks in France and Germany, in particular (e.g., Credit Agricole, Landesbanken), is often passed of as a major hurdle for these banks to initiate and pursue a successful M&A (Wrighton 2003). But exogenous economic borders may also make cross-border bank M&As result in complex holding structures (Dermine 2003), possibly further complicating future M&A activity (see also Barros, Berglof, Fulghieri, Gual, Mayer, and Vives 2005).

The impact of endogenous (informational) economic borders on cross-border bank M&A activity is less researched. It is possible that the domestic merger activity, we have observed until now in Europe, for example, creating so-called "National Champions" is partly made possible by the existence of informational borders (possibly in addition to state efforts to promote them through favorable mergers expanding scale and market share as in Carbó Valverde, Humphrey, and López del Paso 2007). Outside banks seeking to acquire a local bank find it more difficult than incumbent banks to assess the value of the loan portfolio of the possible target banks. As a result, outside banks refrain from stepping in, and most M&A activity, driven by, for example, (revenue and cost) scale and scope considerations, occurs between domestic banks. However, as the domestic banks increase in size and possibly partly refocus their lending toward larger firms they become easier-to-value targets. Moreover, national competition policy concerns may hinder further domestic consolidation. Hence, one could argue that informational borders may have a tendency to partly and endogenously self-destruct and that "National Champions" will almost inevitably metamorphose into "European Champions." Consequently, national competition authorities may have a key role to play in preventing further domestic consolidation (see Vives 2005) and also enhance the transparency of the process of decision making on bank M&As (e.g., recent work by Carletti, Hartmann, and Ongena 2006).

A natural question is then how borrowers will be affected by cross-border bank M&As. It is possible that "in the first round" small local firms serviced by domestic target banks suffer somewhat as with domestic mergers (Sapienza 2002; Bonaccorsi di Patti and Gobbi 2007; Karceski, Ongena, and Smith 2005). Eventually, niche banks may arise taking over part of the lending activities ceased by the merged bank (Berger, Saunders, Scalise, and Udell 1998).

To conclude, a potential source of credit rationing are the effects of physical distance and presence of borders on the conduct and strategies of the financiers. These effects will differ among many dimensions providing an interesting topic for further empirical research.

6

The Macroeconomic Consequences of Financial Imperfections

6.1. Introduction

This chapter assesses the empirical linkages between financial intermediation and real activity. Banks tackle and mitigate the asymmetric information frictions present in imperfect capital markets, and may therefore enhance the supply and allocation of credit. Consequently, financial intermediation may determine economic growth. Cull, Davis, Lamoreaux, and Rosenthal (2005), for example, show that the financial intermediaries present in the economies of the North Atlantic core during the nineteenth century were able to "tap into local information networks" and thereby extend credit to firms that were too young or small to secure funds from large regional or national institutions. Also, by raising the return to savings for local households, they propagated new resources for economic development.

The importance of the intermediation–growth nexus has led to a recent surge of studies trying to determine empirically the association and causality between finance and economic growth.[1] As comprehensively summarized in Levine (2005), Aghion (2006), and Papaioannou (2008), the findings generally suggest that finance, and financial intermediation, in particular, plays a key role in spurring and propagating economic growth through the facilitation of the problems inherent in imperfect capital markets.

---

1. Not all theoretical models imply that financial intermediation contributes to growth (e.g., Bencivenga and Smith 1991). We return to this point toward the end of this chapter when we discuss the effects of other financing possibilities on growth.

6.2. Methodology

6.2.1. Growth Regression

The empirical studies on finance and growth generally use the following form:

$$G = \alpha + \beta F + \gamma X + \mu, \tag{6.1}$$

where G is the average growth rate of a country, F is a vector of indicators of financial development of the country, X represents various conditioning variables to control for other factors associated with growth, and μ is a disturbance term. The major differences among the numerous studies concern the level of detail at which the models are estimated, the measurement of the indicators of financial development (F), the econometric sophistication in the treatment of the potential endogeneity and measurement errors of the financial development indicators, and the type of data sets used.

The level of detail runs from the country level (King and Levine 1993), through regional level (Guiso, Sapienza, and Zingales 2004), to industry level (Rajan and Zingales 1998), and down to firm level (Demirgüç-Kunt and Maksimovic 1998). The various data sets employed are cross-section, time series, and panel data.

When empirically investigating the effect of the various variables associated with banking and financial development, on economic development and growth, we may face the multiple problem of what we usually refer to as omitted variables or measurement errors problem. A potential concern with the results which are generated from our empirical specification is that they may be driven by unobserved changes in industry structure or conditioning factors that are correlated with changes in the intrinsic structure of the financial markets in general and those of the banking industry in particular. Thus, there is a danger that what we discover amounts at best to spurious relationships.

Consider, for instance, the Schumpeterian view of the relationship between financial regulation, financial development, and growth that may indicate that a more developed financial sector is more efficient in reallocating capital to its best use. It is possible, of course, that the various forms and characteristics of banking markets are a response to greater levels of economic activity, including entrepreneurship, rather than the cause of them. Growth itself may lead to better financial institutions, deregulation, and so forth. Thus, this simultaneity problem or direction-of-causality affects our ability to assess the effects financial and banking development and deepening may have on the variables of interest such as growth. Additionally, measurement errors problems can bias the parameter estimates and render them inconsistent when variables are measured incorrectly, especially so when many of the variables we use are just proxies for the unobservable or hard-to-measure ones implied by theory.

The problems of simultaneity, omitted variables, and measurement errors all will introduce an attenuation bias in the relevant parameter estimates when ordinary least squares (OLS) estimator is applied. Technically, attenuation bias results from the regressors not being orthogonal to the regression's disturbance term.

The conventional and by now standard remedy for ameliorating attenuation bias problems is the application of the instrumental variables (IV) technique. In this technique, a set of instruments is used to extract the exogenous components of the system of relationships. Thus, an instrumental variable is one that correlates with the endogenous variable of concern but is orthogonal to the regression's disturbance term. The Hansen test for overidentifying restrictions (see, e.g., Davidson and MacKinnon 1993) is then applied in order to test for overidentifying restrictions, that is, a test of the validity of the instruments used. The hypothesis being tested is that the instruments used are uncorrelated with the residuals. If we are unable to reject the null hypothesis, then the instruments used are appropriate. The particular instruments used are research specific and depend on the particular investigation.

6.2.2. Instrumental Variable Estimation

To be more precise, the OLS slope estimator (when the independent variables x_i are measured in deviations form) is

$$\hat{\beta} = \frac{\sum_i x_i y_i}{\sum_i x_i^2},$$
(6.2)

where

$$y_i = \beta x_i + \mu_i,$$
(6.3)

and μ_i are identically and independently distributed disturbances. Substituting equation 6.3 in equation 6.2 yields

$$\hat{\beta} = \frac{\beta \sum_i x_i^2 + \sum_i x_i \mu_i}{\sum_i x_i^2} = \beta + \frac{\sum_i x_i \mu_i}{\sum_i x_i^2}. \tag{6.4}$$

As is well known only when the second right-hand-side term in equation 6.4 has zero expected value the estimator $\hat{\beta}$ is an unbiased estimator of β as required. When, however, there is a correlation between any independent variable and the disturbance term, $\hat{\beta}$ will be an inconsistent and biased estimator of β. Such is the case when the x_i are measured with an error. Assume that

$$x_i^* - x_i + \xi_i, \tag{6.5}$$

where x_i is the true value and the x_i^* is the variable we actually use. The true regression model is in equation 6.3, while the actual regression we work with is

$$y_i = \beta x_i^* + \mu_i - \beta \xi_i = \beta x_i^* + \mu_i^*. \tag{6.6}$$

It is straightforward to see that the disturbance μ_i^* and the variable x_i^* have nonzero covariance, meaning they are correlated. Specifically,

$$Cov(\mu_i^*, x_i^*) = E[(\mu_i - \beta \xi_i)(x_i + \xi_i)] = -\beta \sigma_\xi^2. \tag{6.7}$$

Hence, the OLS estimates of the regression parameters will be biased and inconsistent with the degree of bias and inconsistency being related to the variance of the measurement error.

Instrumental variable (IV) estimation offers us the remedy for such a problem. This, by now standard, technique involves the search for a variable, say, z, which is highly correlated with the erroneously measured and perhaps endogenous independent variable but orthogonal to the disturbance term of the regression and the measurement errors. In our example, the proper instrumental variable estimator will be

$$\beta^* = \frac{\sum_i y_i z_i}{\sum_i x_i^* z_i}. \tag{6.8}$$

Thus, the relationship between the instrumental variable estimator and the true slope parameter is

$$\beta^* = \frac{\sum\limits_i y_i z_i}{\sum\limits_i x_i^* z_i} = \frac{\beta \sum\limits_i x_i^* z_i + \sum\limits_i \mu_i^* z_i}{\sum\limits_i x_i^* z_i} = \beta + \frac{\sum\limits_i \mu_i^* z_i}{\sum_i x_i^* z_i}. \qquad (6.9)$$

The choice of the z instrument guarantees that β^* will approach β asymptotically, that is,

$$\underset{n \to +\infty}{Cov(z, \mu^*)} \longrightarrow 0 \qquad\qquad (6.10)$$

(n is number of observations), and hence will be a consistent estimator of β.

The practical difficulty, though, is in the detection and specification of such an instrumental variable that is rather often a function of the specific researcher's ingenuity. However, once a proper instrument is determined one can proceed to consistent estimation by the instrumental variable procedure.

To be concrete, in the context of the finance–growth nexus, when using cross-country data, for instance, one must find instrumental variables z that can explain cross-country differences in financial development, but that are uncorrelated with economic growth beyond their association with financial development and other growth determinants.

Levine, Loayza, and Beck (2000), for example, employ the La Porta, Lopez-de-Silanes, Shleifer, and Vishny (1998) measures of legal origin, as such instruments, relying on the idea that since most countries obtained their legal systems through occupation and colonization, the legal origin variables may plausibly be exogenous and hence uncorrelated with the disturbance term. Thus, these instruments imply that legal origin affects growth only through the financial development indicators and the conditioning variables x.

Another example is Levine (1999), who employs the legal and regulatory determinants of financial development as instruments. His findings are consistent with the view that improvements in creditor rights, contract enforcement, and the information content of corporate financial statements induce improvements in the functioning of financial intermediaries that enhance economic growth.

A recent inspiring approach is offered by Guiso et al. (2004), who investigate the financial development–growth paradigm in the local/regional context using Italian regional data. They instrument their indicator of financial development (access to credit, which is obviously endogenous) with variables that describe regional characteristics of the banking system in 1936, such as branch entry restrictions that had been applied differentially to savings versus national banks in 1936 and that resulted in differential composition of credit availability in the 1990s, when the industry was completely deregulated. They report that their instruments are correlated with the variable of interest (local access to credit), but uncorrelated with the disturbance in their regressions relating economic performance to financial development. They do so by showing that the number of bank branches per inhabitant in 1936 is not very highly correlated with the level of economic development of the region. Further evidence on the finance–growth relationship is discussed in the following section.

6.2.3. Interaction Variables

Recently interaction terms between financial development and other variables of interest K have been added to equation 6.1, resulting in the specification

$$G = \alpha + \beta F_i + \gamma X + \delta F_i K + \mu. \tag{6.11}$$

Rajan and Zingales (1998), for example, interact external dependence and financial development, Aghion (2006) introduces interaction effects between financial development and technological or macro variables, while Deidda and Fattouh (2007) interact an indicator of banking development with a measure of stock market development.[2]

The approach first suggested by Rajan and Zingales (1998) was subsequently applied to firm level data by Bertrand, Schoar, and Thesmar (2007), for example. In another application, Giannetti and Ongena (in press) argue that firms in Eastern European countries that are more dependent on external finance should be those that benefit to a larger extent from foreign bank presence (if foreign banks indeed improve lending policies). They distinguish the effect of foreign bank presence across firms belonging to industries with different degree of financial dependence. They measure bank dependence in a sector with the ratio of short-term loans and long-term debt to

---

2. When the interaction term is between continuous variables, it may be preferable to center these variables around their respective means. This procedure enables each of the parameters estimates to affect the independent variable conditionally on the other's mean value rather than on the other's zero value.

total liabilities (as in Bertrand et al. 2007). Notice that they employ U.K. data [*sic*] to measure financial dependence (1) to ensure the exogeneity of their financial dependence proxy and (2) to have a measure of the propensity to use bank loans in a financially developed country where financing constraints are less likely to be binding. They then test whether the impact of foreign bank lending is larger for firms in sectors that are more bank-dependent by including an interaction variable between the proxy for bank dependence and foreign lending.

6.3. Evidence

6.3.1. Banks and Growth

In their influential study of a panel of 77 countries over the 1960–89 period, King and Levine (1993) document all β values to be positive in equation 6.1, statistically significant, and economically relevant. Their indicators for the development of financial intermediation are the size of financial intermediaries, the relative importance of commercial banks versus the central bank in allocating credit, and the degree to which intermediaries allocate credit to the private sector versus the government or public enterprises.

Demirgüç-Kunt and Maksimovic (1998) show that firms in countries with better developed financial systems grow faster than these firms would have without this access. Jayaratne and Strahan (1996) also document an association between financial intermediation and growth. They show that when individual states of the United States relaxed intrastate branching restrictions, the quality of bank loans rose and per capita GDP growth accelerated (for other examples of within-country regional studies, see Carbó-Valverde, Rodríguez-Fernández, and Udell 2005; Carbó Valverde, López del Paso, and Rodríguez Fernández 2007).

Kerr and Nanda (2007) have studied how the entry rate, the distribution of entry sizes, and survival rates for firms respond to changes in banking competition; that is, they investigate how changes in financial markets impact the entry and exit of nonfinancial firms in product markets. Kerr and Nanda (2007) documents that branching deregulation in the United States reduced financing constraints, particularly among small startups, and improved allocative efficiency across the entire firm size distribution.[3]

---

3. Kerr and Nanda (2007) use U.S. Census Bureau's Longitudinal Business Database ranging from 1976 to 1999. The panel nature of their data enables them to track individual

Moreover, and very interesting, they provide strong evidence that the deregulation reduced financing constraints benefiting mostly startup firms that tend to have fewer sources of external finance and hence are more sensitive to increases in interest rates or credit rationing. This evidence is important because it provides yet an additional mechanism through which financial sector (reforms) contributes to and propagates product markets (on banks and innovation in Italian firms, see also Benfratello, Schiantarelli, and Sembenelli (2008).

6.3.2. Causality: Banks to Growth?

While the already mentioned studies, and many others, document a strong association between intermediation and growth, they do not resolve the issue of causality. Levine (1999) not only extends King and Levine (1993) but also further investigates the issue of causality. Levine (1999) employs measures of the legal and regulatory environment as instruments for financial development. Using GMM (generalized methods of moments) estimates, he then tests for overidentifying restrictions to find out whether the instruments are associated with growth beyond their effect on the cross-country variation in financial intermediary development. The legal and regulatory environment matters for financial development and growth. In particular, legal and regulatory attention to the sovereignty of creditors rights, contract enforcement and information disclosure determine financial development, and perhaps more important, these variables are also positively associated with economic growth. Levine et al. (2000), for example, corroborate these findings. They use a GMM dynamic panel estimator, a technique that may mitigate simultaneity and omitted variable biases, including those originating from unobserved country-specific effects.

To the best of our knowledge, Rousseau and Wachtel (1998) are the only ones in this literature explicitly testing for causality between banking and growth. They examine the nature of the links between the intensity of financial intermediation and growth in the United States, the United Kingdom, Canada, Norway, and Sweden during the 1870–1929 period. Studying their time series data employing vector error correction models reveals the quantitative importance of long-run relationships among measures of financial intensity and growth in real per capita levels of output and the monetary base. The authors clearly point out that Granger causality tests suggest a

---

establishments over time, thereby allowing for differential analyses of entry rates vs. changes in entry sizes.

leading role for the intermediation variables in explaining real sector activity, while feedback effects seem largely insignificant. These results suggest an important role for intermediation in determining growth.

Using data on value added across sectors, Claessens and Laeven (2003) confirm the importance of property rights for financial development and real growth. They show that optimal resource allocation within the firm is crucially dependent on the strength of property rights. Asset allocation is an important channel through which property rights affect firm growth. A very interesting aspect of their study is their differentiation between tangible and intangible assets. Intangible assets almost by definition are most in need of protection by property rights. Consequently, if "new economy" growth is "intangible intensive," efficient financial intermediation will remain crucially important in determining future growth.

Our knowledge regarding the causality nature running from financial intermediation to economic growth is further enhanced by a recent study by Kroszner, Laeven, and Klingebiel (2007). They analyze the links between financial shocks and real activity. The rationale behind their study is straightforward: if banks ameliorate credit constraints, then a (negative) shock to their activities in environments where banks are dominant should exert a disproportionately contractionary impact on those sectors owing their development to the financial intermediary sector. Employing data from 38 developed as well as developing countries that have experienced banking crises, the authors confirm the aforementioned rationale. They find that in noncrisis periods, intermediation-intensive sectors benefit from positive differential growth in countries with "deep financial systems," as in Rajan and Zingales (1998). But results are the opposite for crisis periods. Of importance is their finding that these results hold only for banking crises and do not hold for other type of crises such as currency crises or general recessions. The authors interpret their results to be consistent with the credit channel running through the banking system.

6.3.3. Banks, Financial Markets, and Growth

As we have seen from the body of literature discussed above, the great majority of empirical studies to date point to a positive association between banks and real growth and to the direction of causality running from banking activity to growth. However, such a relationship may be nonlinear. Allen and Gale (1997), for example, claim that banks effectiveness is dependent on the competition they face from other financial institutions, while Boot and Thakor (1997) show that equilibrium financial structure consists of an optimal mix of banks as well as market finance. As financial markets develop, market finance expands relative to bank finance.[4]

Rousseau and Wachtel (2000) estimate vector autoregressions (VARs) for a set of 47 countries using annual data for 1980–95. Their panel VARs indicate that increases in both the intensity of activity in traditional intermediaries and the market value of equity traded on organized exchanges have a strong effect on output, while the effects of market capitalization are weaker. This study in fact points to the important interaction of subsectors of the financial sector (banking and equity markets) and their differential, perhaps nonlinear effects on growth.[5]

Deidda and Fattouh (2007) develop a theoretical model that predicts a nonlinear relationship between banking development, stock market development and growth. In particular, they predict that a move from a bank-based system toward a combination of bank- and market-based system should have a negative impact on the effects of bank development. They test their model on the (often employed) cross-country data set originated by Demirgüç-Kunt and Levine (2001). In addition, they find that the interaction term between banking and stock market development is significantly negative, which implies that the effect of banking development on growth tends to be less positive as stock markets develop. It is in this sense that the finance growth nexus may be subject to various sorts of nonlinear relationships. Moreover, this result holds subject to instrumental variables estimation and the conditioning on the various conventional controls.

The notion of nonlinearities in the relationship between finance and growth is discussed in Ciccone and Papaioannou (2006). They consider the conjecture that some countries experience faster aggregate productivity growth than others, because their high levels of financial development lead to capital being reallocated rapidly to industries with superior investment opportunities. They embed this capital reallocation hypothesis in a multiindustry world equilibrium model to test it with international data on industry value-added growth.

---

4. There are possibly three key types of information asymmetries: (1) asymmetry regarding project quality, (2) postlending moral hazard, and (3) individual borrowers' moral hazard. The third asymmetry is better resolved by financial markets, as opposed to the first two, which are potentially better handled by banks. Consequently, a combination of both banks and financial markets may exist in equilibrium.

5. Levine and Zervos (1998) show a positive association (but not causality) between stock market development and long-run growth in a sample of 42 countries over the period 1976–1993. They claim that the links among stock markets, banks, and growth is productivity growth rather than physical capital accumulation.

Consequently, Ciccone and Papaioannou (2006) test the cross-country industry growth implication of the capital reallocation hypothesis using a two-stage least-squares approach. In the first-stage regression they relate actual industry capital growth in a financially developed country (the United States) to the estimated world-average industry opportunities (excluding the United States). In the second stage, they use global industry investment opportunities (predicted industry capital growth from the first stage) to estimate the effect of financial development on growth in industries with global investment opportunities to estimate the effect of financial development on growth in industries with global investment opportunities.

Their empirical results using only the U.S. proxy for global investment opportunities indicate a significantly positive effect of financial development on growth in industries with investment opportunities using data on 28 manufacturing industries in 67 countries during the 1980s. This effect of financial development on growth in industries with investment opportunities becomes larger and statistically stronger when they implement the two-stage least squares approach to focus on industry growth in response to global opportunities.

The overall picture emerging from the Ciccone and Papaioannou (2006) study is in line with Fisman and Love (2004a, 2004b), who emphasize the role of financial development for the speed of interindustry resource reallocation and test it using industry data. Fisman and Love (2004b) document that industry value-added growth patterns are more closely correlated for country pairs with similar levels of financial development, even when they control for economic development and other factors.

Fisman and Love (2004a) test whether countries with high levels of financial development grow faster in industries with global growth opportunities proxied by U.S. sales growth. Their results show that industries with global growth opportunities grow faster in financially developed countries, and that this finding prevails when they control for the external finance intensity of industries. Bekaert, Harvey, Lundblad, and Siegel (2007) find that country-level growth opportunities predict output and investment growth, and also that this relation is strongest in countries that have liberalized their capital accounts, equity markets, and banking systems (in this context, see also Giannetti and Ongena in press).

As has already emerged from the aforementioned research, the association between finance and development is quite complex and hosts numerous important determinants. This complexity is further apparent when one considers such a macroeconomic fundamental as inflation. Rousseau and Wachtel (2000), for example, discover the complex interactions between financial development and inflation that affect economic growth.[6] Their major finding is quite striking: the finance to growth nexus holds only when inflation falls below a threshold that varies between a 5-year average inflation rate of 13 percent to 25 percent, depending on the measure of financial depth. The effects become significantly positive when inflation falls below a threshold of about 6 percent to 8 percent.

The important implication of this research is that although deeper financial intermediation may be a significant causal factor in economic growth, one cannot infer that any expansion in intermediary activity will be beneficial. As succinctly put by Wachtel (2001): "Financial sector expansion that results from inflationary liquidity creation or deterioration in lending standards will not enhance long-run growth prospects." (p.357).

Wachtel's caveat regarding the varying effects of the types and forms of financial depth on economic growth is supported by the findings of La Porta, Lopez-de-Silanes, and Shleifer (2002), who show, for instance, that higher degree of public ownership of banks is associated with lower level of bank development and slower growth.[7] This important insight reinforces those reached earlier by Jayaratne and Strahan (1996), who documented that the quality of banks' loan portfolios improves significantly after deregulatory reform and that these improvements in lending quality and efficiency and not sheer volumes of credit are the key elements in the channel through which finance propagates growth (King and Levine 1993).[8] This is also in line with theoretical endogenous growth models, showing that higher quality investment can contribute to long-run growth (Lucas 1988; Romer 1986).

Does the finance–growth nexus also apply for less developed countries and fast growing economies? Only a handful of studies consider developing countries. Haber (1991, 1997), for example, examine the role of financial liberalization for economic growth in Brazil and Mexico, contending that financial liberalization allows a greater number of firms access to external finance. He argues that political institutions play an important role in determining the degree of financial liberalization and concludes that Brazil did

---

6. The data from Rousseau and Wachtel (2000) cover 84 countries from 1960 to 1995.

7. The claim is that publicly owned banks are inferior in corporate governance, risk management, and information collection efforts.

8. Jayaratne and Strahan (1996, 1998) provide some evidence that improved screening and monitoring of borrowers were responsible for the dramatic decline in nonperforming loans after the branch-restrictions deregulation. The ratio of nonperforming loans to total loans declines by 0.24–0.77 percentage points.

better in financial liberalization than did Mexico because of better political institutions.

The finance and growth issue in China have only recently received attention, so as yet there is no consensus on the impact of financial development. One view holds that finance promotes growth in China. Employing a province-level data set for the period 1985–98, Li and Liu (2001) find that growth of provincial aggregate output is positively related to the growth in lending of the largest banks and self-raised funds. Cheng and Degryse (2007) show that only bank development contributes to province growth in China whereas development of nonbank financial institutions does not have an impact. They attribute this to financial reforms only at work for banks.

Hasan, Wachtel, and Zhou (2006), analyze the issue more broadly, using panel data covering 31 Chinese provinces for the period 1986–02. They find that the extent of development of financial markets is associated with growth (along with the legal environment, awareness of property rights, and political pluralism). A recent study of Ayyagari, Demirgüç-Kunt, and Maksimovic (2007) examines finance and growth in China using micro-level data. Employing the World Bank 2003 survey data covering 2,400 firms, they find that despite its weaknesses, higher growth of firms is associated with financing from the formal financial system, and that fund raising from alternative channels is not.

Other papers take the view that China is a counterexample of the finance–growth nexus. Allen, Qian, and Qian (2005), for example, observing the coexistence of weak legal and financial systems and high economic growth in China, question whether development of financial institution actually plays much of a role in China's growth (see also Boyreau-Debray 2003). Through a close examination of the relationship of law, finance, and growth in China, they reveal that the relatively poor legal system and the underdeveloped financial sector contribute little to private-sector growth, the oft-touted motor of China's growth. Allen et al. (2005) conclude that the private sector must have access to alternative financing channels besides financial institutions.

To conclude, a broad body of knowledge documents a positive correspondence between the development of the financial intermediary sector and economic growth. Causality seems to run from finance to growth, as well. However, future work needs to broaden and deepen our understanding of the determinants of financial intermediary development. Additional measures of the legal, supervisory, and regulatory environment that may determine and deepen financial intermediary development should be considered. The

possible effects of financial sector development on the differential allocation of credit to productive versus unproductive firms as well as its effects on
entry and exist of firms is of great interest as these may have important implications for important channels of growth. The analysis of the potentially
nonlinear relationship between finance and growth and the interaction of
market structure in the intermediary and nonintermediary financial sectors
and their effects on the real sector performance also seems very promising.

7

Individual Bank Runs and Systemic Risk

7.1. Introduction

So far in this book we have dealt with issues concerning the notion of market structure, competition, and efficiency and the multidimensional character associated with each of these concepts. An additional issue, and a particularly pressing one for policy makers around the world, is the potential instability of the banking system. This instability may find its roots in various market failures, such as information asymmetries, moral hazard, adverse selection, scale and scope economies, and a host of externalities but may also stem from contagion.

Are market structure and efficiency considerations at odds with system stability, and is there a unidirectional association between competition and fragility? Is the banking system inherently unstable with recurring bank runs and contagion? What happens to the banking sector and the economy as a whole after a banking crisis? A thorough understanding of the aforementioned, even preliminary answers to some of these basic questions is essential when analyzing the various regulatory and supervisory interventions and policies. But such exploration may nevertheless barely scratch the surface of the complex issues at hand.[1]

---

1. For an excellent and exceptionally thorough treatment of the main theoretical perspective on this subject, see Allen and Gale (2007). Claessens and Forbes (2001) provide an extensive empirical review.

Some brief historical anecdotes are in place. Miron (1986) estimates that during the period 1890–1908, the probability of a bank panic in a given year to be almost one in three. Moreover, when he takes out the years in which a bank panic occurred, the average yearly rate of growth of GNP would have been 6.8 percent compared to only 3.8 percent when years with a panic are included. If the only major anomalies pertaining to these years are due to bank panics, then it is indeed a very important phenomenon deserving much attention.

Freixas and Rochet (1997) note that a strong negative impact of a panic is a defining characteristic for the periods prior to the founding of the U.S. Federal Reserve System, the establishment of the U.K. Central Bank, and the creation of central banks in other European countries. This may hint to the importance of these institutions that are in charge of regulating this sector of the economy since it seems that without regulation, bank runs and bank panics are inherent to the nature of banking and to the fractional reserve system on which it relies.

It is important to distinguish between bank runs that affect individual banks and contagion and bank panics that concerns part of the sector or the sector in its entirety and consequently the entire payment system and potentially the real economy.[2] There have been many financial crises in the past two decades, despite the regulatory scrutiny imposed by central banks and associated institutions. In the early 1990s, there was a banking crisis in Scandinavia, first in Norway[3] and then in Sweden and Finland; after the European Exchange Rate Mechanism crisis of the fall of 1992, there was the Mexican crisis of 1994/95, the East Asian crisis of 1997, followed by the financial crises in Russia and Brazil in 1998. In the past couple of years, there has been a very severe crisis in Argentina and financial turmoil in Brazil, to name just a few major non-U.S. countries.[4]

The 1980s was a troublesome period for the U.S. banking system, as well. Demirgüç-Kunt (1989), for example, calculates that since the establishment of the FDIC in 1933, more then 1,500 banks were declared officially insolvent, with more than 800 of these closures taking place during the 1980s and 200 being closed in 1988 alone.

---

2. The term "contagion" may in general describe situations where economic phenomena move more closely together than otherwise. No consensus seems to exist on a more precise definition. See Rigobon (2002) and Forbes and Rigobon (2002) for a discussion.

3. See Moe, Solheim, and Vale (2004) for a comprehensive and detailed description of the Norwegian banking crisis, its resolution, and the costs to tax payers.

4. Caprio (2003) compiles information regarding scope and estimated losses or costs on 117 systemic banking crises in 93 countries since the late 1970s.

Preventing banking crises has thus far been a frustrating exercise, as the frequency and number of crises seem to have been increasing. Thus, our understanding of the reasons behind and the consequences of bank runs and panics is of utmost importance.[5]

This chapter explores the basics of the phenomena known as bank runs, contagion, and panics in banking. In doing so, we attempt to explain the probable reasons for individual bank runs and the association and perhaps causation between market structure and contagion. We ultimately want to evaluate the effects of banking crises on the economy as a whole and assess its effects on the propagation and prolongation of recessions.

The conventional explanation for a bank run is that when depositors observe large withdrawals from their bank, they fear bankruptcy and respond by also withdrawing their own deposits (see Diamond and Dybvig 1983; Freixas and Rochet 1997). Withdrawals in excess of current expected demand for liquidity generate a negative externality for the bank experiencing the liquidity shortage, since these withdrawals imply an increase in the bank's probability of failure. But withdrawals can also generate an externality for the whole banking system if the agents view the failure as a symptom of difficulties occurring throughout the industry. In such a case, a bank run may induce contagion and develop into a bank panic (Freixas and Parigi 1998; Freixas, Parigi, and Rochet 2000; Allen and Gale 2000b; Aghion, Bolton, and Dewatripont 2000).

The transformation by banks of illiquid assets into liquid claims is one of their major contributions to economic activity. This "task" is performed by banks through the supply of demand-deposit contracts that enable depositors to withdraw their deposits when they are hit by liquidity shocks. This task is sustainable as long as these shocks are specific to the depositor, that is, "idiosyncratic." However, when withdrawals are no longer idiosyncratic, as in cases where the shocks are either marketwide, that is, "fundamentals-based contagion" as in Calvo and Reinhart (1996), or are due to coordination failure of investors' exercising panic-type beliefs concerning the banking sector as a whole, banks are forced to liquidate their long-run investments at a loss, potentially causing bank failure.

In their seminal contribution, Diamond and Dybvig (1983) show that while demand-deposit contracts enable banks to provide liquidity, they simultaneously expose banks to panic-based bank runs. However, a trade-off may exist between the benefits from liquidity and the costs emanating

---

5. For a comprehensive summary of the contagion phenomenon, see Dornbusch, Park, and Claessens (2000).

from bank runs. In fact, Goldstein and Pauzner (2005) in a recent and related paper modify and extend the Diamond and Dybvig (1983) contribution, and find conditions under which banks can increase overall welfare and construct a demand-deposit contract that trades off the benefits from liquidity against the cost of runs.

7.2. Evidence

7.2.1. Determinants of Banking Crises: Market and Economic Conditions

There is a widely held view among policy makers that reduced competition in banking may be desirable, because softening competition may result in higher stability of the system. Such a widely held view may stem from the "charter value hypothesis," which conjectures that a competitive banking system is prone to instability and increased failure rates. The theoretical literature is not unanimous though regarding the effect of competition on failure. Earlier contributions conclude that when confronted with increased competition, moral hazard is exacerbated and banks intentionally take more risk (e.g., Allen and Gale 2000a, 2000b, 2004b).

However, some recent theoretical models based on an "optimal contracting hypothesis" point in the opposite direction. Boyd and De Nicolo (2005), for example, present a moral hazard model in which risk of failure unambiguously declines as the banking sector become more competitive. The reasoning is that the optimal contract between bank and borrower should leave enough money on the table to lower the moral hazard problem of the borrower. Sufficient banking competition lowering interest rates therefore dampens moral hazard problems.

Extending Boyd and De Nicolo (2005), Boyd, De Nicolo, and Jalal (2006) allow for competition in both loan and deposit markets and allow banks to hold risk-free bonds. Their model then predicts a negative relationship between the number of banks and banks' risk of failure, contrary to the predictions generated by the "charter value hypothesis." Martinez-Miera and Repullo (2008), however, show that when taking into account the impact of lower loan rates on revenues from nondefaulting loans, a U-shaped relationship between competition and the risk of bank failure is obtained.

The mixed theoretical results are reflected in the empirical literature, as well. There exists quite a large body of empirical evidence; however, the evidence is mixed. Keeley (1990), for example, provides evidence that the relaxation of state branching restrictions in the 1980s that increased competition, reduced monopoly rents and hence "charter value," and induced large U.S. bank holding companies to increase their risk taking.[6] This increased risk taking caused the increase in bank failures during the 1980s. Similarly, Dick (2006) shows that following the deregulation of the 1990s there was an increase in loan loss provisions. On the other hand, Jayaratne and Strahan (1998) document that deregulation was followed by sharp reduction in loan losses.

Beck, Demirgüç-Kunt, and Levine (2006a)—motivated by public policy debates about bank consolidation and conflicting theoretical predictions about the relationship among bank concentration, bank competition, and banking system fragility—study the impact of national bank concentration, bank regulations, and national institutions on the likelihood of a country suffering a systemic banking crisis. Using data on 69 countries from 1980 to 1997, they find that crises are less likely in economies with more concentrated banking systems (even after controlling for differences in commercial bank regulatory policies, national institutions affecting competition, macroeconomic conditions, and shocks to the economy). Furthermore, the data used in their study indicate that regulatory policies and institutions that thwart competition are associated with greater banking system fragility.

Boyd et al. (2006) tests whether the "charter value hypothesis" or the "optimal contracting hypothesis" applies by employing two different data sets, one comprising 2,500 U.S. banks in 2003 and the other a panel of 18,000 bank-year observations from 134 nonindustrialized countries for the 1993–04 time period. Specifying regressions that relate measures of concentration to measures of risk of failure, and loan-to-asset ratios, they document that the probability of failure is positively and significantly related to concentration, and this result is present in both data sets. Consequently, their results are more in line with the "optimal contracting hypothesis" and invalidate the "charter value hypothesis." To conclude the relationship between competition and stability is complex: it is quite difficult, if not impossible, to assert a definitive relationship between market structure and fragility.

---

6. This phenomenon may have emanated from a known agency problem. Bank owners and their agents/managers have an increased incentive to take on extra risk: if their choices turn out to be successful, they would collect the rewards; if not, the costs would be borne by the deposit insurance fund (or ultimately the tax payers).

Also, it is not impossible that the conflicting results which emerge from the various studies discussed so far emanate from (1) the use of different proxies for risk of failure, (2) the use of the Herfindahl Hirshman Index or other measures of concentration to measure the intensity of competition in general and market power in particular, or (3) the abstraction from nonstationarity possibly present in the time series data.

An earlier strand of the empirical literature was interested in the effects the macroeconomic environment had on the probability of the occurrence of a banking crisis. Demirgüç-Kunt and Detragiache (1998), for example, study the major macroeconomic factors which are associated with systemic banking crises. They use a multivariate logit model to study panel data of between 45 and 65 market economies (excluding those in transition) for the 1980–94 time period.[7] They find that there is high degree of association between banking crisis and low GDP growth, high inflation, high real interest rates, explicit deposit insurance, and weak law enforcement. Their findings do not reveal much about market structure effects, coordination problems, and other idiosyncratic elements that may contribute to bank runs.

7.2.2. Implications of Banking Crises

Aside from our need to study the determinants of crises, it is also important to understand the various implications of crises, in other words, what happens to the banking sector and the economy at large in the period following the crisis. For example, monetary shocks that have adverse effects on the credit supplied by the banking system and on the borrowing firms may enhance and prolong the adverse effects of a crisis on aggregate economic activity (Bernanke 1983).

Calomiris and Mason (2003) examine the effects of banking distress on the real economy during the Great Depression in order to ascertain whether banks propagated demand shocks through their loan supply. They find that the variation in the supply of bank credit indeed explains most of the variation in income growth.

Banking crises may not be limited to domestic economic activity only, but can transmit their adverse effects through the loan supply channel onto foreign countries, as well. Peek and Rosengren (2000), for example, document

---

7. See section 3.2.2.4, on structural demand models, for a description of the multinomial logit specification.

that the dramatic declines in Japanese equity and real estate prices in the early 1990s had exerted strong downward pressure on the capital positions of Japanese banks, which in turn responded by reducing their lending in the United States. This fact enabled the authors to test the extent to which a (foreign) loan supply shock can affect real (domestic) economic activity. Since the shock was exogenous to U.S. credit markets and at the same time connected to it through the substantial penetration into U.S. commercial real estate loan markets by Japanese banks, this enabled the identification of this exogenous loan supply shock and linked it to construction activity in major commercial real estate markets in the United States. Peek and Rosengren (2000) established conclusively that loan supply shocks that had emanated from Japan had real effects on economic activity in the United States.

Demirgüç-Kunt, Detragiache, and Gupta (2006) use aggregate as well as bank-level data on 36 banking crises in 35 countries to study what happens to the banking system following a banking crisis.[8] The methodology used by the authors tries to ascertain how certain banking and macroeconomic variables of interest are affected following the occurrence of a crisis.

The first question Demirgüç-Kunt et al. (2006) address is whether bank distress propagates adverse shocks thereby prolonging recessions (Bernanke 1983). Their second question relates to depositors' runs. That is, they study whether deposits decline after a crisis. They estimate ordinary least squares regressions where each variable of interest is regressed on four time dummies, one for the crisis year, and one each for the three periods following the crisis. Country dummies are included, as well. As recognized by Demirgüç-Kunt et al. (2006), their results may discover association rather than causation between crises and the aftermath.

Moreover, their results (as well as other results present in this field of research) may be subjected to misspecification in the sense that there is no attention given to the usual nonstationarity character of the time series behavior of the various variables of interest. As is well known, nonstationarity invalidates conventional statistical inferences and thus the alleged result may be spurious.

Notwithstanding the aforementioned problems, the results documented by Demirgüç-Kunt et al. (2006) are quite illuminating: in that the banking crisis is accompanied by a sharp decline in output growth (four percentage

---

8. They consider a crisis to be systemic if nonperforming loans reached at least 10 percent of total loans or if the cleaning up operations' costs were at least 2 percent of GDP.

points) but growth rebounds back to the precrisis period in the second year after the crisis. Thus, the effect of a crisis on the real economy seems to be short-lived, strengthening the earlier findings of Kaminsky and Reinhart (1999).

Furthermore, crises are not accompanied by a significant decline in aggregate bank deposits relative to GDP, although depositors do substitute strong banks for weaker ones—a cleansing effect. This result is quite encouraging since they may indicate either the workings of well functioning safety nets or market discipline, and the emergence of a healthier and more efficient postcrisis banking system. Credit slows substantially, but credit to GDP ratio is higher after crisis. Output recovery begins in the second year after the crisis, while credit still stagnates. Banks, including healthier ones, reallocate their asset portfolio away from loans, suggesting a lack of loan demand or collateral.

The "after crisis cleansing effect" is also documented in Cornett, McNutt, and Tehranian (2005), who examine the impact of bank failures on the long-term performance of rival banks.[9] They show that the postcrisis effect is heterogeneous, depending on whether bank failure is due to idiosyncratic reasons or is due to a general economic decline. If a failure is unique to the failing bank it has a positive effect on operating performance of rival banks but when failure is due to a general economic decline this finding no longer holds. Thus, their results may indicate that panic-based behavior resulting in contagion may not be present in their data and that the distinction stressed by theory between "coordination problems" versus "fundamentals-based contagion" is indeed important.

The above results are in contrast to those documented by Boyd, Kwak, and Smith (2005), who attempt to assess real output losses associated with modern crises. These authors criticize previous research by pointing out real output losses were underestimated as only contemporaneous output losses during and immediately after crises were typically being considered. Boyd et al. (2005) in contrast document very large output losses, which can anywhere between 63 percent and 302 percent of real per capita GDP, reflecting the very slow recovery period. However, they do corroborate previous research results pointing to quite diverse experiences, where in mature and highly developed countries banking crises were not associated

---

9. They extend a study by Aharony and Swary (1996), who did not distinguish among the types of failure. Aharony and Swary (1996) find that the contagion effect is stronger (1) the closer the rival bank is to the failing bank, (2) the larger is the rival bank and, (3) the higher is the rival banks' leverage.

with any significant reduction in real per capita GDP.[10] This in sharp contrast to other countries where crises caused considerable output losses which could amount to several years of lost GDP.[11]

Strengthening the aforementioned findings of differential impact of crises, a recent study by Dell'Ariccia, Detragiache, and Rajan (2007) revisit the "real effect of banking crises" problem trying to find whether banking sector problems have independent (of a concurrent economic downturn) negative real effects. They use a difference-in-difference approach (on which we elaborate in chapter 9) and apply it to panel data from 41 countries for the 1980–00 period, controlling for industry-year, country-year, and industry-country fixed effects. In particular, they run the following specification for country i, industry j and time t:

$$Real\ output\ growth_{ijt} = \sum_{i,j} \alpha_{ij}d_{ij} + \sum_{i,t} \beta_{it}d_{it} + \sum_{j,t} \gamma_{jt}d_{jt}$$

$$+ \delta FINDEP_j * Bank\ crisis_{it} + \lambda Controls + \varepsilon_{ijt}, \quad (7.1)$$

where growth measures the real output growth, $FINDEP$ captures the degree of external financial dependence and $Bank\ crisis_{it}$ is a dummy variable equal to one for the years and countries in which a financial crisis took place. Three sets of interactive fixed effects are included to control for shocks to firm performance.

The hypothesis put forth by Dell'Ariccia et al. (2007) is that if banking crises exogenously hamper real activity, the sectors more dependent on external finance should perform relatively worse during banking crises. They find that this is indeed the case, particularly in developing countries, in countries with lower access to foreign finance, and in countries that experience more severe banking crises. In particular, they find that an industry at the 25th percentile in terms of external financial dependence compared to an industry of the 75th percentile exhibits a 1.1 percentage point lower value added growth per year of crisis. Their results are robust when controlling for recessions, currency crises and various proxies for bank dependence.

---

10. Norway, e.g., is such a case; see also Ongena et al. (2003).

11. Their results are based on a sample of countries with reasonably well-developed financial markets. They exclude very poor as well as the Eastern European transitional nations, and consider only countries with at least ten years of stock market data.

Thus, the adverse effects of banking crises are present independently of a concurrent general economic downturn.

Overall, results indicate that crises have a strongly negative effect on output and growth, but even more so in "weaker" developing nations, hence the importance of strong and healthy institutional environment that can foster proper national safety nets and regulatory scrutiny (that are both often lacking in less developed nations).

7.2.3. Regulation and Banking Crises

We stress that the distinction between coordination and fundamentals-based contagion is of crucial importance for policy and intervention purposes, and might even have resulted from these. As alluded to earlier, results emerging from the empirical literature concerning the various effects of market structure and inherent characteristics of banking on fragility, failure, panic, and contagion may affect and be affected by the existence (or perhaps absence) of proper public policy interventions in the banking sector. It may very well be the case that policies that intend to alleviate problems associated with failure actually propagate and contribute to such.

Deposit insurance is one such policy that has been favored by policy makers and has been subject to controversy among economists due to its moral hazard nature, which may induce banks to take more projects with correlated risks, thereby inducing more bank failure. In their very influential contribution, Diamond and Dybvig (1983) show that deposit insurance is optimal where self-fulfilling depositor runs bring about instability. On the other hand, Matutes and Vives (1996) reflect the ambiguous welfare effect of deposit insurance when market structure is endogenous.

Thus, empirical work is required to determine the actual contribution of deposit insurance to banking system stability. A recent contribution by Demirgüç-Kunt and Detragiache (2002) employs panel data from 61 countries for the 1980–97 time period. The task of disentangling the effect of deposit insurance from other potential "contributors" to instability is quite formidable. Moreover, deposit insurance schemes may vary significantly in their characteristics and arrangements (e.g., de facto vs. de jure) across countries and through time, providing empirical opportunities but also drawing general conclusions from the analysis even more problematic and challenging.

To tackle these problems, Demirgüç-Kunt and Detragiache (2002) use several strategies. Building on their earlier work (Demirgüç-Kunt and Detragiache 1997), they first employ multivariate logit specifications where the dependent variable is a crisis dummy variable and the independent variables include a deposit insurance dummy (presence or no presence of deposit insurance) and various controls. The authors then replace the deposit insurance dummy by a more refined set of variables that capture the various characteristics of the deposit insurance system. To further sharpen their results they add various indices of the institutional quality and legal environment. Lastly, they deal with simultaneity biases that may arise if the decision to adopt insurance is affected by the system's fragility.

The results documented by these authors are quite striking: explicit deposit insurance is detrimental to stability, and this effect is enhanced when interest rates are deregulated and the institutional environment is weak. Moreover, the adverse effects of deposit insurance is stronger the wider the insurance coverage is, and if it is run by the government rather than the private sector. These findings point to the importance of healthy and strong institutional environments that are more effective in mitigating moral hazard and other related problems.

7.2.4. Contagion

As is well known, interbank markets play an essential role in a well func-tioning and integrated financial system through the provision of liquidity among banks. However, the intrinsic interconnections and type of exposures among banks in the interbank markets may also be a channel of contagion: problems affecting one bank may spread to other banks and even to banking systems across international borders.

This problem has been studied in the theoretical literature by Rochet and Tirole (1996), Allen and Gale (2000b), and Freixas et al. (2000), among others. Furthermore, modern banking and financial markets have been very innovative, creating new financial instruments and opening new markets, thereby creating new channels for increased liquidity and risk sharing and exposure. However, this increase in liquidity and superior diversification have also been accompanied by an increase in credit risk transfers, especially since the creation and spread of numerous credit structures and derivatives, as well as collateralized debt obligations that may have exacerbated the probability for contagion. As has been recently shown by Allen and Carletti (2006), when banks face idiosyncratic liquidity risk and hedge it in the interbank market, contagion may emerge.

Should we be concerned about the possibility of interbank contagion? Are different interbank market structures prone to contribute more to the risk of interbank contagion? The answer to these questions lies in the empirical regularity or its absence regarding this phenomenon and consequently may indicate different measures for regulatory interventions to be applied in order to limit and deal with interbank contagion.

There are four basic market structures pertaining to the interbank markets (Allen and Gale 2000b):

1. The complete structure where banks are symmetrically linked to all other banks
2. The incomplete structure where banks are only linked to neighboring banks
3. The disconnected incomplete structure where two disconnected markets coexist
4. The money center, which is symmetrically linked to all the other banks, which are themselves not linked to each other (Freixas et al. 2000)

Empirical work on the interplay between the structure of the interbank market and the risk of contagion has mainly focused on national banking systems. Table 7.1 provides an overview of the results. Two recent papers on this important issue do highlight some of the methodological difficulties involved. Degryse and Nguyen (2007) employ individual banks time series data on interbank exposures from the Belgian system over the period 1993–02 to investigate the evolution and determinants of contagion risk for that market. They find that a move from a complete structure toward a multiple money-center structure has decreased the risk and impact of contagion that is consistent with a theoretical prediction in Freixas et al. (2000). They further show that the increase in the relative importance of cross-border interbank exposure has lowered local contagion risk as well. How the increased reliance on cross-border exposures affects the potential of global contagion through interbank exposures is an open question for future research.

Mistrulli (2007) assessing the risk of contagion for the Italian interbank system on the basis of 2003 data and using simulations, concludes that moving from a complete structure to a multiple-money center structure has increased its risk of contagion that seems at odds with results for the Belgian system documented by Degryse and Nguyen (2007). However, this difference in findings may stem from the fact that Mistrulli's analysis does not account for the decrease in the degree of internalization that has actually brought the Italian interbank market to become rather local, contributing to an increased risk of contagion. Future work that relies on micro bank–bank data is required to solve these seemingly conflicting findings.

Table 7.1. Interbank Contagion and Financial Stability

Paper	Country, Time Period	Interbank Exposure Matrix Source	Exposures Included	Importance of Contagion for 100% LGD (If Available)
Amundsen and Arnt (2005)	Denmark 2004	Large-Scale Payment System	Overnight Loans between Domestic Counterparts with Maturity <1 Year	1–4% of Danish Banking Assets
Blavarg and Nimander (2002)	Sweden 1999/9–2001/9	Supervisory Report on 15 Largest Exposures of Top 4 Banks	Deposits, Securities, and Derivatives; FX Settlement Exposures	16 of 108 Cases with Potential of Contagion
Degryse and Nguyen (2007)	Belgium 1992/12–2002/12	Aggregate Exposures and Register on Large Exposures	All on Balance Exposures	3–85% of Total Banking Assets (Depends on Time and Market Structure)
Elsinger et al. (2006a)	Austria 2001/9	ME and Credit Register	Loans to Domestic Banks	70% of All Banks When LGD of 100%
Elsinger, Lehar, and Summer (2006b)	United Kingdom 2003	Supervisory Report and Stock Market Prices	Large Exposures Include Off-Balance Sheet Instruments	Probability of Contagious Default Is Close to Zero
Furfine (2003)	United States 1998/2–1998/3	Fedwire Payments	Federal funds transactions	Less than 3.5% of Total Assets
Lublóy (2005)	Hungary 50 days in 2003	Supervisory Reports	Uncollateralized	Limited
Mistrulli (2005)	Italy 1990/12–2003/12	Supervisory Reports	All On-Balance Sheet Exposures Excluding Equity	About 16% of Total Banking Assets

(continued)

Table 7.1. (*Continued*)

Paper	Country, Time Period	Interbank Exposure Matrix Source	Exposures Included	Importance of Contagion for 100% LGD (If Available)
Müller (2006)	Switzerland 2003/12	Supervisory Reports	All Exposures Including Credit Lines	About 3%/20% of Total Assets Become Insolvent/Illiquid
Sheldon and Maurer (1998)	Switzerland	ME for Bank Categories (Not Individual Banks)	Loans to Domestic Banks	Limited First-Round Effects
Upper and Worms (2004)	Germany 1998/12	ME, Using Breakdown by Maturity and Type of Counterpart	Loans to Domestic Banks	Up to 85% of Total Assets
Van Lelyveld and Liedorp (2006)	Netherlands 2002/12	ME, Large Exposures, Supervisory Reports for Largest Banks	On-Balance Sheet Exposures, Foreign Banks Grouped by Regions	Up to 96% of Total Assets
Wells (2004)	United Kingdom 2000/12	ME and Supervisory Reports on Largest 20 Exposures	Large Exposures Include Off-Balance Sheet Instruments	Up to 25% of Total Assets

The table summarizes the results from studies on contagion in the interbank market. The first two columns list the paper citation, the country, and the studied time period. The fourth column identifies where the interbank exposure matrix is obtained from. The fifth column indicates which exposures are included. The sixth column reports the importance of the contagion for 100 percent loss given default, if this result is available in the study. FX, foreign exchange; LGD, loss given default; ME, medium-sized enterprises.

Source: based on Upper (2006).

The aforementioned empirical findings point to the extreme difficulty in the assessment of risk of contagion in interbank markets. Interbank structures across nations evolve differently and consequently empirical regularities may be hard to establish. The task for regulators thus is quite demanding in that frequent monitoring may be required.

To conclude, after presenting the various theoretical arguments and reviewing the empirical evidence, the safest stand to take with respect to the relationship between market structure and stability, is to exert caution and careful consideration of all known factors that take part in this complex interplay. As Allen and Gale (2004b) show, a large number of possibilities exist concerning the relationship between market structure and financial stability. Thus, as both efficiency arguments and stability ones are of utmost importance and as there are trade-offs between these aspects of the banking system, we need various forms and intensities of prudential regulatory intervention and supervision. These regulatory interventions are more effective in alleviating both instability problems and some of the by-products of regulation itself by accompanying it with effective prudential regulation, depending on the general health of the surrounding economic legal, and perhaps political institutions. We discuss banking regulation in chapter 9.

Contagion has also been measured more broadly by taking into account different shocks. Elsinger, Lehar, and Summer (2006a) simulate the joint impact of interest rate shocks, exchange rate shocks, and stock market movements on interbank payment flows of Austrian banks. These states of the world determine the net value of the bank and the feasibility of interbank payments. They distinguish between insolvency due to correlated exposures and due to domino effects. Their simulations indicate that although the probability of contagious default is low compared to the total default probability, there are situations in which up to 75 percent of the defaults are due to contagion.

Another method that assesses contagion taking into account a larger variety of shock is to investigate banks' stock price behavior. Lehar (2005), for example, estimates correlations between bank portfolios to compute different measures of systemic risk. Gropp and Vesala (2003) use the tail properties of distance to default to study contagion risk and find that both domestic and cross-border contagion is present within Europe, with domestic more important than cross-border.

8

Managing Risks in the Banking Firm

8.1. Introduction

In maximizing profits and shareholders' wealth, banks also take risks. Banks manage risks on their own behalf, but also on behalf of their clients. They act as market makers in risks, holding an inventory of risks (see Ho and Saunders 1981). Financial institutions are specialists in measuring and managing risks. The risks financial intermediaries are running should be measured and managed carefully, as these risks may threaten the solvency of each individual financial institution and, through contagion or exposure to common shocks, the stability of the banking and entire financial system.

In this chapter, we discuss the most important methods and findings in measuring and managing risks in the banking firm. The purpose is not to provide an overview of all specific products that banks can employ to manage risks, such as futures, swaps, collars, and options. We refer the reader to Saunders and Cornett (2002), for example, for an extensive review of how banks use these derivatives to manage banking risks.

In chapter 7 we argue that banks may fail and that such failure could put the entire banking system under stress, for example, through interbank linkages and to exposures through common shocks. In this chapter, we highlight how risks at financial institutions are measured and managed; we do not focus on how distress at one institution may spread to other institutions or to the entire financial system. The potential for spillover effects implies that prudence is needed in banking.

Bank managers deal with transactions that may be reported on balance but also off-balance. First, they should manage their assets, or practice asset management. Banks optimally choose assets that are well diversified and also include low-risk assets in their portfolio. Second, banks' liability management should aim for cheap funding, but without too important maturity mismatches. The latter aspect reflects the liquidity management of firms, which incorporates aspects from both asset and liability side of banks. Fourth, banks should keep sufficient capital as a buffer against unexpected losses. This capital management reflects both economic capital—what banks would voluntarily hold—and regulatory capital—as required by regulators. Finally, financial institutions decide on their on-balance and off-balance sheet activities. The off-balance-sheet management is also important for banks as often assets and liabilities are contingent, implying that many risks are not visible on the books but are latently present off the books.

Banks incur many types of risks. We follow Freixas and Rochet (1997) and distinguish among default or credit risks, liquidity risks, and market risks.[1] In the methodology section, we discuss the most commonly employed method to measure market risks—value at risk—but also discuss credit risk measurement.

8.2. Methodology: Value at Risk and Credit Risk Measurement

Banks are leading developers of risk management techniques. This leadership mainly stems from the nature of their business. Banks have developed many (internal) models to measure banking risks. Examples include JP Morgan's CreditMetrics, Credit Suisse Financial Product's Credit Risk+, or Credit Monitor by Moody's KMV.

A commonly employed tool to measure market risks in the banking sector is value at risk (VaR). VaR aims to determine how much can be lost in a trading portfolio by the next day's close. Under the "internal models approach" of the Basle Accord on capital requirements, financial institutions enjoy the freedom to specify and develop their own VaR model.

The VaR is a probabilistic/statistical approach that quantifies into one number the potential losses of a bank stemming from the variability of portfolio values due to changes in market prices, such as interest rates,

---

1. See Saunders and Cornett (2002) for treatment of other risks, e.g., operational and technological risks.

exchange rates, or stock prices. The VaR of a portfolio is the worst-case loss expected over a certain period with a certain probability as given by the chosen confidence interval.

To define the VaR more formally, recall the basic properties of the normal distribution, which is fully defined by two parameters: the mean, μ, and the standard deviation, σ. The VaR also hinges on the chosen confidence interval, that is, the α percent probability of an even worse outcome for a day. We denote the α percent VaR by $VaR_{\alpha\%}$. For example, $VaR_{1\%}$ denotes a daily loss that will be exceeded only in 1 percent of the time.

To illustrate the application of VaR, consider a bank having a market portfolio of $1 billion on the S&P500 index, and consider the mean return per day to be 0 percent and the per day standard deviation to be 100 bp. $VaR_{5\%}$ then, for example, equals $VaR_{5\%} = \$1 billion * 1.645 * 100\, bp = \$1,645 million$, where 1.645 stems from the 5 percent cumulative probability from the normal distribution. So for the portfolio of $1 billion, the loss of $1,645 million should be exceeded in only 5 percent of the time.

We considered up to now only daily VaR and applied VaR to only one security. Depending on the time to liquidation, the holding period, and other determinants, banks and regulators may want to be informed about the VaR over a certain period of time—a week, a month or a year. The N-day $VaR_{\alpha\%}$ then becomes $\sqrt{N} x VaR_{\alpha\%}$, where the implicit assumption is made that returns are not predictable (or the random walk assumption), and volatility is not time varying. VaR can also easily be extended to include several (types of) securities allowing to benefit from diversification advantages. For changes in interest rates, for example, VaR calculations need to account for the effect of duration D. That is, a 1-bp change in interest rates leads to a $-D$ basis point move in the value of the bond.

The VaR approach presented above starts from a number of assumptions that may not necessarily hold. Moreover, appropriate estimation approaches of the input variables are important in order to obtain an unbiased VaR number. We now highlight some issues related to the inputs of VaR and its application.

8.2.1. Assumptions

VaR starts from the normal distribution of asset returns. In reality, however, asset returns may deviate from normality. One deviation is that asset returns have fat tails—more probability weight in the tails relative to the normal distribution. So while the true distribution has the same mean and variance, the probability mass at the extreme tails of the probability distribution is larger. This is an important concern for risk managers as the normal distribution underestimates the true impact of extreme events when the true distribution exhibits fat tails. A related issue concerns the fact that distributions may be skewed: declines in asset prices are more severe than increases such that the distribution is not symmetric. Finally, the parameters characterizing the normal distribution may be unstable, for example, stemming from varying market conditions. Illustrations are the regime-switching volatility model, where the conditional volatility is normal but exhibit different states. Then, asset returns are conditionally normally distributed.

8.2.2. Estimation Approaches

VaR can be estimated employing different approaches. We make the following categorization in approaches (for an elaborate discussion and a similar categorization, see Allen, Boudoukh, and Saunders 2004). The historical-based approaches are a first important category. These approaches employ historical time-series data to infer the shape of the conditional distribution. The shape can be inferred using a parametric approach, which imposes a specific distributional assumption on the conditional asset returns. An example is the normal distribution with time-varying volatility. The volatility and correlations are then estimated using recent data and making a number of parametric assumptions. A nonparametric approach is also possible. Then, historical data are employed directly without further parametric estimation or restrictions. Historic or back simulation is an illustration of this. The main idea is to take the current portfolio of assets and revalue these assets on the basis of observed prices in the past. On this basis, the $VaR_{\alpha\%}$ can be computed by looking at the α percent worst case: only α percent of the time, the value of the portfolio will fall below this number based on the recent historic financial series. Finally, within the historical-based approaches, we have the hybrid approaches that combine elements of the parametric and nonparametric approaches.

A second important category is the implied volatility approaches. In contrast to using historical data, this approach employs derivative prices to impute an implied volatility. The implied volatility is often derived from the Black-Scholes option pricing model. So this implied volatility method uses all available market information and therefore also contains forward looking information.

8.2.3. Nontradable Loans, Herding, and VaR Use

While the VaR can quite easily be implemented for traded securities, it is less straightforward to implement it for nontradable or less frequently traded loans. The reason is that credit events such as downgrades or defaults are rare. Next to more traditional models like expert systems, rating systems and credit scoring models, banks have nevertheless adapted the VaR models to measure credit risk exposure when the time interval is longer.

Credit risk measurement has aimed to estimate the probability of default (PD) using a set of traditional approaches and more modern approaches. There are a set of different traditional approaches. Expert systems are the first approach. Examples include the 5C's: character (reputation), capital (degree of leverage), capacity (earnings volatility), collateral, and (business) cycle conditions. These 5C's can be processed by individuals but may also be assessed employing neural networks.

A second approach is the use of internal rating systems. Many banks have installed internal rating systems since the announcement of the Basle II capital agreement. The idea is that each loan receives an individual rating based on its PD. Often also the loss given default (LGD, which equals 1 − the recovery rate) is assessed (for an overview for the United States, see Treacy and Carey 2000). A third approach are credit scoring models initiated by Altman (1968). Financial variables are linked to default using different approaches like discriminant analysis or logit models.

Credit risk measurement is more recently underpinned by two more modern, theoretical approaches to obtain the default probabilities needed as input for the VaR models. A first modern approach that underpins the default probabilities is the options-theoretic structural models of credit risk measurement. The theoretical model is Merton (1974), which models a firm's equity as a call option on the firm's assets with a strike price equal to the amount to be repaid. In particular, Merton shows that the equilibrium default risk premium can be expressed as

$$r_l - i = \left(\frac{-1}{\tau}\right) \ln \left[N(h_2) + \left(\frac{1}{d}\right) N(h_1) \right]. \tag{8.1}$$

r_l is the required yield on risky debt, i the risk-free rate on debt of equivalent maturity, τ the time to maturity of loan, and d the "quasi" debt-to-asset ration (equal to the discounted value of the value of the bond B divided by the assets A (i.e., $Be^{-i\tau}/A$). $N(h_2)$ can be interpreted as the risk-adjusted probability of survival at T (a value computed from the standardized normal distribution statistical tables).

To implement this model, the modeler needs information on the market value of the firm's assets A and the asset risk, both of them are not directly observed. Different assumptions may lead to estimates of both asset risk and firm's assets (e.g., KMV's credit monitor uses databases containing historical experience).

A second modern approach is a reduced form of credit risk measurement. A reduced form does not model the economic process leading to default but models default as a point process. Observed credit spreads represent the expected cost of default, which is determined by the PD and the LGD. Formally:

$$r_l = i + PD_t * LGD_t, \tag{8.2}$$

where the time index t indicates that both the PD and the LGD are time dependent.

Almost all financial institutions are applying similar quantitative techniques such as VaR to manage their risks. This widespread implementation has raised concerns that model similarities could lead to herding across banks. This then could imply higher volatility during stress times and ultimately lead to simultaneous failures of banks or systemic risk (for a theoretical underpinning of this argument, see Basak and Shapiro 2001).

VaR has a number of limitations and shortcomings. VaR measures are subject to model risks. VaR approaches need therefore be evaluated by back testing, that is, comparing historical VaR measures with actual losses. As already indicated above, past return and volatility need not be good indicators of future values due to, for example, unusual chocks or structural changes. The Basle Committee, under the supervisory review process (second pillar of the Basle II Accord) that supervises the use of internal models, subjects internal models to back testing and stress testing (for a review of backtesting and backtesting procedures, see Campbell 2005).

Although VaR is the standard most commonly applied, it is not without shortcomings as a risk measure for defining economic capital. For example, it does not provide information on the magnitude of the loss incurred in the event that you are in the tails of the distribution. The expected shortfall provides such an estimate and is the expected loss conditional on being in the tail. Regulators themselves might be interested in the expected excess loss, that is, the loss above the economic capital held by banks.

8.3. Evidence

We structure our discussion on the evidence on managing risks in the banking firm according to the different risks they are incurring, default or credit risk, liquidity risk, and market risks.

8.3.1. Default or Credit Risks

Loan losses or losses on counterparties are the most frequent cause of losses in the banking sector. Banks have traditionally managed credit risks employing a set of standard procedures such as ceilings on exposures to individual lenders (to avoid name concentration), as well as ceilings on a single sector or highly correlated sectors (sector concentration). Banks also face credit risk in nonloan financial instruments such as bonds, options, futures, and securitized products.

In contrast to the wholesale market where credit risk models can employ a rich information set concerning companies financial health, retail borrowers tend to be informationally opaque. These loans are therefore often illiquid and do not frequently trade in the secondary market. Only a few academic papers have estimated the credit risk for retail borrowers and small and medium-sized enterprises, even though banks have a relatively high share of such exposures in their loan portfolios. Notable exceptions in this regard are Dietsch and Petey (2004), who provide a methodology to deal with this type of credit risk; Dullman and Masschelein (2006), who study concentration risk; and Jiménez, Ongena, Peydró, and Saurina (2007) and Ioannidou, Ongena, and Peydró (2007), who employ time-varying duration models on the performance of individual bank loans to assess the impact of monetary policy on bank risk taking.

8.3.2. Liquidity Risks

Banks are liquidity providers on demand. This function exposes them to sudden liquidity withdrawals and bank runs (à la Diamond and Dybvig 1983). Banks provide liquidity on demand not only to the liability side but also on the asset side, for example, by providing loan commitments. Indeed, Kashyap, Rajan, and Stein (2002) argue that there are synergies between the two sides of the balance sheet: if deposit withdrawals and takedowns of loan commitments are not too highly correlated, then both activities can share the costs of holding sufficient liquid assets. The predictions of their model are that banks relative to other institutions should have relatively more loan commitments, and also within banks, banks with relatively more demand deposits should have relatively more loan commitments.

Kashyap et al. (2002) report evidence supporting these theoretical conjectures. They test this using the 1993 NSSBF data set and the Call reports, regressing the commitment ratio [loan commitments/(loan commitments plus loans)] on a constant and the deposit ratio (transaction deposits/total deposits). They find that a 1 standard deviation increase in the deposit ratio can explain about an 18 percent of a standard deviation in the commitment ratio. Similar results hold when studying the securities to assets ratio.

Gatev, Schuermann, and Strahan (2007) further investigate the theoretical predictions in Kashyap et al. (2002), in particular, whether liquidity risks stemming from asset-side liquidity risks and liability-side liquidity risks yield a diversification benefit. To do this, they focus on publicly listed banks and study the determinants of bank's stock-return volatility. They find that the bank's stock-return volatility increases in unused loan commitments, but this does not hold for banks having high levels of transaction deposits. This suggests that there is a hedging synergy. They further find that the hedging synergy is stronger when market liquidity (as proxied by the commercial paper-treasury bill spread) is low. At times that firms want to take up unused lines of credit, banks obtain an inflow of transaction deposits (see also Gatev and Strahan 2006).

8.3.3. Market Risks

While VaR is widely employed by financial and nonfinancial firms, the proprietary nature of data and risk models has prevented the creation of an important empirical literature in the public domain. Berkowitz and O'Brien (2002) provide the first direct evidence on the performance of VaR models in banking for six large U.S. banks. They have daily profit and loss data for the period January 1998 to March 2000, as well as the reported daily VaR estimates.[2] These estimates are maintained by the banks for the purpose of back testing.

Berkowitz and O'Brien (2002) find that for five of the six banks the average VaR lies outside the 99th percentile of the daily profits and losses. This suggests that the VaR estimates are quite conservative. When the actual loss is larger than the forecasted VaR, the mean violation is surprisingly large (e.g., for two banks it is two standard deviations beyond the VaR). To evaluate forecasting performance, violations should not only occur one percent of the time but these violations should also be identically and independently distributed "(i.i.d)" over time. Berkowitz and O'Brien (2002) study forecasting performance by putting the bank's internally produced

---

2. Perignon, Deng, and Wang (2008) confirm this conservatism for a sample of Canadian banks. They find that the historical VaR have a risk overstatement ranging between 19 percent and 79 percent. They attribute this to extreme cautiousness and underestimation of diversification benefits when aggregating business lines.

VaR into competition with a time-series VaR based on a ARMA + GARCH model. While such a simple ARMA + GARCH model does not take into account existing portfolio information and correlations across securities, it may give some information on time varying volatility.

Their results show that the average time-series VaR is close to the 99th percentile VaR coverage—removing some of the conservativeness of the internal VaR, and not at the expense of creation larger (maximum) deviations. Thus the time-series VaR allows for lower capital requirements than the internally produced VaR, and performs equally well, lower than the internal VaR. In sum, this shows that accurately measuring a structural VaR model that takes into account thousands of market risk factors is challenging. Also, the structural VaR do not take into account time-varying volatility.

O'Brien and Berkowitz (2006) complement Berkowitz and O'Brien (2002) by evaluating VaR models with desk-level data from one large, international commercial bank. They obtain daily profit and loss generated by four business lines all involved in securities trading, as well as the 1-day-ahead VaR$_{1\%}$ forecasts. They employ an extensive toolkit to investigate how well the VaR forecast performs. In particular, they argue that violations of VaR forecasts should be unpredictable. They set up a series of martingale tests to evaluate this unpredictability. For example, they test for uncorrelatedness by estimating the sample autocovariances and employing the Ljung-Box test. In particular, under the null hypothesis, all autocorrelations are zero:

$$H_0 : \gamma_k = 0, \quad k > 0, \tag{8.3}$$

with k the autocorrelation lag number. The alternative hypothesis of interest is that

$$H_1 : \gamma_k \neq 0, \quad \textit{for some } k. \tag{8.4}$$

The Ljung-box statistic then is a joint test of whether the first m-autocorrelations are zero:

$$LB(m) = T(T+2) \sum_{k=1}^{m} \frac{\gamma_k^2}{T-k} \tag{8.5}$$

The statistic is asymptotically chi square with m degrees of freedom.

They also investigate whether violations/nonviolations hinge on their lagged values and lagged variables such as previous VaR forecasts (in the spirit of Campbell and Shiller 1987). Furthermore, they check whether the number of days separating violations (durations) are unpredictable (as in Christoffersen and Pelletier 2004).

O'Brien and Berkowitz (2006) find strong evidence of volatility dynamics and nonnormality in profits and losses for the four business lines. While they find that the VaR forecasts move quite rapidly, there is still clustering in VaR violations. As in Berkowitz and O'Brien (2002), they suggest that GARCH modeling may be desirable to remove clustering of VaR violations.

But how useful are publicly disclosed VaR measures? Since 1995, under pressure from the Basel Committee on Banking Supervision and later the Basel Accord, banks often provide VaR estimates in their financial reports. Jorion (2002) studies the informativeness of VaR disclosures in financial reports employing data from eight major U.S. commercial banks. He investigates the relation between these publicly disclosed VaR measures and the volatility of trading revenues also stemming from quarterly and annual financial reports. He finds that VaR measures can be employed to predict the variability of banks' trading revenues.

It is clear from the above applications and review of methods that the methodology to measure risk has improved dramatically over the last decades. At the same time, academic researchers are often confronted with the lack of detailed bank level and desk level data to perform independent analysis. Internal models have been developed by definition by banks themselves. The market turmoil at the occasion of the subprime crisis as well as the Société Générale rogue trader case in 2007 highlight the necessity for continuous improvements in this field and to subject the internal models to further academic and supervisory scrutiny.

9

The Regulation of Banks

9.1. Introduction

Banking is an industry that in most countries is subject to a tight set of regulations (for reviews, see, e.g., Vives 1991; Fischer and Pfeil 2004). Some of the regulations tend to soften competition. Examples include restrictions on the entry of new banks or limitations of the free deployment of competitive tools by banks. Other regulations restrict banking activities in space and scope, putting limitations on the bank's potential to diversify and exploit scale/scope economies. Finally, there is prudential regulation that alters the competitive position of banks vis-à-vis other nonbank institutions (see, e.g., Dewatripont and Tirole 1994).

In the last two decades, several countries including the European Union countries and the United States have implemented a series of deregulatory changes with the objective to stimulate competition and to enhance financial integration.

We first review key methodologies that can be used in investigating the effects of regulation, and focus our attention to the difference-in-difference methodology. We then turn to empirical work on the impact of regulation on (1) market structure, (2) bank conduct, (3) bank strategy, and (4) financial stability and development.

9.2. Methodology: Difference in Difference

The difference-in-difference approach (DD) aims to identify the impact of a specific treatment, for example, the impact of deregulation. The idea is that outcomes are observed for two groups for two time periods. One group is exposed to a treatment in the second period but not in the first period, whereas the second group does not receive a treatment at all.

Denote A as the control group and B as the treatment group and y the variable of interest. Then, we can write

$$y = \beta_0 + \beta_1 dB + \delta_0 d2 + \delta_1 d2dB + u, \qquad (9.1)$$

where dB is a dummy that captures the possible differences between the treatment group B and control group A before the policy change. Similarly, $d2$ is a dummy that captures changes in period 2 that would take place even without a policy change. The coefficient of interest is δ_1. This DD estimate equals

$$\hat{\delta}_1 = (\bar{y}_{B,2} - \bar{y}_{B,1}) - (\bar{y}_{A,2} - \bar{y}_{A,1}). \qquad (9.2)$$

The DD methodology can be easily extended when having more than two periods by simply adding time dummies to the equation. The maintained assumption, then, is that the treatment has the same effect in every year.

Further extensions are called the difference-in-difference-in-differences (DDD) approach. This builds on a further refinement of the treatment and control groups. Suppose that within the groups A and B there is a subset of subjects for which we expect the treatment to work and call this group E. Let dE then be a dummy equal to one for someone in group E. Then, we have

$$y = \beta_0 + \beta_1 dB + \beta_2 dE + \beta_3 dBdE + \delta_0 d2 + \delta_1 d2dE + \delta_3 d2dBdE + u. \quad (9.3)$$

The coefficient on the triple interaction term $d2dBdE$ is now of interest. The estimate equals

$$\hat{\delta}_3 = (\bar{y}_{B,E,2} - \bar{y}_{B,E,1}) - (\bar{y}_{A,E,2} - \bar{y}_{A,E,1}) - (\bar{y}_{B,N,2} - \bar{y}_{B,N,1}), \qquad (9.4)$$

with N being those who are not in group E.

Jayaratne and Strahan (1996) study the intrastate branch banking reform in the United States, where in the early 1970s about 35 states introduced a "treatment" by relaxing restrictions on intrastate branching. They apply a generalization of the DD method to investigate the change in economic growth rates before and after the branch reform relative to a control group of states that were unaffected by the reform. In particular, they estimate the following fixed effects model:

$$y_{i,t} = \alpha_t + \beta_i + \gamma D_{it} + \varepsilon_{it}, \tag{9.5}$$

where i and t denote the states and years, respectively, and y is the per capita economic growth.

The treatment here is branching deregulation. In particular, D_{it} is a branching indicator equal to one for states permitting branching via mergers and acquisitions and zero otherwise. The fixed time and states effects should control for state specific and time specific growth shocks. It is therefore as if the control group is constructed from the average of all states, rather than from a set of states not experiencing a deregulation. The parameter γ measures the increase in growth resulting from bank-branch deregulation. They find a 0.94** percentage point increase in growth after bank-branch deregulation.

Huang (2008) goes one step further in applying the DD methodology. In particular, he creates a natural "regression discontinuity" setup by comparing economic performance of contiguous counties on opposite side of state borders, where only one state experienced the bank-branch deregulation treatment. This geographic matching may improve the control group in observable characteristics in that the differences between control group and treatment groups are much smaller. Also in unobservable characteristics, the geographic matching procedure may be an improvement as contiguous counties are less likely to differ from each other. His empirical results show that only 5 out of 23 deregulation events exhibit an empirically significant growth acceleration.

9.3. Evidence

9.3.1. Regulation and Market Structure

A number of papers investigate whether specific deregulatory initiatives have changed competition. Angelini and Cetorelli (2003), for example, consider the impact of the Second European Banking Directive on competition within the Italian banking industry, by analyzing data over the period 1983–1997. Using a conjectural-variations model they compute a Lerner index L for bank i:

$$L \equiv \frac{p_i - MC_i}{p_i} = \frac{-\theta_i/\tilde{\varepsilon}}{p_i},$$

with θ_i is the conjectural elasticity of total industry output with respect to the output of bank i, and $\tilde{\varepsilon} = \frac{\partial Q/\partial p}{Q}$ is the market demand semielasticity to the price. The computed Lerner index remained constant during the 1983–1992 period but steadily decreased thereafter, suggesting a substantial increase in the degree of competition after 1993.

Angelini and Cetorelli (2003) further explore whether the changes in the Lerner index after 1993 can be attributed to the second banking directive. After controlling for changes in market structure (HHI, number of banks operating in each regional market, number of branches per capita) and some other exogenous variables, they find that a dummy variable equal to one for years in the period 1993–1997 explains a considerable fraction of the drop in the Lerner index. The Lerner index drops from about 14 percentage points before 1992 to about 6 percentage points after 1992. The deregulation dummy can explain about 5 percentage points of this drop.

Gual (1999) studies the impact of European banking deregulation over the period 1981–1995 on the European banking market structure. He computes the elasticity of concentration to competition (which is directly measured by deregulation): evaluated at the sample means, an increase in deregulation of 10 percent leads to an increase in the CR5 ratio of 0.86 percent.

Finally, in a widely cited study Spiller and Favaro (1984) look at the effects of entry regulation on oligopolistic interaction in the Uruguayan banking sector. Before June 1978 entry was totally barred. They find unexpectedly that following the relaxation of the legal entry barriers the degree of oligopolistic interaction among the leading banks actually reduces, pointing to less competition.

9.3.2. Regulation and Bank Conduct

How does banking regulation contribute to bank interest margins? Jayaratne and Strahan (1998) find that permitting statewide branching and interstate banking in the United States decreased operating costs and loan losses, reductions that were ultimately passed on to borrowers in lower loan rates. And using data from banks covering 72 countries a recent paper by Demirgüç-Kunt, Laeven, and Levine (2004) examines the impact of banking regulation on bank net interest margins. The information on commercial banking regulation is taken from Barth, Caprio, and Levine (2001). Regulatory variables include the fraction of entry that is denied, a proxy for the degree to which banks face regulatory restrictions on their activities in, for example, securities markets and investment banking, and a measure of reserve requirements. They also employ an indicator of "banking freedom," taken from the Heritage Foundation, which provides an overall index of the openness of the banking industry and the extent to which banks are free to operate their business. The different regulatory variables are entered one at a time in a regression that also features bank-specific and macroeconomic controls.

The results in Demirgüç-Kunt et al. (2004) indicate that restrictive banking regulation substantially hikes net interest margins. For example, a 1 standard deviation increase in entry or activity restrictions, reserve requirements, or banking freedom, result respectively in 50***, 100***, 51*, and 70*** bp extra for the incumbent banks. However, when including, in addition to the bank-specific and macroeconomic controls, also an index of property rights, the regulatory restrictions turn insignificant and do not provide any additional explanatory power. Demirgüç-Kunt et al. (2004) interpret this result as indicating that banking regulation reflects something broader about the competitive environment. Their interpretation fits with findings in Kroszner and Strahan (1999) and Garrett, Wagner, and Wheelock (2004), who investigate the political and economic drivers of bank branching deregulation across U.S. states.

9.3.3. Regulation and Bank Strategy

How does the presence of foreign banks influence competition? Foreign-owned banks may not only compete in different ways than domestically owned institutions but could also be affected differently by domestic regulation. Levine (2003) distinguishes between entry restrictions for foreign versus domestic banks (he thus further refines the analysis by Demirgüç-Kunt et al. 2004). Levine substantiates that foreign bank entry restrictions determine interest rate margins,[1] while domestic bank entry restrictions do not. Foreign banks that are often more efficient than domestic banks could enter in many transition or developing countries, for example, because

---

1. Magri, Mori, and Rossi (2005), e.g., document that foreign banks successfully entered the Italian banking market following the lowering of the regulatory barriers under the Second Directive enacted in 1992.

government officials did not try to encourage private, domestic institutions to combine into "National Champions" by delaying or denying foreign entry (Berger 2007b). In contrast to the contribution, then, of foreign ownership of domestic banks on the banking efficiency in these nations, the fraction of the domestic banking industry held by foreign banks does not determine bank interest margins.

State-owned banks may also compete in different ways than privately owned institutions. Government ownership of banks remains pervasive around the world, in particular in developing countries (La Porta, Lopez-de-Silanes, and Shleifer, 2002). Cross-country exercises indicate that more state ownership of the banking sector leads to less competition (Barth, Caprio, and Levine 2004) and slower subsequent financial development (La Porta et al. 2002). However, firms that actually borrow from state-owned banks pay less than the firms that borrow from the privately owned banks (Sapienza 2004). If this relatively lower interest rate is actually granted to the less productive firms, then state-owned banks may in fact contribute to the misallocation of credit, eventually propagating stagnation and negatively affecting economic growth.[2]

In general bank supervisory policies could also affect the availability of credit. Beck, Demirgüç-Kunt, and Levine (2006b), for example, show that mandating official supervisory agencies to monitor, discipline and influence banks directly may actually increase the degree to which bank corruption is an obstacle to firms raising external finance. On the other hand, facilitating private monitoring by enforcing public disclosure of accurate information by banks tends to dissipate corruption as an obstacle.

9.3.4. Regulation and Financial Stability and Development

Do regulatory restrictions offer benefits in other dimensions? Beck, Demirgüç-Kunt, and Levine (2004) examine the link with financial stability. They study the impact of bank concentration, bank regulation, and national institutions fostering, for example, competition or property rights on the likelihood of experiencing a banking crisis. They find that fewer regulatory restrictions—lower barriers to bank entry and fewer restrictions on bank activities—lead to less banking fragility, suggesting that regulatory restrictions are not beneficial in the stability dimension. Black and Strahan

---

2. This issue is related to the so-called Zombie lending phenomenon (Caballero, Hoshi, and Kashyap in press).

(2002) find that the deregulation of restrictions on branching and interstate banking stimulated rates of incorporation in the United States, suggesting that access to finance increases following deregulation. Similarly, Kerr and Nanda (2007) show that access to finance following deregulation in the United States facilitated the entry of small startups. Allocative efficiency improved across the entire firm size distribution. "Creative destruction" by the surviving young startups displacing incumbents also intensified.

Deregulation also generates interesting dynamic effects. When deregulation induces a more competitive outcome, then we can expect that "good banks" should survive and grow faster, whereas "weak banks" should shrink and eventually exit. Stiroh and Strahan (2003), for example, assess the competitive dynamics in terms of market share and industry exits after the deregulation in the U.S. banking industry. Banks that are performing well are more likely to gain market share after deregulation. Moreover, they find an interesting heterogeneity in line with deregulatory forces: the strengthening in the performance-market share link is strongest in unit-banking states and in more concentrated markets. Branching deregulation had the largest impact for small banks whereas interstate deregulation had its greatest impact for large banks. They also find that the poorest performing banks were shrinking after deregulation, that the exit rate increased by 3.6 percent after a state removed its interstate banking restrictions, and that the relative profitability of banks exiting increased after deregulation. Finally, Buch (2003b) explores the impact of deregulation on gross financial assets of banks. She finds that the E.U. single market program and the Basel Capital Accord have a positive impact on intra-E.U. asset holdings and lending to OECD countries, respectively.

To conclude, despite decades of deregulation in many countries, bank market structure, conduct, strategy, stability, and development remain to a substantial extent determined by the regulatory framework. More research seems warranted to further highlight the most harmful effects of regulation also on macroeconomic outcomes such as income distribution (e.g., Beck, Levine, and Levkov 2007).

10
Conclusion

Any attempt to summarize the many methodological issues, applications, and empirical results present in this vast literature we labeled "the microeconometrics of banking" is bound to fail and to ignore the many subtleties involved. Nevertheless, we aim to offer here a very crude and simple summary of the many studies we canvassed.[1] A few broad results seem to emerge, which we outline below.

More methodological and empirical research in banking seems warranted. We realize that "setting out directions in this regard for future research often results in not much more than myopic and highly individual lists of current interests and never-finished projects, lists that are bound to be either ill-directed from the start or outdated the moment they are in print" (Degryse and Ongena 2008, p541).

Nevertheless, our "Christmas list" would definitely include issues such as the following:

- The effect of the two-stage "purchasing process" in credit markets (application then offer / approval) on the estimated relationships say between measures of competition and loan rates
- The development of loan conditions throughout the life-cycle of the bank—firm relationship and the differences in these relationships across countries and time
- Bank organization and its impact on competition, both in deposit and loan markets, both domestically and internationally

---

1. Our discussion is based partly on Degryse and Ongena (2008).

- And related, the geography of bank financing: "Is distance dead?" or "Will it die another day?" (but hopefully not before we can analyze its effects)
- The impact of technology on bank organization (e.g., and incentives of loan officers), banking geography, and banking activities, in particular, the supply of relationship versus transactional banking products
- The role banks (may or may fail to) play in the development of emerging economies, such as China and India, and the provision of different financial solutions there
- The effects of monetary policy on bank behavior, risk-taking in particular
- The impact of the development of the regulatory and wider institutional framework (e.g., competition policy) on competition and bank rents
- The interrelationships between social capital, trust, and the functioning of financial markets, in particular, the relationship between trust and loan rates, collateral, and other characteristics of interest
- And finally, the causes and consequences of the banking crisis that started in August 2007 on the development of banking products and banking in general (see also chapter 11)

Given the speed at which evidence in empirical banking is currently being collected, we suspect that we may have to start working on a second edition of *Microeconometrics of Banking* the moment this first edition is out. Wish us the courage to do so!

11

Epilogue: The Banking Crisis of 2007–2008

Major problems in the credit markets first surfaced in the summer of 2007.[1] Since then, liquidity recurrently evaporated almost entirely from the inter-bank markets, and central banks intervened worldwide on a scale not often seen before. Large reputable banks, such as UBS and Citibank, had to write down substantial portions of their loan portfolios. Many bank CEOs were forced to resign.

Market commentators immediately argued that during the long period of very low interest rates and abundant liquidity,[2] stretching from 2001 to 2005, banks had softened their lending standards and taken on excessive credit risk.[3] Consequently, market participants started clamoring for central

---

1. Our discussion is based partly on Jiménez et al. (2007) and the December 2007 *Financial Stability Review* (pp. 163–167) of the European Central Bank.

2. The root cause of this credit correction was the Federal Reserve's willingness to keep money too easy for too long. The federal funds rate was probably negative in real terms for close to two years between 2003 and 2005. This led to a misallocation of capital ... An emergency rate cut, as some in the market seem to be anticipating or hoping for, carries the risk of introducing even greater moral hazard into the financial system. (*Wall Street Journal*, August 11, 2007).

3. Nominal rates were the lowest in almost four decades and below Taylor rates in many countries while real rates were negative (see, e.g., the multiple editorials and op-eds in the *Wall Street Journal*, *Financial Times*, and *Economist* and Ahrend, Cournède, and Price 2008; Taylor 2007). Expansionary monetary policy and credit risk taking followed by restrictive monetary policy possibly led to the financial crisis during the 1990s in Japan (see, e.g., Allen and Gale 2004a).

banks to reduce interest rates again to alleviate their financial predicament.[4] Observers also pointed in the direction of the increased financial complexities and interlinkages as a contributing factor. Financial innovation, the originate-and-distribute model, and securitization, in particular, further altered the financial players' incentive structures, observers argued.

> Underlying the deterioration of confidence [during the crisis] has been a constellation of three broad factors which, although already individually known to market participants and policy makers alike well in advance of the turmoil, have reinforced one another in a way that almost nobody could have foreseen. These factors included an abundance of liquidity that underpinned a build up of leverage in the financial system, an increasingly interwoven and complex financial system the growth of which was fed by financial innovation and some financial agents' incentives that were aligned against prudent practices. (Trichet 2008)

In this epilogue, we briefly discuss empirical work that directly or indirectly investigates one of the root causes of the banking crisis, that is, the abundance of liquidity and low short-term interest rates. Given the recent nature of the events, most of this work is still unpublished.

Jiménez et al. (2007) use discrete choice models, within borrower comparison models and duration analyses, to investigate whether short-term interest rates prior to loan origination influence credit risk taking by banks. They analyze the Credit Register of the Banco de España (CIR). The CIR records detailed monthly information on all, new and outstanding, commercial/industrial and financial loans (>6,000 Euros) to nonfinancial firms by all credit institutions in Spain during the last 23 years—generating almost

---

4. The Fed has a new problem: convincing investors it does not need to cut interest rates yet... A rate cut does not just increase the supply of cash; it directly influences people's calculations about risk. Cheaper money makes other assets look more attractive—an undesirable consequence at a moment when risk is being repriced after many years of lax lending. (*Economist*, August 23, 2007)

    A cut in the Fed funds rate, in contrast, would do little to solve the interbank problem. The main effect could be to reawaken banks' appetite for risk. (*Financial Times*, September 8, 2007)

    But knowing that the political pressure to intervene is asymmetric, asserted far more strongly when markets turn illiquid and asset prices fall than when markets are excessively liquid and asset prices booming, central banks ought also to avoid bringing such situations upon themselves. Better to lean against the wind with prudential norms, tightening them as liquidity exceeds historical levels, than to ignore the boom and be faced with the messy political reality of forcibly picking up the pieces after the bust. (Raghuram G. Rajan in *Financial Times*, September 7, 2007).

23 million bank loan records in total. Monetary conditions in Spain were fairly exogenous and basically "set in Frankfurt," first through the fixed exchange rate policy with the Deutsche Mark and as of January 1, 1999, within the Eurosystem. Consequently, they can use the German and then Euro overnight interbank rates as an exogenous measure of the stance of monetary policy (alternatively, they instrument the Spanish by the German overnight rate, a strong instrument our later reported results clearly indicate).

Lower interest rates prior to the origination of the loans precede more lending to borrowers with either a bad or no credit history, they find. More important, banks also grant more loans with a higher hazard rate (which is a default probability normalized per time, a normalization that is desirable as loan maturity may also be affected). In striking contrast, once loans are outstanding lower interest rates imply lower hazard rates conform to standard theoretical predictions. In sum, when monetary policy is expansive, not only do banks give more loans to borrowers with either a bad or no credit history, but also the new loans themselves are more hazardous.

Jiménez et al. (2007) also find robust evidence, confirming theoretical predictions, that smaller banks' incentives and ability for risk taking are more affected by the stance of monetary policy than larger banks' incentives. The effect of the stance of monetary policy on credit risk taking further depends on bank liquidity and ownership type, and on the level of banking competition and new borrower entry in the local area. All in all, their results suggest that the stance of monetary policy and, in particular, the level of short-term interest rates influences banks' appetite for credit risk.

Ioannidou et al. (2007) use the Credit Register from Bolivia—where the banking system is almost completely dollarized—from 1999 to 2003. When the federal funds rate decreases, they find, not only do banks take more risk, but they also reduce their loan spreads. Despite using credit registers covering different countries, time periods, and monetary policy regimes, both papers find strikingly similar results.

Dell'Ariccia, Igan, and Laeven (2008) "provide hints" [*sic*] on the potential effects of monetary policy on banks' risk taking. Their results are consistent with the idea that low interest rates in the United States may have loosened lending standards both directly and through their effect on real estate prices (see also Cerqueiro, Degryse, and Ongena 2007). Similarly, Den Haan, Sumner, and Yamashiro (2007) find that restrictive monetary policy reduces consumer and real estate lending in particular and argue that high short-term rates could imply a decline in bank risk taking. Black and Rosen (2008) show that a lowering of the federal funds rate lengthens loan maturity and reallocates lending from large to small firm. And in a different setting, Bernanke and Kuttner (2005) find that higher unanticipated interest rates reduce equity prices. One of their interpretations of this finding is that tight money may reduce the willingness of stock investors to bear risk. Rigobon and Sack (2004) show that higher interest rates reduce equity prices, especially on NASDAQ, where arguably more risky firms are listed.

There are a number of natural extensions to these papers. First, the papers currently focus on the impact of monetary policy on the probability of default of individual bank loans but overlook the correlations between loan default and the impact on each individual bank's portfolio or the correlations between all the banks' portfolios and the resulting systemic impact of monetary policy. Herding between banks may particularly occur during periods of risk taking (as "there may be safety in the herd"). Second, bank ownership and control, in particular board independence and ownership dispersion for listed banks and the type of political control for state-owned banks, for example, may also matter for risk-taking incentives. Finally, credit risk taking by banks may be amplified by certain types of financial innovation, for example by loan securitization.

Clearly, the dramatic events in the banking sector in 2007–2008 will be a fertile ground for study for many years to come.

References

Agarwal, R., and J.A. Elston (2001) Bank-Firm Relationships, Financing and Firm Performance in Germany, *Economics Letters* 72, 225–232.

Agarwal, S., and R. Hauswald (2006) Distance and Information Asymmetries in Lending Decisions, Mimeo, American University.

Agarwal, S., and R. Hauswald (2007) The Choice between Arm's-Length and Relationship Debt: Evidence from eLoans, Mimeo, American University.

Aghion, P. (2006) Interaction Effects in the Relationship between Growth and Finance, *Capitalism and Society* 1, 1–26.

Aghion, P., P. Bolton, and M. Dewatripont (2000) Contagious Bank Failures in a Free Banking System, *European Economic Review* 44, 713–718.

Aharony, J., and I. Swary (1996) Additional Evidence on the Information-Based Contagion Effects of Bank Failures, *Journal of Banking and Finance* 20, 57–69.

Ahrend, R., B. Cournède, and R. Price (2008) Monetary Policy, Market Excesses and Financial Turmoil, Economics Department Working Paper, Organisation for Economic Co-operation and Development.

Aintablian, S., and G.S. Roberts (2000) A Note on Market Response to Corporate Loan Announcements in Canada, *Journal of Banking and Finance* 24, 381–393.

Alegria, C., and K. Schaeck (2008) On Measuring Concentration in Banking Systems, *Finance Research Letters* 5, 59–67.

Alem, M. (2003) Insurance Motives in Lending Relationships: Evidence from Argentina, Mimeo, University of Chicago.

Allen, F., and E. Carletti (2006) Credit Risk Transfer and Contagion, *Journal of Monetary Economics* 53, 89–111.

Allen, F., and D. Gale (1997) Financial Markets, Intermediaries and Intertemporal Smoothing, *Journal of Political Economy* 105, 523–546.

Allen, F., and D. Gale (2000a) *Comparing Financial Systems*, MIT Press, Cambridge, MA.

Allen, F., and D. Gale (2000b) Financial Contagion, *Journal of Political Economy* 108, 1–33.

Allen, F., and D. Gale (2004a) Asset Price Bubbles and Monetary Policy, in Meghnad Desai and Yahia Said (eds.), *Global Governance and Financial Crises*, Routledge, London, 19–42.

Allen, F., and D. Gale (2004b) Competition and Financial Stability, *Journal of Money, Credit and Banking* 36, 453–480.

Allen, F., and D. Gale (2007) *Understanding Financial Crises*, Oxford University Press, New York, NY.

Allen, F., H. Gersbach, J.P. Krahnen, and A.M. Santomero (2001) Competition among Banks: Introduction and Conference Overview, *European Finance Review* 5, 1–11.

Allen, F., J. Qian, and M. Qian (2005) Law, Finance and Economic Growth in China, *Journal of Financial Economics* 77, 57–116.

Allen, L., J. Boudoukh, and A. Saunders (2004) *Understanding Market, Credit and Operational Risk*, Blackwell Publishing, Oxford.

Allen, L., and A. Rai (1996) Operational Efficiency in Banking: An International Comparison, *Journal of Banking and Finance* 20, 655–672.

Altman, E.I. (1968) Financial Ratios, Discriminant Analysis and the Prediction of Corporate Bankruptcy, *Journal of Finance* 23, 589–610.

Amundsen, E., and H. Arnt (2005) Contagion Risk in the Danish Interbank Market, Working Paper, Danmark Nationalbank.

Anderson, S.P., A. de Palma, and J.F. Thisse (1989) Demand for Differentiated Products, Discrete Choice Models, and the Characteristics Approach, *Review of Economic Studies* 56, 21–35.

Andre, P., R. Mathieu, and P. Zhang (2001) A Note On: Capital Adequacy and the Information Content of Term Loans and Lines of Credit, *Journal of Banking and Finance* 25, 431–444.

Angelini, P., and N. Cetorelli (2003) Bank Competition and Regulatory Reform: The Case of the Italian Banking Industry, *Journal of Money, Credit, and Banking* 35, 663–684.

Angelini, P., R. Di Salvo, and G. Ferri (1998) Availability and Cost of Credit for Small Businesses: Customer Relationships and Credit Cooperatives, *Journal of Banking and Finance* 22, 925–954.

Anvari, M., and V.V. Gopal (1983) A Survey of Cash Management Practises of Small Canadian Firms, *Journal of Small Business Management* 83, 53–58.

Arping, S. (2002) Banking, Commerce, and Antitrust, Mimeo, University of Amsterdam.

Ausubel, L.M. (1991) The Failure of Competition in the Credit Card Market, *American Economic Review* 81, 50–76.

Ayyagari, M., A. Demirgüç-Kunt, and V. Maksimovic (2007) Formal versus Informal Finance: Evidence from China, Mimeo, World Bank.

Azofra-Palenzuela, V., F.J. López Iturriaga, and F. Tejerina-Gaite (2009) Banks as Shareholders: The Spanish Model of Corporate Governance, in Frank J. Columbus (ed.), *Corporate Governance: Issues and Challenges*, Nova Science Publishers.

Bae, K.H., J.K. Kang, and C.W. Lim (2002) The Value of Durable Bank Relationships: Evidence from Korean Banking Shocks, *Journal of Financial Economics* 64, 181–214.

Bain, J. (1956) *Barriers to New Competition*, Harvard University Press, Cambridge, MA.

Barros, P.P. (1999) Multimarket Competition in Banking, with an Example from the Portuguese Market, *International Journal of Industrial Organization* 17, 335–352.

Barros, P.P., E. Berglof, P. Fulghieri, J. Gual, C. Mayer, and X. Vives (2005) *Integration of European Banks: The Way Forward*, Centre for Economic Policy Research, London.

Barth, J.R., G. Caprio, and R. Levine (2001) The Regulations and Supervision of Banks around the World: A New Database, Mimeo, World Bank.

Barth, J.R., G. Caprio, and R. Levine (2004) Bank Regulation and Supervision: What Works Best? *Journal of Financial Intermediation* 13, 205–248.

Basak, S., and A. Shapiro (2001) Value-at-Risk Based Risk Management: Optimal Policies and Asset Prices, *Review of Financial Studies* 14, 371–405.

Bebczuk, R.N. (2004) What Determines the Access to Credit by SMEs in Argentina? Working Paper, Universidad Nacional de la Plata.

Becher, D.A. (2000) The Valuation Effects of Bank Mergers, *Journal of Corporate Finance* 6, 189–214.

Beck, T., A. Demirgüç-Kunt, and R. Levine (2004) Bank Concentration and Crises, Mimeo, World Bank.

Beck, T., A. Demirgüç-Kunt, and R. Levine (2006a) Bank Concentration, Competition and Crises: First Results, *Journal of Banking and Finance* 30, 1581–1603.

Beck, T., A. Demirgüç-Kunt, and R. Levine (2006b) Bank Supervision and Corruption in Lending, *Journal of Monetary Economics* 53, 2131–2163.

Beck, T., R. Levine, and A. Levkov (2007) Big Bad Banks? The Impact of U.S. Branch Deregulation on Income Distribution, Policy Research Working Paper, World Bank.

Beggs, A., and P. Klemperer (1992) Multi-period Competition with Switching Costs, *Econometrica* 60, 651–666.

Beitel, P., D. Schiereck, and M. Wahrenburg (2004) Explaining M&A Success in European Banks, *European Financial Management* 10, 109–140.

Bekaert, G., C.R. Harvey, C. Lundblad, and S. Siegel (2007) Global Growth Opportunities and Market Integration, *Journal of Finance* 62, 1081–1137.

Bencivenga, V.R., and B.D. Smith (1991) Financial Intermediation and Endogenous Growth, *Review of Economics Studies* 58, 195–209.

Benfratello, L., F. Schiantarelli, and A. Sembenelli (2008) Banks and Innovation: Microeconometric Evidence on Italian Firms, *Journal of Financial Economics*. 90, 197–217.

Berg, S.A., and M. Kim (1994) Oligopolistic Interdependence and the Structure of Production in Banking: An Empirical Evaluation, *Journal of Money, Credit, and Banking* 26, 309–322.

Berg, S.A., and M. Kim (1998) Banks as Multioutput Oligopolies: An Empirical Evaluation of the Retail and Corporate Banking Markets, *Journal of Money, Credit, and Banking* 30, 135–153.

Berger, A.N. (1995) The Profit-Structure Relationship in Banking. Tests of Market-Power and Efficient-Structure Hypotheses, *Journal of Money, Credit, and Banking* 27, 404–431.

Berger, A.N. (2003) The Efficiency Effects of a Single Market for Financial Services in Europe, *European Journal of Operational Research* 150, 466–481.

Berger, A.N. (2007a) International Comparisons of Banking Efficiency, *Financial Markets, Institutions and Instruments* 16, 119–144.

Berger, A.N. (2007b) Obstacles to a Global Banking System: "Old Europe" versus "New Europe," *Journal of Banking and Finance* 31, 1955–1973.

Berger, A.N., Q. Dai, S. Ongena, and D.C. Smith (2003) To What Extent Will the Banking Industry Be Globalized? A Study of Bank Nationality and Reach in 20 European Nations, *Journal of Banking and Finance* 27, 383–415.

Berger, A.N., A. Demirgüç-Kunt, R. Levine, and J.G. Haubrich (2004a) Bank Concentration and Competition: An Evolution in the Making, *Journal of Money, Credit, and Banking* 36, 433–451.

Berger, A.N., R. Demsetz, and P. Strahan (1999) The Consolidation of the Financial Services Industry: Causes, Consequences, and Implications for the Future, *Journal of Banking and Finance* 23, 135–194.

Berger, A.N., and R. DeYoung (2001) The Effects of Geographic Expansion on Bank Efficiency, *Journal of Financial Services Research* 19, 163–184.

Berger, A.N., R. DeYoung, H. Genay, and G. Udell (2000) Globalization of Financial Institutions: Evidence from Cross-Border Banking Performance, *Brookings-Wharton Papers on Financial Services* 3, 23–120.

Berger, A.N., and A. Dick (2007) Entry into Banking Markets and the Early-Mover Advantage, *Journal of Money, Credit, and Banking* 39, 775–807.

Berger, A.N., M. Espinosa-Vega, W.S. Frame, and N.M. Miller (2005a) Debt Maturity, Risk, and Asymmetric Information, *Journal of Finance* 60, 2895–2924.

Berger, A.N., and T.H. Hannan (1989) The Price-Concentration Relationship in Banking, *Review of Economics and Statistics* 71, 291–299.

Berger, A.N., I. Hasan, and L.F. Klapper (2004b) Further Evidence on the Link between Finance and Growth: An International Analysis of Community Banking and Economic Performance, *Journal of Financial Services Research* 25, 169–202.

Berger, A.N., and D.B. Humphrey (1997) Efficiency of Financial Institutions: International Survey and Directions for Future Research, *European Journal of Operational Research* 98, 175–212.

Berger, A.N., L.F. Klapper, M.S. Martinez Peria, and R. Zaida (2006) Bank Ownership Type and Banking Relationships, Mimeo, Board of Governors of the Federal Reserve System.

Berger, A.N., L.F. Klapper, and G.F. Udell (2001) The Ability of Banks to Lend to Informationally Opaque Small Businesses, *Journal of Banking and Finance* 25, 2127–2167.

Berger, A.N., N.M. Miller, M.A. Petersen, R.G. Rajan, and J.C. Stein (2005b) Does Function Follow Organizational Form? Evidence from the Lending Practices of Large and Small Banks, *Journal of Financial Economics* 76, 237–269.

Berger, A.N., R.J. Rosen, and G.F. Udell (2002) Does Market Size Structure Affect Competition? The Case of Small Business Lending, Mimeo, Board of Governors of the Federal Reserve System.

Berger, A.N., A. Saunders, J.M. Scalise, and G.F. Udell (1998) The Effects of Bank Mergers and Acquisitions on Small Business Lending, *Journal of Financial Economics* 50, 187–230.

Berger, A.N., and D.C. Smith (2003) Global Integration in the Banking Industry, *Federal Reserve Bulletin* 90, 451–460.

Berger, A.N., and G.F. Udell (1992) Some Evidence on the Empirical Significance of Credit Rationing, *Journal of Political Economy* 100, 1047–1077.

Berger, A.N., and G.F. Udell (1995) Relationship Lending and Lines of Credit in Small Firm Finance, *Journal of Business* 68, 351–381.

Berger, A.N., and G.F. Udell (1998) The Economics of Small Business Finance: The Roles of Private Equity and Debt Markets in the Financial Growth Cycle, *Journal of Banking and Finance* 22, 613–673.

Berger, A.N., and G.F. Udell (2002) Small Business Credit Availability and Relationship Lending: The Importance of Bank Organisational Structure, *Economic Journal* 112, 32–53.

Berger, A.N., and G.F. Udell (2006) A More Complete Conceptual Framework for SME Finance, *Journal of Banking and Finance* 30, 2945–2966.

Berglöf, E., and H. Sjögren (1998) Combining Arm's-Length and Control Oriented Finance—Evidence from Main Bank Relationships in Sweden, in K.J. Hopt, H. Kanda, M.J. Roe, E. Wymeersch, and S. Prigge (eds.), *Comparative Corporate Governance: The State of the Art and Emerging Research*, Clarendon Press, Oxford, 787–808.

Bergstresser, D. (2001a) Banking Market Concentration and Consumer Credit Constraints: Evidence from the Survey of Consumer Finances, Mimeo, MIT.

Bergstresser, D. (2001b) Market Concentration and Loan Portfolios in Commercial Banking, Mimeo, MIT.

Bergström, R., L. Engwall, and E. Wallerstedt (1994) Organizational Foundations and Closures in a Regulated Environment: Swedish Commercial Banks 1831–1990, *Scandinavian Journal of Management* 10, 29–48.

Berkowitz, J., and J. O'Brien (2002) How Accurate are Value-at-Risk Models at Commercial Banks? *Journal of Finance* 57, 1093–1111.

Berlin, M. (1996) For Better and For Worse: Three Lending Relationships, *Federal Reserve Bank of Philadelphia Business Review* November, 3–12.

Berlin, M., and L.J. Mester (1999) Deposits and Relationship Lending, *Review of Financial Studies* 12, 579–607.

Bernanke, B.S. (1983) Nonmonetary Effects of the Financial Crisis in the Propagation of the Great Depression, *American Economic Review* 73, 257–276.

Bernanke, B.S. (1993) Credit in the Macroeconomy, *Federal Reserve Bank of New York Quarterly Review* 18, 50–70.

Bernanke, B.S., and K.N. Kuttner (2005) What Explains the Stock Market's Reaction to Federal Reserve Policy? *Journal of Finance* 60, 1221–1258.

Berry, S., J. Levinsohn, and A. Pakes (1995) Automobile Prices in Market Equilibrium, *Econometrica* 63, 841–890.

Bertrand, M., A. Schoar, and D. Thesmar (2007) Banking Deregulation and Industry Structure: Evidence from the French Banking Reforms of 1985, *Journal of Finance.* 62, 597–628

Best, R., and H. Zhang (1993) Alternative Information Sources and the Information Content of Bank Loans, *Journal of Finance* 48, 1507–1522.

Bharath, S., S. Dahiya, A. Saunders, and A. Srinivasan (2007) So What Do I Get? The Bank's View of Lending Relationships, *Journal of Financial Economics* 58, 368–419.

Bhattacharya, S., and G. Chiesa (1995) Proprietary Information, Financial Intermediation, and Research Incentives, *Journal of Financial Intermediation* 4, 328–357.

Bhattacharya, S., and A.V. Thakor (1993) Contemporary Banking Theory, *Journal of Financial Intermediation* 3, 2–50.

Biais, B., and C. Gollier (1997) Trade Credit and Credit Rationing, *Review of Financial Studies* 10, 903–937.

Bianco, M., T. Jappelli, and M. Pagano (2005) Courts and Banks: Effects of Judicial Enforcement on Credit Markets, *Journal of Money, Credit, and Banking* 37, 223–244.

Biehl, A.R. (2002) The Extent of the Market for Retail Banking Deposits, *Antitrust Bulletin* 47, 91–106.

Bikker, J., L. Spierdijk, and P. Finnie (2006) Misspecification of the Panzar Rosse Model: Assessing Competition in the Banking Industry, Working Paper, De Nederlandsche Bank.

Bikker, J.A., and K. Haaf (2002) Competition, Concentration and Their Relationship: An Empirical Analysis of the Banking Industry, *Journal of Banking and Finance* 26, 2191–2214.

Billett, M.T., M.J. Flannery, and J.A. Garfinkel (1995) The Effect of Lender Identity on a Borrowing Firm's Equity Return, *Journal of Finance* 50, 699–718.

Binks, M.R., and C.T. Ennew (1997) The Relationship between U.K. Banks and Their Small Business Customers, *Small Business Economics* 9, 167–178.

Black, L.K., and R.J. Rosen (2008) The Effect of Monetary Policy on the Availability of Credit: How the Credit Channel Works, Mimeo, Board of Governors of the Federal Reserve System.

Black, S.E., and P.E. Strahan (2002) Entrepreneurship and Bank Credit Availability, *Journal of Finance* 57, 2807–2834.

Blackwell, D.W., and D.B. Winters (1997) Banking Relationships and the Effect of Monitoring on Loan Pricing, *Journal of Financial Research* 20, 275–289.

Blavarg, M., and P. Nimander (2002) Inter-bank exposures and Systemic Risk, *Sveriges Riksbank Economic Review* 2, 19–45.

Bodenhorn, H. (2003) Short-Term Loans and Long-Term Relationships: Relationship Lending in Early America, *Journal of Money, Credit, and Banking* 35, 485–505.

Bodenhorn, H. (2007) Usury Ceilings and Bank Lending Behavior: Evidence from Nineteenth Century New York, *Explorations in Economic History* 44, 179–202.

Boldt-Christmas, M., F.S. Jacobsen, and A.E. Tschoegl (2001) The International Expansion of the Norwegian Banks, *Business History* 43, 79–104.

Bolton, P., and D.S. Scharfstein (1996) Optimal Debt Structure and the Number of Creditors, *Journal of Political Economy* 104, 1–25.

Bonaccorsi di Patti, E., and G. Dell'Ariccia (2004) Bank Competition and Firm Creation, *Journal of Money, Credit, and Banking* 36, 225–252.

Bonaccorsi di Patti, E., and G. Gobbi (2007) Winners or Losers? The Effects of Banking Consolidation on Corporate Borrowers, *Journal of Finance* 62, 669–695.

Bonin, J.P., and M. Imai (2007) Soft Related Lending: A Tale of Two Korean Banks, *Journal of Banking and Finance* 31, 173–1729.

Boone, J. (2008) A New Way to Measure Competition, *Economic Journal* 118, 1245–1261.

Boone, J., J.C. van Ours, and H. van der Wiel (2007) How (Not) to Measure Competition, Discussion Paper, Centre for Economic Policy Research.

Boot, A.W.A. (2000) Relationship Banking: What Do We Know? *Journal of Financial Intermediation* 9, 3–25.

Boot, A.W.A., and A.V. Thakor (1994) Moral Hazard and Secured Lending in an Infinitely Repeated Credit Market Game, *International Economic Review* 35, 899–920.

Boot, A.W.A., and A.V. Thakor (1997) Financial System Architecture, *Review of Financial Studies* 10, 693–733.

Boot, A.W.A., and A.V. Thakor (2000) Can Relationship Banking Survive Competition? *Journal of Finance* 55, 679–713.

Bornheim, S.P., and T.H. Herbeck (1998) A Research Note on the Theory of SME–Bank Relationships, *Small Business Economics* 10, 327–331.

Bos, J.W.B., and J.W. Kolari (2005) Large Bank Efficiency in Europe and the United States: Are There Economic Motivations for Geographic Expansion in Financial Services?, *Journal of Business* 78, 1555–1592.

Boscaljon, B., and C.C. Ho (2005) Information Content of Bank Loan Announcements to Asian Corporations during Periods of Economic Uncertainty, *Journal of Banking and Finance* 29, 369–389.

Boyd, J., G. De Nicolo, and A. Jalal (2006) Bank Risk-Taking and Competition Revisited: New Theory and New Evidence, Working Paper, International Monetary Fund.

Boyd, J.H., and G. De Nicolo (2005) The Theory of Bank Risk Taking and Competition Revisited, *Journal of Finance* 60, 1329–1343.

Boyd, J.H., S. Kwak, and B.D. Smith (2005) The Real Output Losses Associated with Modern Banking Crises, *Journal of Money Credit and Banking* 37, 977–999.

Boyd, J.H., and E.C. Prescott (1986) Financial Intermediary Coalitions, *Journal of Economic Theory* 38, 211–232.

Boyreau-Debray, G. (2003) Financial Intermediation and Growth: Chinese Style, Working Paper, World Bank.

Braggion, F. (2004) Credit Market Constraints and Financial Networks in Late Victorian Britain, MimeoNorthwestern University.

Braverman, A., and J.E. Stiglitz (1989) Credit Rationing, Tenancy, Productivity, and the Dynamics of Inequality, in Pranab Bardhan (ed.), *The Economic Theory of Agrarian Institutions*, Oxford University Press, Oxford, 185–203.

Brealey, R.A., and E.C. Kaplanis (1996) The Determination of Foreign Banking Location, *Journal of International Money and Finance* 15, 577–597.

Bresnahan, T. (1982) The Oligopoly Solution Is Identified, *Economics Letters* 10, 87–92.

Bresnahan, T. (1989) Empirical Studies of Industries with Market Power, in R. Schmalensee and R.D. Willig (eds.), *Handbook of Industrial Organization*, Elsevier, Amsterdam, 1011–1057.

Bresnahan, T., and P. Reiss (1994) Measuring the Importance of Sunk Costs, *Annales d'Economie et de Statistique* 34, 181–217.

Bresnahan, T.F., and P.C. Reiss (1991) Entry and Competition in Concentrated Markets, *Journal of Political Economy* 99, 977–1009.

Brewer, E., H. Genay, W.C. Hunter, and G.G. Kaufman (2003) The Value of Banking Relationships during a Financial Crisis: Evidence from Failures of Japanese Banks, *Journal of Japanese and International Economies* 17, 233–262.

Brick, I.E., and D. Palia (2007) Evidence of Jointness in the Terms of Relationship Lending, *Journal of Financial Intermediation* 16, 452–476.

Bris, A., and I. Welch (2005) The Optimal Concentration of Creditors, *Journal of Finance* 60, 2193–2212.

Brito, P., and A.S. Mello (1995) Financial Constraints and Firm Post-entry Performance, *International Journal of Industrial Organization* 13, 543–565.

Brunner, A., and J.P. Krahnen (2008) Multiple Lenders and Corporate Distress: Evidence on Debt Restructuring, *Review of Economic Studies*. 75, 415–442.

Buch, C.M. (2000) Why Do Banks Go Abroad? Evidence from German Data, *Financial Markets, Institutions and Instruments* 9, 33–67.

Buch, C.M. (2002) Financial Market Integration in the U.S.: Lessons for Europe, *Comparative Economic Studies* 44, 46–71.

Buch, C.M. (2003a) Information or Regulation: What Is Driving the International Activities of Commercial Banks? *Journal of Money, Credit, and Banking* 35, 851–869.

Buch, C.M. (2003b) What Determines Maturity? An Analysis of German Commercial Banks' Foreign Assets, *Applied Financial Economics* 13, 337–351.

Buch, C.M., and G.L. DeLong (2004) Cross-Border Bank Mergers: What Lures the Rare Animal? *Journal of Banking and Finance* 28, 2077–2102.

Buch, C.M., J.C. Driscoll, and C. Ostergaard (2003) International Diversification in Bank Asset Portfolios, Mimeo, Kiel Institute of World Economics.

Buch, C.M., and S.M. Golder (2001) Foreign versus Domestic Banks in Germany and the U.S.: A Tale of Two Markets? *Journal of Multinational Financial Management* 11, 341–361.

Buch, C.M., and S.M. Golder (2002) Domestic and Foreign Banks in Germany: Do They Differ? *Kredit und Kapital* 19–53.

Buch, C.M., and A. Lipponer (2005) Clustering or Competition? The Foreign Investment Behavior of German Banks, Mimeo, University of Tubingen.

Burkart, M., T. Ellingsen, and M. Giannetti (in press) What You Lend Is How You Lend? Explaining Trade Credit Contracts, *Review of Financial Studies*.

Byrd, D.T., and M.S. Mizruchi (2005) Bankers on the Board and the Debt Ratio of Firms, *Journal of Corporate Finance* 11, 129–173.

Caballero, R.J., T. Hoshi, and A.K. Kashyap (in press) Zombie Lending and Depressed Restructuring in Japan, *American Economic Review*.

Cabral, L., and S. Greenstein (1990) Switching Costs and Bidding Parity in Government Procurement of Computer Systems, *Journal of Law, Economics and Organization* 6, 453–469.

Calem, P.S., and G.A. Carlino (1991) The Concentration/Conduct Relationship in Bank Deposit Markets, *Review of Economics and Statistics* 73, 268–276.

Calem, P.S., and L.I. Nakamura (1998) Branch Banking and the Geography of Bank Pricing, *Review of Economics and Statistics* 80, 600–610.

Calem, P.S., and J.A. Rizzo (1992) Banks as Information Specialists: The Case of Hospital Lending, *Journal of Banking and Finance* 16, 1123–1141.

Calomiris, C.W., and C.M. Kahn (1991) The Role of Demandable Debt in Structuring Optimal Banking Arrangements, *American Economic Review* 81, 497–513.

Calomiris, C.W., and J.R. Mason (2003) Consequences of Bank Distress during the Great Depression, *American Economic Review* 93, 937–947.

Calvo, S., and C. Reinhart (1996) Capital Flows to Latin America: Is There Evidence of Contagion Effect? in Guillermo Calvo, Morris Goldstein, and Eduard Hochreiter (eds.), *Private Capital Flows to Emerging Markets After the Mexican Crisis*, Institute for International Economics, Washington, DC., 151–171.

Cameron, A., and P. Trivedi (1990) Regression Based Tests for Overdispersion in the Poisson Model, *Journal of Econometrics* 31, 255–274.

Cameron, A.C., and P.K. Trivedi (1986) Econometric Models Based on Count Data: Comparisons and Applications of Some Estimators, *Journal of Applied Econometrics* 1, 1–16.

Cameron, A.C., and P.K. Trivedi (2005) *Microeconometrics: Methods and Applications*, Cambridge University Press, New York.

Caminal, R., and C. Matutes (1990) Endogenous Switching Costs in a Duopoly Model, *International Journal of Industrial Organization* 8, 353–373.

Campa, J.M., and I. Hernando (2004) Shareholder Value Creation in European M&As, *European Financial Management* 10, 47–81.

Campbell, J.Y., and R.J. Shiller (1987) Cointegration and Tests of Present Value Models, *Journal of Political Economy* 95, 1062–1088.

Campbell, S.D. (2005) A Review of Backtesting and Backtesting Procedures, Finance and Economics Discussion Series, Board of Governors.

Campbell, T.S. (1979) Optimal Investment Financing Decisions and the Value of Confidentiality, *Journal of Financial and Quantitative Analysis* 14, 232–257.

Cantillo, M., and J. Wright (2000) How Do Firms Choose Their Lenders? An Empirical Investigation, *Review of Financial Studies* 13, 155–189.

Caprio, J. (2003) Episodes of Systemic and Borderline Financial Crises, Data Set, World Bank.

Carbo, S., D. Humphrey, J. Maudos, and P.Y. Molyneux (in press) Cross-Country Comparisons of Competition and Pricing Power in European Banking, *Journal of International Money and Finance*.

Carbó Valverde, S., D.B. Humphrey, and R. López del Paso (2007) Do Cross-Country Differences in Bank Efficiency Support a Policy of "National Champions"? *Journal of Banking and Finance* 31, 2173–2188.

Carbó Valverde, S., R. López del Paso, and F. Rodríguez Fernández (2007) Financial Innovations in Banking: Impact on Regional Growth, *Regional Studies* 41, 311–326.

Carbó Valverde, S., F. Rodriguez Fernández, and G.F. Udell (2006) Bank Market Power and SME Financing Constraints, Proceedings of the 42nd Annual Conference on Bank Structure and Competition, Federal Reserve Bank of Chicago.

Carbó-Valverde, S., F. Rodríguez-Fernández, and G.F. Udell (2005) Bank Market Power and SME Financing Constraints, Mimeo, University of Granada.

Carletti, E. (2004) The Structure of Bank Relationships, Endogenous Monitoring, and Loan Rates, *Journal of Financial Intermediation* 13, 58–86.

Carletti, E. (2008) Competition and Regulation in Banking, in Anjan V. Thakor and Arnoud W.A. Boot (eds.), *Handbook of Financial Intermediation and Banking*, North Holland, London, 449–482.

Carletti, E., V. Cerasi, and S. Daltung (2007) Multiple-Bank Lending: Diversification and Free-Riding in Monitoring, *Journal of Financial Intermediation* 16, 425–451.

Carletti, E., P. Hartmann, and S. Ongena (2006) The Economic Impact of Merger Control: What Is Special about Banking? Mimeo, Tilburg University.

Carling, K., and S. Lundberg (2005) Asymmetric Information and Distance: An Empirical Assessment of Geographical Credit Rationing, *Journal of Economics and Business* 57, 39–59.

Carmignani, A., and M. Omiccioli (2007) Costs and Benefits of Creditor Concentration: An Empirical Approach, Working Paper, Banca d'Italia.

Casolaro, L., and P.E. Mistrulli (2007) Distance, Organizational Structure and Loan Rates, Mimeo, Bank of Italy.

Castelar Pinheiro, A., and A. Moura (2003) Segmentation and the Use of Information in Brazilian Credit Markets, in M.J. Miller (ed.), *Credit Reporting Systems and the International Economy*, MIT Press, Cambridge, MA, 335–396.

Castelli, A., G.P. Dwyer, Jr., and I. Hasan (2006) Bank Relationships and Small Firms' Financial Performance, Working Paper, Federal Reserve Bank of Atlanta.

Cavallo, L., and S. Rossi (2001) Scale and Scope Economies in the European Banking Systems, *Journal of Multinational Financial Management* 11, 515–531.

Cavalluzzo, K.S., L.C. Cavalluzzo, and J.D. Wolken (2002) Competition, Small Business Financing, and Discrimination: Evidence from a New Survey, *Journal of Business* 75, 641–680.

Cerasi, V., B. Chizzolini, and M. Ivaldi (2002) Branching and Competition in the European Banking Industry, *Applied Economics* 34, 2213–2225.

Cerqueiro, G., H. Degryse, and S. Ongena (2007) Rules versus Discretion in Loan Rate Setting, Mimeo, Tilburg University.

Cesarini, F. (1994) The Relationship between Banks and Firms in Italy: A Banker's View, *Review of Economic Conditions in Italy* 29–50.

Cetorelli, N. (2001) Does Bank Concentration Lead to Concentration in Industrial Sectors, Working Paper, Federal Reserve Bank of Chicago.

Cetorelli, N. (2003a) Bank Concentration and Competition in Europe, Mimeo, Federal Reserve Bank of Chicago.

Cetorelli, N. (2003b) Life-Cycle Dynamics in Industrial Sectors: The Role of Banking Market Structure, *Review of the Federal Reserve Bank of St. Louis* 85, 135–147.

Cetorelli, N., and M. Gambera (2001) Banking Market Structure, Financial Dependence and Growth: International Evidence from Industry Data, *Journal of Finance* 56, 617–648.

Cetorelli, N., and P.E. Strahan (2006) Finance as a Barrier to Entry: Bank Competition and Industry Structure in Local U.S. Markets, *Journal of Finance* 61, 867–892.

Chakraborty, A., and C.X. Hu (2006) Lending Relationships in Line-of-Credit and Nonline-of-Credit Loans: Evidence from Collateral Use in Small Business, *Journal of Financial Intermediation* 15, 86–107.

Chakravarty, S., and J.S. Scott (1999) Relationships and Rationing in Consumer Loans, *Journal of Business* 72, 523–544.

Chen, Y., and R.W. Rosenthal (1996) Dynamic Duopoly with Slowly Changing Customer Loyalties, *International Journal of Industrial Organization* 14, 269–296.

Cheng, X., and H. Degryse (2007) The Impact of Banks and Non-bank Financial Institutions on Local Economic Growth in China, Mimeo, Katholieke Universiteit Leuven.

Chiou, I. (1999) Daiwa Bank's Reputational Crisis: Valuation Effects on Bank–Firm Relationships, Mimeo, New York University Stern School of Business.

Christoffersen, P., and D. Pelletier (2004) Backtesting Value-at-Risk: A Duration-Based Approach, *Journal of Financial Econometrics* 2, 84–108.

Ciamarra, E.S. (2006) Monitoring by Affiliated Bankers on Board of Directors: Evidence from Corporate Financing Outcomes, Mimeo, New York University.

Ciccone, A., and E. Papaioannou (2006) Adjustment to Target Capital, Finance, and Growth, Mimeo, Universitat Pompeu Fabra.

Claessens, S., and K.J. Forbes (2001) International Financial Contagion: An Overview of the Issues and the Book, in Stijn Claessens and Kristin J. Forbes (eds.), *International Financial Contagion*, Kluwer Academic Press, Boston, MA. 3–17.

Claessens, S., T. Glaessner, and D. Klingebiel (2002) Electronic Finance: Reshaping the Financial Landscape around the World, *Journal of Financial Services Research* 22, 29–61.

Claessens, S., and L. Laeven (2003) Financial Development, Property Rights and Growth, *Journal of Finance* 58, 2401–2436.

Claessens, S., and L. Laeven (2004) What Drives Bank Competition? Some International Evidence, *Journal of Money, Credit, and Banking* 36, 563–583.

Claessens, S., and N. Van Horen (2007) Location Decisions of Foreign Banks and Competitive Advantage, Working Paper, Worldbank.

Claeys, S., and R. Vander Vennet (2005) Determinants of Bank Interest Margins in Central and Eastern Europe: A Comparison with the West, Mimeo, Ghent University.

Cocco, J.F., F.J. Gomes, and N.C. Martins (2003) Lending Relationships in the Interbank Market, Mimeo, London Business School.

Cohen, A., and M. Mazzeo (2003) Market Structure and Competition among Retail Depository Institutions, Mimeo, Northwestern University.

Cohen, A., and M. Mazzeo (2004) Competition, Product Differentiation and Quality Provision: An Empirical Equilibrium Analysis of Bank Branching Decisions, Mimeo, Northwestern University.

Cole, R. (1998) The Importance of Relationships to the Availability of Credit, *Journal of Banking and Finance* 22, 959–977.

Cole, R.A., L.G. Goldberg, and L.J. White (2004) Cookie-Cutter versus Character: The Micro Structure of Small Business Lending by Large and Small Banks, *Journal of Financial and Quantitative Analysis* 39, 227–252.

Coleman, A.D.F., N. Esho, and I.G. Sharpe (2004) Does Bank Monitoring Influence Loan Contract Terms? Mimeo, Australian Prudential Regulation Authority.

Conigliani, C., G. Ferri, and A. Generale (1997) The Impact of Bank-Firm Relations on the Propagation of Monetary Policy Squeezes: An Empirical Assessment for Italy, *Banca Nazionale del Lavoro* 202, 271–299.

Cornett, M.M., J.J. McNutt, and H. Tehranian (2005) Long-Term Performance of Rival Banks around Bank Failures, *Journal of Economics and Business* 57, 411–432.

Corts, K.S. (1999) Conduct Parameters and the Measurement of Market Power, *Journal of Econometrics* 88, 227–250.

Corvoisier, S., and R. Gropp (2001) Contestability, Technology, and Banking, Mimeo, European Central Bank.

Corvoisier, S., and R. Gropp (2002) Bank Concentration and Retail Interest Rates, *Journal of Banking and Finance* 26, 2155–2189.

Cosci, S., and V. Meliciani (2002) Multiple Banking Relationships: Evidence from the Italian Experience, *Manchester School Supplement* 37–54.

Cox, D. (1972) Regression Models and Life Tables, *Journal of the Royal Statistical Society* 24, 187–201.

Craig, S.G., and P. Hardee (2007) The Impact of Bank Consolidation on Small Business Credit Availability, *Journal of Banking and Finance* 31, 1237–1263.

Crystal, J.S., B.G. Dages, and L.S. Goldberg (2002) Has Foreign Bank Entry Led to Sounder Banks in Latin America? *Current Issues in Economics and Finance* 8, 1–6.

Cull, R., L.E. Davis, N.R. Lamoreaux, and J.-L. Rosenthal (2005) Historical Financing of Small and Medium-Sized Enterprises, Working Paper, National Bureau for Economic Research.

Cyrnak, A.W., and T.H. Hannan (1999) Is the Cluster Still Valid in Defining Banking Markets? Evidence from a New Data Source, *Antitrust Bulletin* 44, 313–331.

Dahiya, S., A. Saunders, and A. Srinivasan (2003) Financial Distress and Bank Lending Relationships, *Journal of Finance* 58, 375–399.

Dahlby, B., and D. West (1986) Price Dispersion in an Automobile Insurance Market, *Journal of Political Economy* 94, 418–438.

Danthine, J.-P., F. Giavazzi, X. Vives, and E.-L. von Thadden (1999) *The Future of European Banking*, Centre for Economic Policy Research, London.

Datta, S., M. Iskandar-Datta, and A. Patel (1999) Bank Monitoring and the Pricing of Corporate Public Debt, *Journal of Financial Economics* 51, 435–449.

D'Auria, C., A. Foglia, and P.M. Reedtz (1999) Bank Interest Rates and Credit Relationships in Italy, *Journal of Banking and Finance* 23, 1067–1093.

Davidson, R., and J.G. MacKinnon (1993) *Estimation and Inference in Econometrics*, Cambridge University Press, New York.

Davis, E.P. (1996) Banking, Corporate Finance, and Monetary Policy: An Empirical Perspective, *Oxford Review of Economic Policy* 10, 49–67.

de Bodt, E., F. Lobez, and J.C. Statnik (2005) Credit Rationing, Customer Relationship, and the Number of Banks: An Empirical Analysis, *European Financial Management* 11, 195–228.

De Haas, R., D. Ferreira, and A. Taci (2007) What Determines Banks' Customer Choice? Evidence from Transition Countries, Mimeo, European Bank for Reconstruction and Development.

De Juan, R. (2003) The Independent Submarkets Model: An Application to the Spanish Retail Banking Market, *International Journal of Industrial Organization* 21, 1461–1487.

De Mello, J.M.P. (2007) Can Lender Market Power Benefit Borrowers? Further Evidence from Small Firm Finance, Mimeo, Stanford.

DeGennaro, R.P., F.A. Elayan, and J.W. Wansley (1999) Information Content in Bank Lines of Credit, in A.H. Chen (ed.), *Research in Finance*, JAI Press, Stamford, CT, 65–80.

Degryse, H., and A. de Jong (2006) Investment and Internal Finance: Asymmetric Information or Managerial Discretion? *International Journal of Industrial Organization* 24, 125–147.

Degryse, H., L. Laeven, and S. Ongena (2007) The Impact of Organizational Structure and Lending Technology on Banking Competition, Mimeo, CentER—Tilburg University.

Degryse, H., N. Masschelein, and J. Mitchell (2004) Belgian SMEs and Bank Lending Relationships, *Financial Stability Review* 3, 121–134.

Degryse, H., N. Masschelein, and J. Mitchell (2006) SMEs and Bank Lending Relationships: The Impact of Mergers, Discussion Paper, Tilburg Law and Economics Center (TILEC), Tilburg University.

Degryse, H., and G. Nguyen (2007) Interbank Exposure: An Empirical Examination of Contagion Risk in the Belgian Banking System, *International Journal of Central Banking* 3, 123–171.

Degryse, H., and S. Ongena (2001) Bank Relationships and Firm Performance, *Financial Management* 30, 9–34.

Degryse, H., and S. Ongena (2002) Bank Relationships and International Banking Markets, *International Journal of the Economics of Business* 9, 401–417.

Degryse, H., and S. Ongena (2003) Distance, Lending Relationships, and Competition, Discussion Paper, Center for Economic Studies, KU Leuven, and CentER—Tilburg University.

Degryse, H., and S. Ongena (2004) The Impact of Technology and Regulation on the Geographical Scope of Banking, *Oxford Review of Economic Policy* 20, 571–590.

Degryse, H., and S. Ongena (2005) Distance, Lending Relationships, and Competition, *Journal of Finance* 60, 231–266.

Degryse, H., and S. Ongena (2007) The Impact of Competition on Bank Orientation, *Journal of Financial Intermediation* 16, 399–424.

Degryse, H., and S. Ongena (2008) Competition and Regulation in the Banking Sector: A Review of the Empirical Evidence on the Sources of Bank Rents, in Anjan V. Thakor and Arnoud W.A. Boot (eds.), *Handbook of Financial Intermediation and Banking*, Elsevier, Amsterdam. 483–542.

Degryse, H., S. Ongena, and G. Tümer-Alkan (2007) Corporate Governance: A Review of the Role of Banks, Mimeo, CentER—Tilburg University.

Degryse, H., and P. Van Cayseele (2000) Relationship Lending within a Bank-Based System: Evidence from European Small Business Data, *Journal of Financial Intermediation* 9, 90–109.

Deidda, L., and B. Fattouh (2008) Banks, Financial Markets and Growth, *Journal of Financial Intermediation*. 17, 6–36.

Delgado, J., V. Salas, and J. Saurina (2007) Joint Size and Ownership Specialization in Bank Lending, *Journal on Banking and Finance* 31, 3563–3583.

Dell'Ariccia, G., D. Igan, and L. Laeven (2008) Credit Booms and Lending Standards: Evidence from the Subprime Mortgage Market, Mimeo, International Monetary Fund.

Dell'Ariccia, G., E. Detragiache, and R.G. Rajan (2008) The Real Effect of Banking Crises, *Journal of Financial Intermediation*. 17, 89–112.

Dell'Ariccia, G., and R. Marquez (2006) Lending Booms and Lending Standards, *Journal of Finance* 61, 2511–2546.

DeLong, G.L. (2001) Stockholder Gains from Focusing versus Diversifying Mergers, *Journal of Financial Economics* 59, 221–252.

Demirgüç-Kunt, A. (1989) Deposit-Institution Failures: A Review of Empirical Literature, *Federal Reserve Bank of Cleveland Economic Review* 25, 2–18.

Demirgüç-Kunt, A., and E. Detragiache (1997) The Determinants of Banking Crises: Evidence from Developed and Developing Countries, Working Paper, World Bank.

Demirgüç-Kunt, A., and E. Detragiache (1998) The Determinants of Banking Crises in Developing and Developed Countries, Staff Paper, International Monetary Fund.

Demirgüç-Kunt, A., and E. Detragiache (2002) Does Deposit Insurance Increase Banking System Stability: An Empirical Investigation, *Journal of Monetary Economics* 49, 1373–1406.

Demirgüç-Kunt, A., E. Detragiache, and P. Gupta (2006) Inside the Crisis: An Empirical Analysis of Banking System in Distress, *Journal of International Money and Finance* 25, 702–718.

Demirgüç-Kunt, A., L. Laeven, and R. Levine (2004) Regulations, Market Structure, Institutions, and the Cost of Financial Intermediation, *Journal of Money, Credit, and Banking* 36, 563–583.

Demirgüç-Kunt, A., and R. Levine (2001) *Financial Structure and Economic Growth: A Cross Country Comparison of Banks, Markets, and Development*, MIT Press, Cambridge, MA.

Demirgüç-Kunt, A., and V. Maksimovic (1998) Law, Finance, Firm Growth, *Journal of Finance* 53, 2107–2137.

Demsetz, H. (1973) Industry Structure, Market Rivalry, and Public Policy, *Journal of Law and Economics* 16, 1–9.

Den Haan, W.J., G. Ramey, and J. Watson (2003) Liquidity Flows and Fragility of Business Enterprises, *Journal of Monetary Economics* 50, 1215–1241.

Den Haan, W.J., S. Sumner, and G. Yamashiro (2007) Bank Loan Portfolios and the Monetary Transmission Mechanism, *Journal of Monetary Economics* 54, 904–924.

Dermine, J. (2003) European Banking: Past, Present, and Future, in V. Gaspar, P. Hartmann, and O. Sleijpen (eds.), *The Transformation of the European Financial System*, European Central Bank (ECB), Frankfurt, 31–95.

Detragiache, E., P.G. Garella, and L. Guiso (1997) Multiple versus Single Banking Relationships, Discussion Paper, Centre for Economic Policy Research.

Detragiache, E., P.G. Garella, and L. Guiso (2000) Multiple versus Single Banking Relationships: Theory and Evidence, *Journal of Finance* 55, 1133–1161.

Dewatripont, M., and E. Maskin (1995) Credit and Efficiency in Centralized and Decentralized Economies, *Review of Economic Studies* 62, 541–555.

Dewatripont, M., and J. Tirole (1994) *The Prudential Regulation of Banks*, MIT, Cambridge, MA.

DeYoung, R., and D.E. Nolle (1996) Foreign-Owned Banks in the United States: Earning Market Share or Buying It? *Journal of Money, Credit, and Banking* 28, 622–636.

DeYoung, R., Frame, W.S., Glennon, D., McMillen, D.P., Nigro, P.J. (2007) Commercial Lending Distance and Historically Underserved Areas, Working Paper No. 2007-11a. Atlanta, GA: Federal Reserve Bank of Atlanta.

Diamond, D.W. (1984) Financial Intermediation and Delegated Monitoring, *Review of Economic Studies* 51, 393–414.

Diamond, D.W. (1991) Monitoring and Reputation: The Choice between Bank Loans and Privately Placed Debt, *Journal of Political Economy* 99, 689–721.

Diamond, D.W., and P.H. Dybvig (1983) Bank Runs, Deposit Insurance and Liquidity, *Journal of Political Economy* 91, 401–419.

Dick, A. (2002) Demand Estimation and Consumer Welfare in the Banking Industry, Finance and Economics Discussion Series Paper, Board of Governors of the Federal Reserve System.

Dick, A. (2007) Market Size, Service Quality and Competition in Banking, *Journal of Money, Credit, and Banking* 39, 49–81.

Dick, A. (2006) Nationwide Branching and Its Impact on Market Structure, Quality and Bank Performance, *Journal of Business* 79, 567–592.

Dietsch, M. (2003) Financing Small Businesses in France, *European Investment Bank Papers* 8, 93–119.

Dietsch, M., and V. Golitin-Boubakari (2002) La Consolidation du Systeme Bancaire et le Financement des PME en France, Mimeo, Institut d' Etudes Politiques de Strasbourg.

Dietsch, M., and J. Petey (2004) Should SME Exposures Be Treated as Retail or Corporate Exposures? A Comparative Analysis of Default Probabilities and Assets Correlations in French and German SMEs, *Journal of Banking and Finance* 28, 773–788.

Dinç, I. (2000) Bank Reputation, Bank Commitment, and the Effects of Competition in Credit Markets, *Review of Financial Studies* 13, 781–812.

Djankov, S.D., J. Jindra, and L. Klapper (2005) Corporate Valuation and the Resolution of Bank Insolvency in East Asia, *Journal of Banking and Finance* 29, 2095–2118.

Dornbusch, R., Y.C. Park, and S. Claessens (2000) Contagion: Understanding How It Spreads, *World Bank Research Observer* 15, 177–197.

Drucker, S., and M. Puri (2005) On the Benefits of Concurrent Lending and Underwriting, *Journal of Finance* 60, 2763–2800.

Du, J. (2003) Why Do Multinational Enterprises Borrow from Local Banks? *Economics Letters* 78, 287–291.

Dullman, K., and N. Masschelein (2006) A Tractable Model to Measure Sector Concentration Risk in Credit Portfolios, Mimeo, Deutsche Bundesbank/National Bank of Belgium.

Eber, N. (1996) Relations de Credit de Long Terme et Structure des Marches Bancaires Locaux, *Revue Economique* 3, 755–764.

Edwards, J., and M. Nibler (2000) Corporate Governance in Germany: The Role of Banks and Ownership Concentration, *Economic Policy* 15, 239–267.

Elsas, R. (2005) Empirical Determinants of Relationship Lending, *Journal of Financial Intermediation* 14, 32–57.

Elsas, R., F. Heinemann, and M. Tyrell (2004) Multiple but Asymmetric Bank Financing: The Case of Relationship Lending, Mimeo, University of Frankfurt.

Elsas, R., and J.P. Krahnen (1998) Is Relationship Lending Special? Evidence from Credit-File Data in Germany, *Journal of Banking and Finance* 22, 1283–1316.

Elsas, R., and J.P. Krahnen (2002) Collateral, Relationship Lending, and Financial Distress: An Empirical Study on Financial Contracting, Mimeo, Center for Financial Studies.

Elsinger, H., A. Lehar, and M. Summer (2006a) Risk Assessment for Banking Systems, *Management Science* 52, 1301–1314.

Elsinger, H., A. Lehar, and M. Summer (2006b) Using Market Information for Banking System Risk Assessment, *International Journal of Central Banking* 2, 137–165.

Elston, J.A. (1995) Investment, Liquidity Constraints and Bank Relationships: Evidence from German Manufacturing Firms, Discussion Paper, Centre for Economic Policy Research.

Elyasiani, E., and L.G. Goldberg (2004) Relationship Lending: A Survey of the Literature, *Journal of Economics and Business* 56, 315–330.

Ergungor, O.E. (2005) The Profitability of Bank-Borrower Relationships, *Journal of Financial Intermediation* 14, 485–512.

Ewert, R., G. Schenk, and A. Szczesny (2000) Determinants of Bank Lending Performance in Germany, *Schmalenbach Business Review* 52, 344–362.

Fabbri, D., and M. Padula (2004) Does Poor Legal Enforcement Make Households Credit Constrained? *Journal of Banking and Finance* 28, 2369–2397.

Fama, E.F. (1985) What's Different about Banks? *Journal of Monetary Economics* 15, 5–29.

Farinha, L.A., and J.A.C. Santos (2002) Switching from Single to Multiple Bank Lending Relationships: Determinants and Implications, *Journal of Financial Intermediation* 11, 124–151.

Farinha, L.A., and J.A.C. Santos (2006) The Survival of Start-ups: Do their Funding Choices and Bank Relationships at Birth Matter? Mimeo, Bank of Portugal.

Felici, R., and M. Pagnini (2005) Distance, Bank Heterogeneity, and Entry in Local Banking Markets, Working Paper, Bank of Italy.

Ferri, G., T.S. Kang, and I.J. Kim (2002) The Value of Relationship Banking during Financial Crises: Evidence from the Republic of Korea, Working Paper, World Bank.

Ferri, G., and M. Messori (2000) Bank-Firm Relationships and Allocative Efficiency in Northeastern and Central Italy and in the South, *Journal of Banking and Finance* 24, 1067–1095.

Fery, J., D. Gasborro, D.R. Woodliff, and J.K. Zumwalt (2003) Market Reaction to Published and Non-published Corporate Loan Announcements, *Quarterly Review of Economics and Finance* 43, 1–10.

Fields, L.P., D.R. Fraser, T.L. Berry, and S. Byers (2006) Do Bank Loan Relationships Still Matter? *Journal of Money, Credit, and Banking* 38, 1195–1209.

Fischer, K. (1990) Hausbankbeziehungen als Instrument der Bindung zwischen Banken und Unternehmen—Eine Theoretische und Empirische Analyse, PhD Dissertation, Universitat Bonn.

Fischer, K.H. (2000) Acquisition of Information in Loan Markets and Bank Market Power: An Empirical Investigation, Mimeo, Johann Wolfgang Goethe University Frankfurt.

Fischer, K.H. (2001) Banken und unvollkommener Wettbewerb. Empirische Beitrage zu einer Industrieokonomik der Finanzmarkte, PhD Dissertation, Goethe University Frankfurt.

Fischer, K.H., and C. Pfeil (2004) Regulation and Competition in German Banking, in J.P. Krahnen and R.H. Schmidt (eds.), *The German Financial System*, Oxford University Press, Frankfurt, 291–349.

Fisman, R., and I. Love (2004a) Financial Development and Growth in the Short and Long Run, Working Paper, National Bureau for Economic Research.

Fisman, R., and I. Love (2004b) Financial Development and Intersectoral Allocation: A New Approach, *Journal of Finance* 54, 2785–2805.

Fluet, C., and P.G. Garella (2007) Relying on the Information of Others: Debt Rescheduling with Multiple Lenders, Working Paper, Université du Québec.

Focarelli, D., and F. Panetta (2003) Are Mergers Beneficial to Consumers? Evidence from the Market for Bank Deposits, *American Economic Review* 93, 1152–1171.

Focarelli, D., and A.F. Pozzolo (2001) The Patterns of Cross-Border Bank Mergers and Shareholdings in OECD Countries, *Journal of Banking and Finance* 25, 2305–2337.

Foglia, A., S. Laviola, and P. Marullo Reedtz (1998) Multiple Banking Relationships and the Fragility of Corporate Borrowers, *Journal of Banking and Finance* 22, 1441–1456.

Fohlin, C. (1998) Relationship Banking, Liquidity, and Investment in the German Industrialization, *Journal of Finance* 53, 1737–1758.

Fok, R.C.W., Y.C. Chang, and W.T. Lee (2004) Bank Relationships and Their Effects on Firm Performance around the Asian Financial Crisis: Evidence from Taiwan, *Financial Management* 33, 89–112.

Forbes, K., and R. Rigobon (2002) No Contagion, Only Interdependence: Measuring Stock Market Co-movements, *Journal of Finance* 57, 2223–2261.

Franks, J., and C. Mayer (2001) Ownership and Control of German Corporations, *Review of Financial Studies* 14, 943–977.

Freixas, X. (2005) Deconstructing Relationship Banking, *Investigaciones Economicas* 29, 3–31.

Freixas, X., and B. Parigi (1998) Contagion and Efficiency in Gross and Net Interbank Payment System, *Journal of Financial Intermediation* 7, 3–31.

Freixas, X., B. Parigi, and J.C. Rochet (2000) Systemic Risk, Interbank Relations and Liquidity Provision by the Central Bank, *Journal of Money, Credit and Banking* 32, 611–638.

Freixas, X., and J.C. Rochet (1997) *Microeconomics of Banking*, MIT Press, Cambridge, MA.

Furfine, C.H. (2003) Interbank Exposures: Quantifying the Risk of Contagion, *Journal of Money, Credit and Banking* 35, 111–128.

Fuss, C., and P. Vermeulen (2006) The Reponse of Firms' Investment and Financing to Adverse Cash Flow Shocks: The Role of Bank Relationships, Mimeo, European Central Bank.

Gan, J. (2007) The Real Effects of Asset Market Bubbles: Loan- and Firm-Level Evidence of a Lending Channel, *Review of Financial Studies* 20, 1941–1973.

Gangopadhyay, S., and B. Mukhopadhyay (2002) Multiple Bank Lending and Seniority in Claims, *Journal of Economics and Business* 54, 7–30.

Garcia-Appendini, E. (2005) Soft Information in Bank Lending: The Use of Trade Credit, Mimeo, Universitat Pompeu Fabra.

Garcia-Marco, T., and C. Ocana (1999) The Effect of Bank Monitoring on the Investment Behavior of Spanish Firms, *Journal of Banking and Finance* 23, 1579–1603.

Garrett, T.A., G.A. Wagner, and D.C. Wheelock (2004) A Spatial Analysis of State Banking Regulation, Working Paper, Federal Reserve Bank of St. Louis.

Gatev, E., T. Schuermann, and P.E. Strahan (in press) Managing Bank Liquidity Risk: How Deposit-Loan Synergies Vary with Market Conditions, *Review of Financial Studies*.

Gatev, E., and P.E. Strahan (2006) Banks' Advantage in Supplying Liquidity: Theory and Evidence from the Commercial Paper Market, *Journal of Finance* 61, 867–892.

Gehrig, T. (1998) Screening, Cross-Border Banking, and the Allocation of Credit, *Research in Economics* 52, 387–407.

Gertler, M. (1988) Financial Structure and Aggregate Economic Activity, *Journal of Money, Credit and Banking* 20, 559–588.

Giannetti, M., and S. Ongena (in press) Financial Integration and Firm Performance: Evidence from Foreign Bank Entry in Emerging Markets, *Review of Finance*.

Gibson, M.S. (1995) Can Bank Health Affect Investment? Evidence from Japan, *Journal of Business* 68, 281–308.

Gibson, M.S. (1997) More Evidence on the Link between Bank Health and Investment in Japan, *Journal of Japanese International Economics* 11, 29–49.

Gilbert, R. (1984) Bank Market Structure and Competition: A Survey, *Journal of Money, Credit, and Banking* 16, 617–644.

Gilbert, R.A., and A.M. Zaretsky (2003) Banking Antitrust: Are the Assumptions Still Valid? *Review of the Federal Reserve Bank of St. Louis* 29–52.

Gobbi, G., and F. Lotti (2004) Entry Decisions and Adverse Selection: An Empirical Analysis of Local Credit Markets, Mimeo, Bank of Italy.

Goddard, J., P. Molyneux, J.O.S. Wilson, and M. Tavakoli (2007) European Banking: An Overview, *Journal of Banking and Finance* 31, 1911–1935.

Goldberg, L.G., and A. Saunders (1981) The Determinants of Foreign Banking Activity in the United States, *Journal of Banking and Finance* 5, 17–32.

Goldstein, I., and A. Pauzner (2005) Demand-Deposit Contracts and the Probability of Bank Runs, *Journal of Finance* 60, 1293–1328.

Gopalan, R., G.F. Udell, and V. Yerramilli (2007) Why Do Firms Switch Banks? Mimeo, Washington University.

Gorton, G., and F.A. Schmid (2000) Universal Banking and the Performance of German Firms, *Journal of Financial Economics* 58, 29–80.

Gorton, G., and A. Winton (2003) Financial Intermediation, in G. Constantinides, M. Harris, and R. Stulz (eds.), *Handbook of the Economics of Finance*, North Holland, Amsterdam 431–552.

Greenbaum, S.I. (1996) Twenty-Five Years of Banking Research, *Financial Management* 25, 86–92.

Greene, W.H. (1997) *Econometric Analysis*, 3rd ed., Prentice Hall, Upper Saddle River, NJ.

Greene, W.H. (2003) *Econometric Analysis*, 5th ed., Prentice Hall, Upper Saddle River, NJ.

Gropp, R., and J. Vesala (2003) Bank Contagion in Europe, Mimeo, European Central Bank.

Grosse, R., and L.G. Goldberg (1991) Foreign Bank Activity in the United States: An Analysis by Country of Origin, *Journal of Banking and Finance* 15, 1093–1112.

Gual, J. (1999) Deregulation, Integration and Market Structure in European Banking, *Journal of Japanese and International Economies* 12, 372–396.

Guiso, L. (2003) Small Business Finance in Italy, *European Investment Bank Papers* 8, 121–147.

Guiso, L., and R. Minetti (2005) Multiple Creditors and Information Rights: Theory and Evidence from U.S. Firms, Mimeo, Ente Luigi Einaudi.

Guiso, L., P. Sapienza, and L. Zingales (2004) Does Local Financial Development Matter? *Quarterly Journal of Economics* 119, 929–970.

Gurley, J., and E. Shaw (1960) *Money in the Theory of Finance*, Brookings Institution, Washington, DC.

Haber, S.H. (1991) Industrial Concentration and the Capital Markets: A Comparative Study of Brazil, Mexico, and the United States, 1830–1930, *Journal of Economic History* 51, 559–580.

Haber, S.H. (1997) Financial Markets and Industrial Development: A Comparative Study of Governmental Regulation, Financial Innovation and Industrial Structure in Brazil and Mexico, 1840–1940, in Stephen H. Haber (ed.), *How Latin America Fell Behind?* Stanford University Press, Stanford, CA, 146–178.

Habyarimana, J. (2006) The Benefits of Banking Relationships: Evidence from Uganda's Banking Crisis, Mimeo, Harvard University.

Hadlock, C., and C. James (1997) Bank Lending and the Menu of Financing Options, Mimeo, University of Florida.

Hadlock, C., and C. James (2002) Do Banks Provide Financial Slack? *Journal of Finance* 57, 1383–1420.

Hainz, C. (2005) The Effects of Bank Insolvency on Corporate Incentives in Transition Economies, *Economics of Transition* 13, 261–286.

Han, L., D.J. Storey, and S. Fraser (2006) The Concentration of Creditors: Evidence from Small Businesses, Mimeo, University of Hull.

Hannan, T. (1997) Market Share Inequality, the Number of Competitors, and the HHI: An Examination of Bank Pricing, *Review of Industrial Organization* 12, 23–35.

Hannan, T.H. (1991) Bank Commercial Loan Markets and the Role of Market Structure: Evidence from Surveys of Commercial Lending, *Journal of Banking and Finance* 15, 133–149.

Hannan, T.H., and R.A. Prager (2004) The Competitive Implications of Multimarket Bank Branching, *Journal of Banking and Finance* 28, 1889–1914.

Hao, L. (2003) Bank Effects and the Determinants of Loan Yield Spreads, Mimeo, York University.

Harhoff, D., and T. Körting (1998a) How Many Creditors Does It Take to Tango? Mimeo, Wissenschaftszentrum Berlin.

Harhoff, D., and T. Körting (1998b) Lending Relationships in Germany— Empirical Evidence from Survey Data, *Journal of Banking and Finance* 22, 1317–1353.

Harm, C. (2001) European Financial Market Integration: The Case of Private Sector Bonds and Syndicate Loans, *Journal of International Financial Markets, Institutions, and Money* 11, 245–263.

Hart, O.D. (1995) *Firms, Contracts, and Financial Structure*, Oxford University Press, Oxford.

Harvey, A. (1976) Estimating Regression Models with Multiplicative Heteroscedasticity, *Econometrica* 44, 461–465.

Hasan, I., P. Wachtel, and M. Zhou (2006) Institutional Development, Financial Deepening and Economic Growth: Evidence from China, Discussion Paper, BOFIT.

Haubrich, J.H. (1989) Financial Intermediation: Delegated Monitoring and Long-Term Relationships, *Journal of Banking and Finance* 13, 9–20.

Hauswald, R., and R. Marquez (2006) Competition and Strategic Information Acquisition in Credit Markets, *Review of Financial Studies* 19, 967–1000.

Heckman, J., and B. Singer (1984a) A Method for Minimizing the Impact of Distributional Assumptions in Econometric Models for Duration Data, *Econometrica* 52, 279–321.

Heckman, J.J., and B. Singer (1984b) Econometric Duration Analysis, *Journal of Econometrics* 24, 63–132.

Heitfield, E.A. (1999) What Do Interest Rate Data Say about the Geography of Retail Banking Markets, *Antitrust Bulletin* 44, 333–347.

Heitfield, E.A., and R.A. Prager (2004) The Geographic Scope of Retail Deposit Markets, *Journal of Financial Services Research* 25, 37–55.

Hellwig, M. (1991) Banking, Financial Intermediation and Corporate Finance, in A. Giovannini and C.P. Mayer (eds.), *European Financial Integration*, Cambridge University Press, Cambridge, MA, 35–63.

Helwege, J., and F. Packer (2003) Determinants of the Choice of Bankruptcy Procedure in Japan, *Journal of Financial Intermediation* 12, 96–120.

Hernandez-Canovas, G., and P. Martinez-Solano (2006) Banking Relationships: Effects on the Debt Terms of the Small Spanish Firms, *Journal of Small Business Management* 44, 315–333.

Herrera, A.M., and R. Minetti (2007) Informed Finance and Technological Change: Evidence from Credit Relationships, *Journal of Financial Economics* 83, 223–269.

Hiraki, T., A. Ito, and F. Kuroki (2003) Single versus Multiple Main Bank Relationships: Evidence from Japan, Mimeo, International University of Japan.

Ho, T.S.Y., and A. Saunders (1981) The Determinants of Bank Interest Margins: Theory and Empirical Evidence, *Journal of Financial and Quantitative Analysis* 16, 581–600.

Hodgman, D.R. (1960) Credit Risk and Credit Rationing, *Quarterly Journal of Economics* 74, 258–278.

Holland, J. (1994) Bank Lending Relationships and the Complex Nature of Bank-Corporate Relations, *Journal of Business Finance and Accounting* 21, 367–391.

Hommel, U., and H. Schneider (2003) Financing the German Mittelstand, *European Investment Bank Papers* 8, 53–90.

Hori, M. (2005) Does Bank Liquidation Affect Client Firm Performance? Evidence from a Main Bank Failure in Japan, *Economics Letters* 88, 415–420.

Horiuchi, T. (1993) An Empirical Overview of the Japanese Main Bank Relationship in Relation to Firm Size, *Rivista Internationale di Scienze Economiche e Commerciale* 40, 997–1018.

Horiuchi, T. (1994) The Effect of Firm Status on Banking Relationships and Loan Syndication, in M. Aoki and H. Patrick (eds.), *The Japanese Main Bank System*, Oxford University Press, Oxford, 258–294.

Horiuchi, T., F. Packer, and S. Fukuda (1988) What Role Has the 'Main Bank' Played in Japan? *Journal of Japanese and International Economies* 2, 159–180.

Hoshi, T., A. Kashyap, and D. Scharfstein (1991) Corporate Structure, Liquidity and Investment: Evidence from Japanese Industrial Groups, *Quarterly Journal of Economics* 106, 33–60.

Houston, J., and C. James (1996) Bank Information Monopolies and the Mix of Private and Public Debt Claims, *Journal of Finance* 51, 1863–1889.

Houston, J., and C. James (2001) Do Relationships Have Limits? Banking Relationships, Financial Constraints and Investment, *Journal of Business* 74, 347–374.

Howorth, C., M.J. Peel, and N. Wilson (2003) An Examination of the Factors Associated with Bank Switching in the UK Small Firm Sector, *Small Business Economics* 20, 305–317.

Huang, R. (2008) The Real Effects of Bank Branching Deregulation: Comparing Contiguous Counties across U.S. State Borders, *Journal of Financial Economics* 87, 678–705.

Huang, W., and S. Zhao (2006) When Debt Is Bad News: Market Reaction to Debt Announcements under Poor Governance, Mimeo, GREMAQ.

Hubert, F., and D. Schafer (2002) Coordination Failure with Multiple-Source Lending, the Cost of Protection against a Powerful Lender, *Journal of Institutional and Theoretical Economics* 158, 256–275.

Hwan Shin, G., D.R. Fraser, and J.W. Kolari (2003) How Does Banking Industry Consolidation Affect Bank-Firm Relationships? Evidence from a Large Japanese Bank Merger, *Pacific-Basin Finance Journal* 11, 285–304.

Ioannidou, V.P., and S. Ongena (2007) "Time for a Change": Loan Conditions and Bank Behavior When Firms Switch, Mimeo, CentER—Tilburg University.

Ioannidou, V.P., S. Ongena, and J.L. Peydró (2007) Monetary Policy and Subprime Lending: "A Tall Tale of Low Federal Funds Rates, Hazardous Loans, and Reduced Loan Spreads," Mimeo, CentER—Tilburg University/European Central Bank.

Iwata, G. (1974) Measurement of Conjectural Variations in Oligopoly, *Econometrica* 42, 947–966.

Jaffee, D., and J.E. Stiglitz (1990) Credit Rationing, in B.M. Friedman and F.H. Hahn (eds.), *Handbook of Monetary Economics*, Elsevier, Amsterdam, 837–888.

James, C. (1987) Some Evidence on the Uniqueness of Bank Loans, *Journal of Financial Economics* 19, 217–235.

James, C., and D.C. Smith (2000) Are Banks Still Special? New Evidence on Their Role in the Corporate Capital Raising Process, *Bank of America—Journal of Applied Corporate Finance* 13, 52–63.

James, C., and P. Wier (1990) Borrowing Relationships, Intermediation and the Cost of Issuing Public Securities, *Journal of Financial Economics* 28, 149–171.

Jaumandreu, J., and J. Lorences (2002) Modelling Price Competition across Many Markets: An Application to the Spanish Loans Market, *European Economic Review* 46, 93–115.

Jayaratne, J., and P.E. Strahan (1996) The Finance-Growth Nexus: Evidence from Bank Branch Deregulation, *Quarterly Journal of Economics* 111, 639–670.

Jayaratne, J., and P.E. Strahan (1998) Entry Restrictions, Industry Evolution, and Dynamic Efficiency: Evidence from Commercial Banking, *Journal of Law and Economics* 41, 239–274.

Jiangli, W., H. Unal, and C. Yom (2008) Relationship Lending, Accounting Disclosure, and Credit Availability during the Asian Financial Crisis, *Journal of Money, Credit and Banking* 40, 25–55.

Jiménez, G., S. Ongena, J.L. Peydró, and J. Saurina (2007) Hazardous Times for Monetary Policy: What Do Twenty-Three Million Bank Loans Say about the Effects of Monetary Policy on Credit Risk? Discussion Paper, Centre for Economic Policy Research.

Jiménez, G., V. Salas, and J. Saurina (2006) Determinants of Collateral, *Journal of Financial Economics* 81, 255–281.

Joeveer, K. (2007) Does Bank Failure Affect Client Firms? Micro Evidence from Estonia, Mimeo, CERGE-EI.

Johnson, S.A. (1997) The Effect of Bank Reputation on the Value of Bank Loan Agreements, *Journal of Accounting, Auditing and Finance* 12, 83–100.

Jorion, P. (2002) How Informative Are Value-at-Risk Disclosures? *Accounting Review* 77, 911–931.

Kalbfleisch, J.D., and R.L. Prentice (1980) *The Statistical Analysis of Failure Time Data*, John Wiley and Sons, New York, NY.

Kaminsky, G.L., and C.M. Reinhart (1999) The Twin Crises: The Causes of Banking and Balance-of-Payments Problems, *American Economic Review* 89, 473–500.

Kane, E.J., and B.G. Malkiel (1965) Bank Portfolio Allocation, Deposit Variability, and the Availability Doctrine, *Quarterly Journal of Economics* 79, 257–261.

Kang, J.K., A. Shivdasani, and T. Yamada (2000) The Effect of Bank Relations on Investment Decisions: An Investigation of Japanese Takeover Bids, *Journal of Finance* 55, 2197–2218.

Kang, J.K., and R.M. Stulz (2000) Do Banking Shocks Affect Borrowing Firm Performance? An Analysis of the Japanese Experience, *Journal of Business* 73, 1–24.

Kano, M., H. Uchida, G.F. Udell, and W. Watanabe (2006) Information Verifiability, Bank Organization, Bank Competition and Bank-Borrower Relationships, Mimeo, Wakayama University.

Kaplan, E.L., and P. Meier (1958) Nonparametric Estimation from Incomplete Observations, *Journal of the American Statistical Association* 53, 457–481.

Kaplan, S.N., and B.A. Minton (1994) Appointments of Outsiders to Japanese Boards: Determinants and Implications for Managers, *Journal of Financial Economics* 36, 225–258.

Karceski, J., S. Ongena, and D.C. Smith (2005) The Impact of Bank Consolidation on Commercial Borrower Welfare, *Journal of Finance* 60, 2043–2082.

Kashyap, A., R.G. Rajan, and J.C. Stein (2002) Banks as Liquidity Providers: An Explanation for the Co-existence of Lending and Deposit-Taking, *Journal of Finance* 57, 33–73.

Kashyap, A.K., J.C. Stein, and D.W. Wilcox (1993) Monetary Policy and Credit Conditions: Evidence from the Composition of External Finance, *American Economic Review* 83, 78–98.

Keeley, M.C. (1990) Deposit Insurance Risk and Market Power in Banking, *American Economic Review* 80, 1183–1200.

Kerr, W., and R. Nanda (2007) Democratizing Entry: Banking Deregulations, Financing Constraints, and Entrepreneurship, Working Paper, Harvard Business School.

Kiefer, N.M. (1988) Economic Duration Data and Hazard Functions, *Journal of Economic Literature* 26, 646–679.

Kim, M. (1986) Banking Technology and the Existence of a Consistent Output Aggregate, *Journal of Monetary Economics* 18, 181–195.

Kim, M., D. Kliger, and B. Vale (2003) Estimating Switching Costs: The Case of Banking, *Journal of Financial Intermediation* 12, 25–56.

Kim, M., E.G. Kristiansen, and B. Vale (2005) Endogenous Product Differentiation in Credit Markets: What Do Borrowers Pay For? *Journal of Banking and Finance* 29, 681–699.

Kim, M., E.G. Kristiansen, and B. Vale (2007) Life-Cycle Patterns of Interest Rate Markups in Small Firm Finance, Working Paper, Norges Bank.

Kim, M., and B. Vale (2001) Non-price Strategic Behavior: The Case of Bank Branches, *International Journal of Industrial Organization* 19, 1583–1602.

Kindleberger, C.P. (1983) International Banks as Leaders or Followers of International Business, *Journal of Banking and Finance* 7, 583–595.

King, R.G., and R. Levine (1993) Finance and Growth: Schumpeter May Be Right, *Quarterly Journal of Economics* 108, 713–737.

Kiser, E.K. (2002) Predicting Household Switching Behavior and Switching Costs at Depository Institutions, *Review of Industrial Organization* 20, 349–365.

Klein, M. (1971) A Theory of the Banking Firm, *Journal of Money, Credit, and Banking* 3, 205–218.

Klemperer, P. (1985) Markets with Consumer Switching Costs, *Quarterly Journal of Economics* 102, 375–394.

Klemperer, P. (1995) Competition When Consumers Have Switching Costs: An Overview with Applications to Industrial Organization, Macroeconomics, and International Trade, *Review of Economic Studies* 62, 515–539.

Klemperer, P.D. (1987) Markets with Consumer Switching Costs, *Quarterly Journal of Economics* 102, 375–394.

Knittel, C., and V. Stango (2004) Compatibility and Pricing with Indirect Network Effects: Evidence from ATMs, Discussion Paper, National Bureau for Economic Research.

Korkeamaki, T.P., and M.W. Rutherford (2006) Industry Effects and Banking Relationship as Determinants of Small Firm Capital Structure Decisions, *Journal of Entrepreneurial Finance and Business Ventures* 11, 7–23.

Kracaw, W.A., and M. Zenner (1998) Bankers in the Boardroom: Good News or Bad News, Mimeo, University of North Carolina–Chapel Hill.

Krahnen, J.P., and R. (2004) Universal Banks and Relationships with Firms, in J.P. Krahnen and R.H. Schmidt (eds.), *The German Financial System*, Oxford University Press, Oxford, 197–233.

Kroszner, R.S., L. Laeven, and D. Klingebiel (2007) Banking Crises, Financial Dependence, and Growth, *Journal of Financial Economics* 84, 187–228.

Kroszner, R.S., and P.E. Strahan (1999) What Drives Deregulation? Economics and Politics of the Relaxation of Bank Branching Restrictions, *Quarterly Journal of Economics* 124, 1437–1467.

Kroszner, R.S., and P.E. Strahan (2001) Bankers on Boards: Monitoring, Conflicts of Interest, and Lender Liability, *Journal of Financial Economics* 62, 415–452.

Kutsuna, K., J.K. Smith, and R.L. Smith (2003) Banking Relationships and Access to Equity Capital Markets: Evidence from Japan's Main Bank System, Mimeo, Kobe University.

La Porta, R., F. Lopez-de-Silanes, and A. Shleifer (2002) Government Ownership of Banks, *Journal of Finance* 57, 265–301.

La Porta, R., F. Lopez-de-Silanes, A. Shleifer, and R.W. Vishny (1998) Law and Finance, *Journal of Political Economy* 106, 1113–1155.

La Porta, R., F. Lopez-de-Silanes, and G. Zamarripa (2003) Related Lending, *Quarterly Journal of Economics* 128, 231–268.

Laeven, L. (2001) Insider Lending and Bank Ownership: The Case of Russia, *Journal of Comparative Economics* 29, 207–229.

Lau, L.J. (1982) On Identifying the Degree of Competitiveness from Industry Price and Output Data, *Economic Letters* 10, 93–99.

Lederer, P., and A.P. Hurter (1986) Competition of Firms: Discriminatory Pricing and Location, *Econometrica* 54, 623–640.

Lefilliatre, D. (2002) La Multibancarite, Cahiers Etudes et Recherches de l'Observatoire des Entreprises, Banque de France.

Lehar, A. (2005) Measuring Systemic Risk: A Risk Management Approach, *Journal of Banking and Finance* 29, 2577–2603.

Lehmann, E., and D. Neuberger (2001) Do Lending Relationships Matter? Evidence from Bank Survey Data in Germany, *Journal of Economic Behavior and Organization* 45, 339–359.

Lehmann, E., D. Neuberger, and S. Rathke (2004) Lending to Small and Medium-Sized Firms: Is There An East-West Gap in Germany, *Small Business Economics* 23, 23–39.

Lehmann, E., and J. Weigand (2000) Does the Governed Corporation Perform Better? Governance Structures and Corporate Performance in Germany, *European Finance Review* 4, 157–195.

Leland, H.E., and D.H. Pyle (1977) Informational Asymmetries, Financial Structure, and Financial Intermediation, *Journal of Finance* 32, 371–387.

Levine, R. (1999) Law, Finance, and Economic Growth, *Journal of Financial Intermediation* 8, 8–35.

Levine, R. (2003) Denying Foreign Bank Entry: Implications for Bank Interest Margins, Mimeo, University of Minnesota.

Levine, R. (2005) Finance and Growth: Theory and Evidence, in Philippe Aghion and Steven N. Durlauf (eds.), *Handbook of Economic Growth*, North Holland, Amsterdam, 865–934.

Levine, R., N. Loayza, and T. Beck (2000) Financial Intermediation and Growth: Causality and Causes, *Journal of Monetary Economics* 46, 31–77.

Levine, R., and S. Zervos (1998) Stock Markets, Banks and Economic Growth, *American Economic Review* 88, 537–558.

Li, K.-W., and T. Liu (2001) Impact of Liberalization of Financial Resources in China's Economic Growth: Evidences from Provinces, *Journal of Asian Economics* 12, 245–262.

Liberti, J.M. (2004) Initiative, Incentives and Soft Information: How Does Delegation Impact the Role of Bank Relationship Managers? Mimeo, Kellogg School of Management Northwestern.

Limpaphayom, P., and S. Polwitoon (2004) Bank Relationship and Firm Performance: Evidence from Thailand before the Asian Financial Crisis, *Journal of Business Finance and Accounting* 31, 1577–1600.

Lublóy, A. (2005) The Domino Effect on the Hungarian Interbank Market, *Magyar Nemzeti Bank Economic Review* 42, 377–401.

Lucas, R.E. (1988) On the Mechanics of Economic Development, *Journal of Monetary Economics* 22, 3–42.

Lummer, S.L., and J.J. McConnell (1989) Further Evidence on the Bank Lending Process and the Capital Market Response to Bank Loan Agreements, *Journal of Financial Economics* 25, 99–122.

Machauer, A., and M. Weber (1998) Bank Behavior Based on Internal Credit Ratings of Borrowers, *Journal of Banking and Finance* 22, 1355–1383.

Machauer, A., and M. Weber (2000) Number of Bank Relationships: An Indicator of Competition, Borrower Quality, or just Size, Discussion Paper, Center for Financial Studies.

Maddala, G.S. (1983) *Limited Dependent Variables and Qualitative Variables in Econometrics*, Cambridge University Press, New York, NY.

Magri, S., A. Mori, and P. Rossi (2005) The Entry and the Activity Level of Foreign Banks in Italy: An Analysis of the Determinants, *Journal of Banking and Finance* 29, 1295–1310.

Mahrt-Smith, J. (2006) Should Banks Own Equity Stakes in their Borrowers? A Contractual Solution to Hold-up Problems, *Journal of Banking and Finance* 30, 2911–2929.

Mallett, T., and A. Sen (2001) Does Local Competition Impact Interest Rates Charged on Small Business Loans? Empirical Evidence from Canada, *Review of Industrial Organization* 19, 437–452.

Martinez Peria, M., and S. Schmukler (2001) Do Depositors Punish Banks for Bad Behavior? Market Discipline, Deposit Insurance, and Banking Crisis, *Journal of Finance* 56, 1029–1051.

Martinez-Miera, D., and R. Repullo (2008) Does Competition Reduce the Risk of Bank Failure? Center for Economics Policy Research (CEPR) Discussion Paper No. DP6669.

Mathieu, R., S. Robb, and P. Zhang (2002) The Impact of Capitalization Level on Lending Commitment after the Introduction of the Basle Accord, Mimeo, Joseph L. Rotman School of Management, University of Toronto.

Matutes, C., and X. Vives (1996) Competition for Deposits, Fragility, and Insurance, *Journal of Financial Intermediation* 5, 184–216.

Maurer, N., and S. Haber (2004) Related Lending and Economic Performance, Mimeo, Stanford University.

Mayer, C. (1988) New Issues in Corporate Finance, *European Economic Review* 32, 1167–1189.

Mayer, C. (1996) The Assessment: Money and Banking, Theory and Evidence, *Oxford Review of Economic Policy* 10, 1–13.

McFadden, D. (1978) Modelling the Choice of Residential Location, in Karlquist A. (ed.), *Spatial Interaction Theory and Residential Location*, North-Holland, Amsterdam, 75–96.

McWilliams, A., and D. Siegel (1997) Event Studies in Management Research: Theoretical and Empirical Issues, *Academy of Management Journal* 40, 626–657.

Menkhoff, L., D. Neuberger, and C. Suwanaporn (2006) Collateral-based Lending in Emerging Markets: Evidence from Thailand, *Journal of Banking and Finance* 30, 1–21.

Menkhoff, L., and C. Suwanaporn (2007) The Rationale of Bank Lending in Pre-crisis Thailand, *Applied Economics* 39, 1077–1089.

Mercieca, S., K. Schaeck, and S. Wolfe (2008) Bank Market Structure, Competition, and SME Financing Relationships in European Regions, Mimeo, Cass Business School.

Merrett, D.T., and A.E. Tschoegl (2004) The Geography of Australian Banking 1942, Mimeo, University of Melbourne.

Merton, R.C. (1974) On the Pricing of Corporate Debt: The Risk Structure of Interest Rates, *Journal of Finance* 29, 449–470.

Mester, L.J. (1993) Efficiency in the Savings and Loan Industry, *Journal of Banking and Finance* 17, 267–286.

Mester, L.J., L. Nakamura, and M. Renault (2007) Transactions Accounts and Loan Monitoring, *Review of Financial Studies* 20, 529–556.

Meyer, S., and R. Prilmeier (2006) The Market vs. Banks—an Event-Study Perspective on the Value Creation of Banks as Blockholders in Germany, Mimeo, European Business School.

Mian, A. (2006) Foreign, Private Domestic, and Government Banks: New Evidence from Emerging Markets, Mimeo, Chicago Graduate School of Business.

Miarka, T. (1999) The Recent Economic Role of Bank-Firm Relationships in Japan, Discussion Paper, Social Science Research Center Berlin (WZB).

Mikkelson, W.H., and M.M. Partch (1986) Valuation Effects of Security Offerings and the Issuance Process, *Journal of Financial Economics* 15, 31–60.

Miron, J. (1986) Financial Panics, the Seasonality of the Nominal Interest Rate, and the Founding of the Fed, *American Economic Review* 76, 125–140.

Mishkin, F.S. (2008) On "Leveraged Losses: Lessons from the Mortgage Meltdown," Speech Presented at U.S. Monetary Policy Forum in New York, Board of Governors of the Federal Reserve System.

Mistrulli, P.E. (2005) Interbank Lending Patterns and Financial Contagion, Mimeo, Banca d' Italia.

Mistrulli, P.E. (2007) Assessing Financial Contagion in the Interbank Market: Maximum Entropy versus Observed Interbank Lending Patterns, Working Paper, Bank of Italy.

Miyajima, H., and Y. Yafeh (2007) Japan's Banking Crisis: An Event-Study Perspective, *Journal of Banking and Finance* 31, 2866–2885.

Moe, T., J.A. Solheim, and B. Vale (2004) The Norwegian Banking Crisis, Occasional Paper, Norges Bank.

Molnár, J. (2007) Market Power and Merger Simulation in Retail Banking, Mimeo, Bank of Finland.

Molnár, J., M. Nagy, and C. Horvath (2007) A Structural Empirical Analysis of Retail Banking Competition: The Case of Hungary, Working Paper, Hungarian National Bank.

Molyneux, P.Y., Y. Altunbas, and E.P.M. Gardener (1996) *Efficiency in European Banking*, John Wiley and Sons, London.

Monti, M. (1972) Deposit, Credit, and Interest Rate Determination under Alternative Bank Objectives, in G.P. Szego and K. Shell (eds.), *Mathematical Methods in Investment and Finance*, North-Holland, Amsterdam, 431–454.

Montoriol Garriga, J. (2006a) The Effect of Relationship Lending on Firm Performance, Mimeo, Universitat Pompeu Fabra.

Montoriol Garriga, J. (2006b) Relationship Lending and Banking Competition: Are They Compatible? Mimeo, Universitat Pompeu Fabra.

Montoriol Garriga, J. (2006c) Relationship Lending in Spain: An Empirical Examination of Cost of Capital and Credit Rationing, Mimeo, Universitat Pompeu Fabra.

Morck, R., and M. Nakamura (1999) Banks and Corporate Control in Japan, *Journal of Finance* 54, 319–339.

Morck, R., M. Nakamura, and A. Shivdasani (2000) Banks, Ownership Structure, and Firm Value in Japan, *Journal of Business* 73, 539–567.

Morgan, D. (2002) How Big are Bank Markets: Evidence Using Branch Sale Premia, Mimeo, Federal Reserve Bank of New York.

Morgan, D.P. (2000) Bank Commitment Relationships, Cash Flow Constraints, and Liquidity Management, Staff Report, Federal Reserve Bank of New York.

Müller, J. (2006) Interbank Credit Lines as a Channel of Contagion, *Journal of Financial Services Research* 29, 37–60.

Nakamura, L.I. (1993a) Commercial Bank Information: Implications for the Structure of Banking, in M. Klausner and L.J. White (eds.), *Structural Change in Banking*, New York University Salomon Center, New York, NY, 131–160.

Nakamura, L.I. (1993b) Monitoring Loan Quality via Checking Account Analysis, *Journal of Retail Banking* 14, 16–34.

Nathan, A., and H. Neave (1989) Competition and Contestability in Canada's Financial System: Empirical Results, *Canadian Journal of Economics* 22, 567–594.

Neuberger, D. (1998) Industrial Organization of Banking: A Review, *International Journal of the Economics of Business* 5, 97–118.

Neuberger, D., M. Pedergnana, and S. Räthke-Döppner (2008) Concentration of Banking Relationships in Switzerland: The Result of Firm Structure or Banking Market Structure, *Journal of Financial Services Research* 33, 101–126.

Neuberger, D., S. Räthke, and C. Schacht (2006) The Number of Bank Relationships of SMEs: A Disaggregated Analysis for the Swiss Loan Market, *Economic Notes* 35, 1–36.

Neuberger, J.A., and G.C. Zimmerman (1990) Bank Pricing of Retail Deposit Accounts and "the California Rate Mystery," *Economic Review Federal Reserve Bank of San Francisco* 3–16.

Neumark, D., and S.A. Sharpe (1992) Market Structure and the Nature of Price Rigidity: Evidence from the Market for Consumer Deposits, *Quarterly Journal of Economics* 107, 657–680.

Norden, L., and M. Weber (2007) Checking Account Information and Credit Risk of Bank Customers, Mimeo, University of Mannheim.

O'Brien, J., and J. Berkowitz (2006) Estimating Bank Trading Risk: A Factor Model Approach, in Rene M. Stulz and Mark S. Carey (eds.), *Risks of Financial Institutions*, University of Chicago Press, Chicago, 59–91.

Ogura, Y. (2006) Endogenous Relationship Banking to Alleviate Excessive Screening in Transaction Banking, Discussion Paper, Institute of Economic Research Hitotsubashi University.

Ongena, S. (1999) Lending Relationships, Bank Default, and Economic Activity, *International Journal of the Economics of Business* 6, 257–280.

Ongena, S., V. Roscovan, and B. Werker (2007a) "Banks and Bonds": The Impact of Bank Loan Announcements on Bond and Equity prices, Mimeo, Tilburg University.

Ongena, S., and D.C. Smith (1998) Quality and Duration of Bank Relationships, in D.F. Birks (eds.), *Global Cash Management in Europe*, Macmillan Press, London, 224–235.

Ongena, S., and D.C. Smith (2000a) Bank Relationships: A Survey, in P. Harker and S.A. Zenios (eds.), *The Performance of Financial Institutions*, Cambridge University Press, London, 221–258.

Ongena, S., and D.C. Smith (2000b) What Determines the Number of Bank Relationships? Cross-Country Evidence, *Journal of Financial Intermediation* 9, 26–56.

Ongena, S., and D.C. Smith (2001) The Duration of Bank Relationships, *Journal of Financial Economics* 61, 449–475.

Ongena, S., D.C. Smith, and D. Michalsen (2003) Firms and their Distressed Banks: Lessons from the Norwegian Banking Crisis (1988–1991), *Journal of Financial Economics* 67, 81–112.

Ongena, S., G. Tümer-Alkan, and N. von Westernhagen (2007b) Creditor Concentration: An Empirical Investigation, Mimeo, CentER—Tilburg University.

Ortiz-Molina, H., and M.F. Penas (2008) Lending to Small Businesses: The Role of Loan Maturity in Addressing Information Problems, *Small Business Economics* 30, 361–383.

Padilla, A.J. (1992) Mixed Pricing in Oligopoly with Consumer Switching Costs, *International Journal of Industrial Organization* 10, 393–411.

Padilla, A.J. (1995) Revisiting Dynamic Duopoly with Consumer Switching Costs, *Journal of Economic Theory* 67, 520–530.

Pagano, M., F. Panetta, and L. Zingales (1998) Why Do Companies go Public? An Empirical Analysis, *Journal of Finance* 53, 27–64.

Panetta, F., F. Schivardi, and M. Shum (2004) Do Mergers Improve Information? Evidence from the Loan Market, Mimeo, Bank of Italy.

Panzar, J.C., and J.N. Rosse (1987) Testing for Monopoly Equilibrium, *Journal of Industrial Economics* 35, 443–456.

Papaioannou, E. (2008) Finance and Growth: A Macroeconomic Assessment of the Evidence from a European Angle, in Xavier Freixas, Philipp Hartmann, and Colin Mayer (eds.), *Handbook of European Financial Markets and Institutions*, Oxford University Press, Oxford, 68–98.

Park, K., and G. Pennacchi (2003) Why Does Institution Size Matter for Banking Market Competition? Mimeo, University of Illinois.

Pawlina, G., and L. Renneboog (2005) Is Investment-Cash Flow Sensitivity Caused by Agency Costs or Asymmetric Information? Evidence from the UK, *European Financial Management* 11, 483–513.

Peek, J., and E.S. Rosengren (2000) Collateral Damage: Effects of the Japanese Bank Crisis on Real Activity in the United States, *American Economic Review* 90, 30–45.

Peltoniemi, J. (2004) The Value of Relationship Banking: Empirical Evidence on Small Business Financing in Finnish Credit Markets, Academic Dissertation, University of Oulu.

Peltoniemi, J. (2007) The Benefits of Relationship Banking: Evidence for Small Business Financing in Finland, *Journal of Financial Services Research* 31, 153–171.

Peltzmann, S. (1977) The Gains and Losses from Industrial Concentration, *Journal of Law and Economics* 20, 229–263.

Perignon, C., Z.Y. Deng, and Z.J. Wang (2008) Do Banks Overstate Their Value-at-Risk, *Journal of Banking and Finance*.32, 783–794.

Petersen, M.A., and R.G. Rajan (1994) The Benefits of Lending Relationships: Evidence from Small Business Data, *Journal of Finance* 49, 3–37.

Petersen, M.A., and R.G. Rajan (1995) The Effect of Credit Market Competition on Lending Relationships, *Quarterly Journal of Economics* 110, 406–443.

Petersen, M.A., and R.G. Rajan (2002) Does Distance Still Matter? The Information Revolution in Small Business Lending, *Journal of Finance* 57, 2533–2570.

Povel, P. (2004) Multiple Banking as a Commitment Not to Rescue, *Research in Finance* 21, 175–199.

Pozzolo, A.F. (2004) The Role of Guarantees in Bank Lending, Mimeo, Ente Luigi Einaudi.

Pozzolo, A.F., and D. Focarelli (2005) Where Do Banks Expand Abroad? An Empirical Analysis, *Journal of Business* 78, 2435–2464.

Preece, D., and D. Mullineaux (1996) Monitoring, Loan Renegotiability, and Firm Value: The Role of Lending Syndicates, *Journal of Banking and Finance* 20, 577–593.

Proust, Y., and D. Cadillat (1996) La Multibancarisation de 1992 a 1995, *Bulletin de la Banque de France Supplement Etudes* 3ème trimestre, 39–51.

Qian, J., and P.E. Strahan (2007) How Law and Institutions Shape Financial Contracts: The Case of Bank Loans, *Journal of Finance* 62, 2803–2834.

Radecki, L.J. (1998) The Expanding Geographic Reach of Retail Banking Markets, *FRBNY Economic Policy Review* 4,(2), 15–34.

Rajan, R.G. (1992) Insiders and Outsiders: The Choice between Informed and Arm's-Length Debt, *Journal of Finance* 47, 1367–1400.

Rajan, R.G., and L. Zingales (1998) Financial Dependence and Growth, *American Economic Review* 559–586.

Ramakrishnan, R.T.S., and A.V. Thakor (1984) Information Reliability and a Theory of Financial Intermediation, *Review of Economic Studies* 51, 415–432.

Rauterkus, A. (2003) Are Bank Lending Relationships Always Beneficial? The Case of Germany, Mimeo, Louisiana State University.

Refait, C. (2002) Les Asymetries d'Information Influencent-Elles le Choix de la Banque entre Soutien et Mise en Failite de l'Entreprise? Une Verification Empirique par un Modele Probit, *Banque et Marche* 59, 6–17.

Refait, C. (2003) La Multibancarite des Entreprises: Choix du Nombre de Banques vs Choix du Nombre de Banques Principales, *Revue Economique* 54, 649–661.

Repetto, A., S. Rodriguez, and R.O. Valdes (2002) Bank Lending and Relationship Banking: Evidence from Chilean Firms, Mimeo, Universidad de Chile.

Rigobon, R. (2002) Contagion: How to Measure It? in Sebastian Edwards and Jeffrey A. Frankel (eds.), *Currency Crises Prevention*, University of Chicago Press, Chicago.

Rigobon, R., and B. Sack (2004) The Impact of Monetary Policy on Asset Prices, *Journal of Monetary Economics* 51, 1553–1575.

Rivaud-Danset, D. (1996) Les Contrats de Credit dans une Relation de Long Terme: De la Main Invisible a la Poignee de Main, *Revue Economique* 4, 937–962.

Roberts, G.S., and N.A. Siddiqi (2004) Collaterilization and the Number of Lenders in Private Debt Contracts: An Empirical Analysis, *Research in Finance* 21, 229–252.

Rochet, J.C., and J. Tirole (1996) Interbank Lending and Systemic Risk, *Journal of Money, Credit and Banking* 28, 733–762.

Romer, P. (1986) Increasing Returns to Scale and Long-Run Growth, *Journal of Political Economy* 154, 1002–1037.

Rosen, R.J. (2003) Banking Market Conditions and Deposit Interest Rates, Working Paper, Federal Reserve Bank of Chicago.

Rosen, R.J. (2007) Banking Market Conditions and Deposit Interest Rates, *Journal of Banking and Finance* 31, 3862–3884.

Rosenfeld, C.M. (2007) The Effect of Banking Relationships on the Future of Financially Distressed Firms, Mimeo, University of Minnesota.

Ross, D.G. (2007) The "Dominant Bank Effect": How High Lender Reputation Affects the Information Content and Terms of Bank Loans, Mimeo, New York University.

Rossignoli, B., and G. Chesini (1995) Multi-banking and Customer Relationships in the Italian Banking System, Research Papers in Banking and Finance, Institute of European Finance.

Roten, I.C., and D.J. Mullineaux (2002) Debt Underwriting by Commercial Bank-Affiliated Firms and Investment Banks: More Evidence, *Journal of Banking and Finance* 26, 689–718.

Rousseau, P.L., and P. Wachtel (1998) Financial Intermediation and Economic Performance: Historical Evidence from Five Industrialized Countries, *Journal of Money, Credit, and Banking* 30, 657–678.

Rousseau, P.L., and P. Wachtel (2000) Equity Markets and Growth: Cross-Country Evidence on Timing and Outcomes, 1980–1995, *Journal of Banking and Finance* 24, 1933–1957.

Salop, S.C. (1987) Symposium on Mergers and Antitrust, *Journal of Economic Perspectives* 1, 3–12.

Samolyk, K. (1997) Small Business Credit Markets: Why Do We Know So Little about Them? *FDIC Banking Review* 10, 14–32.

Santos, J., and A. Rumble (2006) The American Keiretsu and Universal Banks: Investing, Voting and Sitting on Nonfinancials Corporate Boards, *Journal of Financial Economics* 80, 419–454.

Saparito, P.A., C.C. Chen, and H.J. Sapienza (2004) The Role of Relational Trust in Bank-Small Firm Relationships, *Academy of Management Journal* 47, 400–410.

Sapienza, P. (2002) The Effects of Banking Mergers on Loan Contracts, *Journal of Finance* 329–368.

Sapienza, P. (2004) The Effects of Government Ownership on Bank Lending, *Journal of Financial Economics* 72, 357–384.

Saunders, A., and L. Allen (2002) *Credit Risk Measurement*, Wiley, New York, NY.

Saunders, A., and M.M. Cornett (2002) *Financial Institutions Management: A Risk Management Approach*, McGraw-Hill Irwin, New York, NY.

Schenone, C. (2005) The Effect of Banking Relationships on the Firm's IPO Underpricing, *Journal of Finance* 60, 2903–2958.

Scholes, M., and J.T. Williams (1977) Estimating Betas from Nonsynchronous Data, *Journal of Financial Economics* 5, 309–327.

Scholtens, L.J.R. (1993) On the Foundations of Financial Intermediation: A Review of the Literature, *Kredit und Kapital* 26, 112–141.

Scott, J.A. (2003) Soft Information, Loan Officers, and Small Firm Credit Availability, Mimeo, Temple University.

Scott, J.A. (2004) Small Business and the Value of Community Financial Institutions, *Journal of Financial Services Research* 25, 207–230.

Scott, J.A., and W.C. Dunkelberg (2001) Competition and Credit Market Outcomes: A Small Firm Perspective, Mimeo, Temple University.

Scott, J.A., and W.C. Dunkelberg (2003) A Note on Loan Search and Banking Relationships, Mimeo, Temple University.

Seger, F. (1997) *Banken, Erfolg und Finanzierung*, Deutscher Universitatsverlag, Wiesbaden.

Selten, R. (1965) Spieltheoretische Behandlung eines Oligopolmodelles mit Nachfrageträgheit, *Zeitschrift für die gesamte Staatswissenschaft* 121, 301–324.

Seth, R., D.E. Nolle, and S.K. Mohanty (1998) Do Banks Follow Their Customers Abroad? *Financial Markets, Institutions, and Instruments* 7, 1–25.

Shaffer, S. (1989) Competition in the U.S. Banking Industry, *Economics Letters* 29, 321–323.

Shaffer, S. (1993) A Test of Competition in Canadian Banking, *Journal of Money, Credit, and Banking* 25, 49–61.

Shaffer, S. (1998) The Winner's Curse in Banking, *Journal of Financial Intermediation* 7, 359–392.

Shaffer, S. (2004) Patterns of Competition in Banking, *Journal of Economics and Business* 56, 287–313.

Shapiro, C., and H. Varian (1998) *Information Rules: A Strategic Guide to Network Economy*, Harvard Business School Press, Cambridge, MA.

Sharpe, S.A. (1990) Asymmetric Information, Bank Lending and Implicit Contracts: A Stylized Model of Customer Relationships, *Journal of Finance* 45, 1069–1087.

Sharpe, S.A. (1997) The Effect of Consumer Switching Costs on Prices: A Theory and Its Applications to the Bank Deposit Market, *Review of Industrial Organization* 12, 79–94.

Sheldon, G., and M. Maurer (1998) Interbank Lending and Systemic Risk: An Empirical Analysis for Switzerland, *Swiss Journal of Economics and Statistics* 134, 685–704.

Shen, C.H., and A.H. Huang (2003) Are Performances of Banks and Firms Linked? And If So, Why? *Journal of Policy Modeling* 25, 397–414.

Shen, C.H., and C.A. Wang (2003) Does Banking Relationship Matter to Firm's Invetsment and Financial Constraints? Evidence from the Taiwan's Case, Mimeo National Chengchi University.

Shepherd, W. (1982) Causes of Increased Competition in the U.S. Economy 1939–1980, *Review of Economics and Statistics* 64, 613–626.

Shikimi, M. (2005) Do Firms Benefit from Multiple Banking Relationships? Evidence from Small and Medium-Sized Firms in Japan, Discussion Paper, Hitotsubashi University.

Shin, G.H., and J.W. Kolari (2004) Do Some Lenders Have Information Advantages? Evidence from Japanese Credit Market Data, *Journal of Banking and Finance* 28, 2331–2351.

Shockley, R., and A.V. Thakor (1998) Bank Loan Commitment Contracts: Data, Theory, and Tests, *Journal of Money, Credit, and Banking* 29, 517–534.

Shy, O. (2002) A Quick-and-Easy Method for Estimating Switching Costs, *International Journal of Industrial Organization* 20, 71–87.

Sjögren, H. (1994) Long-Term Financial Contracts in the Bank-Orientated Financial System, *Scandinavian Journal of Management* 10, 315–330.

Slovin, M.B., S.A. Johnson, and J.L. Glascock (1992) Firm Size and the Information Content of Bank Loan Announcements, *Journal of Banking and Finance* 16, 35–49.

Slovin, M.B., M.E. Sushka, and C.D. Hudson (1988) Corporate Commercial Paper, Note Issuance Facilities, and Shareholder Wealth, *Journal of International Money and Finance* 7, 289–302.

Slovin, M.B., M.E. Sushka, and J.A. Polonchek (1993) The Value of Bank Durability: Borrowers as Bank Stakeholders, *Journal of Finance* 48, 289–302.

Slovin, M.B., and J.E. Young (1990) Bank Lending and Initial Public Offerings, *Journal of Banking and Finance* 14, 729–740.

Soenen, L.A., and R. Aggarwal (1989) Cash and Foreign Exchange Management: Theory and Corporate Practice in Three Countries, *Journal of Business Finance and Accounting* 16, 599–617.

Sohn, W. (2002) Banking Relationships and Conflicts of Interest: Market Reactions to Lending Decisions by Korean Banks, Mimeo, Columbia University.

Spiegel, M.M., and N. Yamori (2003) Financial Turbulence and the Japanese Main Bank Relationship, *Journal of Financial Services Research* 23, 205–223.

Spiller, P.T., and E. Favaro (1984) The Effects of Entry Regulation on Oligopolistic Interaction: The Uruguayan Banking Sector, *RAND Journal of Economics* 15, 244–254.

Stango, V. (1998) Price Dispersion and Switching Costs: Evidence from the Credit Card Market, Mimeo, University of Tennessee.

Stanley, T.O., C. Roger, and B. McManis (1993) The Effects of Foreign Ownership of U.S. Banks on the Availability of Loanable Funds to Small Businesses, *Journal of Small Business Management* 31.

Stein, J. (2002) Information Production and Capital Allocation: Decentralized versus Hierarchical Firms, *Journal of Finance* 57, 1891–1922.

Steinherr, A., and C. Huveneers (1994) On the Performance of Differently Regulated Financial Institutions: Some Empirical Evidence, *Journal of Banking and Finance* 18, 271–306.

Sterken, E., and I. Tokutsu (2003) What Are the Determinants of the Number of Bank relations of Japanese Firms? Mimeo, CSOS Centre for Economic Research.

Stiglitz, J.E., and A. Weiss (1981) Credit Rationing in Markets with Imperfect Information, *American Economic Review* 71, 393–410.

Stiroh, K., and P. Strahan (2003) Competitive Dynamics of Deregulation: Evidence from U.S. Banking, *Journal of Money, Credit, and Banking* 35, 801–828.

Strahan, P. (2008) Bank Structure and Lending: What We Do and Do Not Know, in A.V. Thakor and A.W.A. Boot (eds.), *Handbook of Corporate*

Finance: Financial Intermediation and Banking, North Holland, London. 107–131.

Streb, J.M., J. Bolzico, P. Druck, A. Henke, J. Rutman, and W.S. Escudero (2002) Bank Relationships: Effect on the Availability and Marginal Cost of Credit for Firms in Argentina, Working Paper, UCEMA, Buenos Aires.

Sussman, O., and J. Zeira (1995) Banking and Development, Discussion Paper, Center for Economic Policy Research (CEPR).

Sutton, J. (1991) *Sunk Cost and Market Structure: Price Competition, Advertising, and the Evolution of Concentration*, MIT Press, Cambridge, MA.

Suzuki, S., and R.W. Wright (1985) Financial Structure and Bankruptcy Risk in Japanese Companies, *Journal of International Business Studies* 16, 97–110.

Swank, J. (1996) Theories of the Banking Firm: A Review of the Literature, *Bulletin of Economic Research* 48, 173–207.

Taylor, J. (2007) Housing and Monetary Policy, Paper Presented at a Symposium Sponsored by the Federal Reserve Bank of Kansas City at Jackson Hole, WY.

Ter Wengel, J. (1995) International Trade in Banking Services, *Journal of International Money and Finance* 14, 47–64.

Thakor, A.V. (1995) Financial Intermediation and the Market for Credit, in R. Jarrow (ed.), *Handbooks in OR and MS*, North-Holland, Amsterdam, 1069–1087.

Thakor, A.V. (1996) The Design of Financial Systems: An Overview, *Journal of Banking and Finance* 20, 917–948.

Thisse, J.F., and X. Vives (1988) On the Strategic Choice of Spatial Price Policy, *American Economic Review* 78, 122–137.

Thompson, R. (1985) Conditioning the Return-Generating Process on Firm-Specific Events: A Discussion of Event Study Methods, *Journal of Financial and Quantitative Analysis* 20, 151–168.

Thomsen, S. (1999) The Duration of Business Relationships: Banking Relationships of Danish Manufacturers 1900–1995, Mimeo, Copenhagen Business School.

Tirri, V. (2007) Multiple Banking Relationships and Credit Market Competition: What Benefits the Firm? Mimeo, Intesasanpaolo.

Tobin, J. (1963) Commercial Banks as Creators of Money, in Dean Carson (ed.), *Banking and Monetary Studies for the Comptroller of the Currency*, U.S. Treasury, Washington, DC, 408–419.

Treacy, W.F., and M.S. Carey (2000) Credit Risk Rating Systems at Large U.S. Banks, *Journal of Banking and Finance* 24, 167–201.

Trichet, J.-C. (2008) Remarks on the Recent Turbulences in Global Financial Markets, Keynote Address at the Policy Discussion "Global Economic Policy Forum 2008," New York University.

Tschoegl, A.E. (2001) Entry and Survival: The Case of Foreign Banks in Norway, *Scandinavian Journal of Management* 18, 131–153.

Tsuru, K. (2001) Bank Relationships and Firm Performance: Evidence from Selected Japanese Firms in the Electrical Machinery Industry, Mimeo, Research Institute of Economy, Trade and Industry.

Tsuruta, D. (2003) Bank Information Monopoly and Trade Credit, Mimeo, University of Tokyo.

Turati, G. (2001) Cost Efficiency and Profitability in European Commercial Banking, Mimeo, *Università Cattolica del S. Cuore*, Milano.

Uchida, H., G.F. Udell, and W. Watanabe (2006a) Bank Size and Lending Relationships in Japan, Mimeo, Wakayama University.

Uchida, H., G.F. Udell, and N. Yamori (2006b) Loan Officers and Relationship Lending, Mimeo, Wakayama University.

Upper, C. (2006) Contagion Due to Interbank Credit Exposures: What Do We Know, Why Do We Know It, and What Should We Know? Mimeo, Bank for International Settlements.

Upper, C., and A. Worms (2004) Estimating Bilateral Exposures in the German Interbank Market: Is There a Danger of Contagion? *European Economic Review* 48, 827–849.

Uzzi, B. (1999) Embeddedness in the Making of Financial Capital: How Social Relations and Networks Benefit Firms Seeking Financing, *American Sociological Review* 64, 481–505.

Vale, B. (1993) The Dual Role of Demand Deposits under Asymmetric Information, *Scandinavian Journal of Economics* 95, 77–95.

Van Damme, E. (1994) Banking: A Survey of Recent Microeconomic Theory, *Oxford Review of Economic Policy* 10, 14–33.

Van Ees, H., and H. Garretsen (1994) Liquidity and Business Investment: Evidence from Dutch Panel Data, *Journal of Macroeconomics* 16, 613–627.

Van Lelyveld, I., and F. Liedorp (2006) Interbank Contagion in the Dutch Banking Sector: A Sensitivity Analysis, *International Journal of Central Banking* 2, 99–133.

van Leuvensteijn, M., J.A. Bikker, A.A.R.J.M. van Rixtel, and C.K. Sørensen (2007) A New Approach to Measuring Competition in the Loan Markets of the Euro Area, Mimeo, De Nederlandsche Bank.

Van Overfelt, W., J. Annaert, M. De Ceuster, and M. Deloof (2006) Do Universal Banks Create Value? Universal Bank Affiliation and Company Performance in Belgium, 1905–1909, Mimeo, University of Antwerp.

Vander Vennet, R. (2002) Cost and Profit Efficiency of Financial Conglomerates and Universal Banks in Europe, *Journal of Money, Credit, and Banking* 34, 254–282.

Vesala, T. (2007) Switching Costs and Relationship Profits in Bank Lending, *Journal of Banking and Finance* 31, 477–493.

Vives, X. (1991) Regulatory Reform in Europe, *European Economic Review* 35, 505–515.

Vives, X. (1999) *Oligopoly Pricing: Old Ideas and New Tools*, MIT Press, Cambridge, MA.

Vives, X. (2000) Lessons from European Banking Liberalization and Integration, in S. Claessens and M. Jansen (eds.), *The Internationalization of Financial Services*, Kluwer Law International, London, 177–198.

Vives, X. (2001) Competition in the Changing World of Banking, *Oxford Review of Economic Policy* 17, 535–547.

Vives, X. (2005) Europe Banks Future on the Urge to Merge, *Wall Street Journal Europe* May, A6.

Volpin, P.F. (2001) Ownership Structure, Banks, and Private Benefits of Control, Mimeo, London Business School.

von Rheinbaben, J., and M. Ruckes (2004) The Number and the Closeness of Bank Relationships, *Journal of Banking and Finance* 28, 1597–1615.

von Thadden, E.L. (1992) The Commitment of Finance, Duplicated Monitoring and the Investment Horizon, Working Paper in Financial Markets, ESF-Center for Economic Policy Research (CEPR).

von Thadden, E.L. (2004) Asymmetric Information, Bank Lending, and Implicit Contracts: The Winner's Curse, *Finance Research Letters* 1, 11–23.

von Weizsäcker, C. (1984) The Cost of Substitution, *Econometrica* 52, 1085–1116.

Wachtel, P. (2001) Growth and Finance: What Do We Know and How Do We Know It? *International Finance* 4, 335–362.

Waheed, A., and I. Mathur (1993) The Effects of Announcements of Bank Lending Agreements on the Market Values of U.S. Banks, *Financial Management* 22, 119–127.

Weill, L. (2004) On the Relationship between Competition and Efficiency in the EU Banking Sectors, *Kredit und Kapital* 37, 329–352.

Weinstein, D.E., and Y. Yafeh (1998) On the Costs of a Bank Centered Financial System: Evidence from the Changing Main Bank Relations in Japan, *Journal of Finance* 53, 635–672.

Wells, S. (2004) Financial Interlinkages in the United Kingdom's Interbank Market and the Risk of Contagion, Working Paper, Bank of England.

Wrighton, J. (2003) Why Unity in Europe Hasn't Yet Extended to the Banking System, *Wall Street Journal Europe*, February 18.

Yafeh, Y., and O. Yosha (2001) Industrial Organization of Financial Systems and Strategic Use of Relationship Banking, *European Finance Review* 5, 63–78.

Yao, J., and H. Ouyang (2007) Dark-Side Evidence on Bank-Firm Relationship in Japan, *Japan and the World Economy* 19, 198–213.

Yosha, O. (1995) Information Disclosure Costs and the Choice of Financing Source, *Journal of Financial Intermediation* 4, 3–20.

Yu, H.-C., A.K. Pennathur, and D.-T. Hsieh (2007) How Does Public Debt Compliment the Interrelationships between Banking Relationships and Firm Profitability, *International Research Journal of Finance and Economics* 12, 36–55.

Zarutskie, R. (2004) New Evidence on Bank Competition, Firm Borrowing and Firm Performance, Mimeo, Duke University.

Zarutskie, R. (2006) Evidence on the Effects of Bank Competition on Firm Borrowing and Investment, *Journal of Financial Economics* 81, 503–537.

Ziane, Y. (2003) Number of Banks and Credit Relationships: Empirical Results from French Small Business Data, *European Review of Economics and Finance* 2, 30–46.

Zineldin, M. (1995) Bank-Company Interactions and Relationships: Some Empirical Evidence, *International Journal of Bank Marketing* 13, 30–40.

Index

CPSIA information can be obtained at www.ICGtesting.com
Printed in the USA
BVOW09*0345190916

462464BV00001B/1/P